AQ2016
AAT ADVANCED DIPLOMA IN
ACCOUNTING LEVEL 3

QUESTION BANK

Synoptic Assessment

2016 Edition

For assessments from September 2016

First edition June 2016

ISBN 9781 4727 4853 9

British Library Cataloguing-in-Publication Data
A catalogue record for this book is available from the British
Library

Published by

BPP Learning Media Ltd
BPP House, Aldine Place
142-144 Uxbridge Road
London W12 8AA

www.bpp.com/learningmedia

Printed in the United Kingdom by Ashford Colour Press Ltd

Unit 600 Fareham Reach
Fareham Road, Gosport
Hapmshire PO13 OFW

Your learning materials, published by BPP Learning
Media Ltd, are printed on paper obtained from traceable
sustainable sources.

We are grateful to the AAT for permission to reproduce the
sample assessment(s). The answers to the sample
assessment(s) have been published by the AAT. All other
answers have been prepared by BPP Learning Media Ltd.

BPP Learning Media is grateful to the IASB for permission to
reproduce extracts from the International Financial Reporting
Standards including all International Accounting Standards,
SIC and IFRIC Interpretations (the Standards). The
Standards together with their accompanying documents are
issued by:

The International Accounting Standards Board (IASB) 30
Cannon Street, London, EC4M 6XH, United Kingdom. Email:
info@ifrs.org Web: www.ifrs.org

Disclaimer: The IASB, the International Financial Reporting
Standards (IFRS) Foundation, the authors and the publishers
do not accept responsibility for any loss caused by acting or
refraining from acting in reliance on the material in this
publication, whether such loss is caused by negligence or
otherwise to the maximum extent permitted by law.

A note about copyright

CONTENTS

INTRODUCTION

This is BPP Learning Media's AAT Question Bank for the *Advanced Diploma in Accounting Level 3 Synoptic Assessment.* It is part of a suite of ground-breaking resources produced by BPP Learning Media for AAT assessments.

This Question Bank has been written in conjunction with the BPP Course Book, and has been carefully designed to enable students to practise all of the learning outcomes and assessment criteria for the units that make up *the Advanced Diploma in Accounting Level 3 Synoptic Assessment.* It is fully up to date as at April 2016 and reflects both the AAT's qualification specification and the sample assessment provided by the AAT.

This Question Bank contains these key features:

- Tasks corresponding to each chapter of the Course Book. Some tasks are designed for learning purposes, others are of assessment standard

- AAT's AQ2016 sample assessment and answers for *the Advanced Diploma in Accounting Level 3 Synoptic Assessment* and further BPP practice assessments

The emphasis in all tasks and assessments is on the practical application of the skills acquired.

VAT

You may find tasks throughout this Question Bank that need you to calculate or be aware of a rate of VAT. This is stated at 20% in these examples and questions.

Test specification for the Level 3 synoptic assessment – Ethics for Accountants, Advanced Bookkeeping, Final Accounts Preparation, Management Accounting: Costing, Indirect Tax and Spreadsheets for Accounting

Assessment method	Marking type	Duration of assessment
Computer based assessment	Partially computer/partial human marked	3 hours, composed of two 90-minute components

Assessment objectives for the Level 3 synoptic assessment	Weighting
1 Demonstrate an understanding of the relevance of the ethical code for accountants, the need to act ethically in a given situation, and the appropriate action to take in reporting questionable behaviour	15%
2 Prepare accounting and VAT records and respond to errors, omissions and other concerns, in accordance with accounting and ethical principles and relevant regulations	16%
3 Demonstrate an understanding of the inter-relationship between the financial accounting and management accounting systems of an organisation and how they can be used to support managers in decision making	14%
4 Apply ethical and accounting principles when preparing final accounts for different types of organisation, develop ethical courses of action and communicate relevant information effectively	15%
5 Demonstrate a range of spreadsheet knowledge and skills when working with accounting data	10%
6 Use relevant spreadsheet skills to analyse, interpret and report management accounting data	16%
7 Prepare financial information, compromising extended trial balances and final accounts for sole traders and partnerships, using spreadsheets	14%
Total	**100%**

Approaching the assessment

When you sit the assessment it is very important that you follow the on screen instructions. This means you need to carefully read the instructions, both on the introduction screens and during specific tasks.

When you access the assessment you should be presented with an introductory screen with information similar to that shown below (taken from the introductory screen from one of the AAT's AQ2016 Sample Assessments for the *Advanced Diploma in Accounting Level 3 Synoptic Assessment*).

Assessment information

- Read the scenario carefully before attempting the questions; you can return to it at any time by clicking on the 'Introduction' button at the bottom of the screen.
- Complete all 7 tasks.
- Answer the questions in the spaces provided. For answers requiring free text entry, the box will expand to fit your answer.
- You must use a full stop to indicate a decimal point. For example, write 100.57 **not** 100,57 or 100 57
- Both minus signs and brackets can be used to indicate negative numbers **unless** task instructions say otherwise.
- You may use a comma to indicate a number in the thousands, but you don't have to. For example, 10000 and 10,000 are both acceptable.
- Where the date is relevant, it is given in the task data.
- **Tasks 1.1 to 1.4** in **Section 1** require you to enter your answer in the assessment environment. **Tasks 2.1 to 2.3** in **Section 2** require you to download files and work outside the assessment environment in a spreadsheet software program. You should ensure that you have uploaded all files required before you finish and submit the assessment.

Information

- The total time for this paper is 3 hours.
- This assessment has a total of **7 tasks** which are divided into subtasks across two sections.
- The total mark for this paper is 100.
- The marks for each sub-task are shown alongside the task.
- The data you need to complete a task is contained within that task or through the pop-up that appears on the task page; you will not need to refer to your answers for previous tasks.

Advice

- Read each question carefully before you start to answer it.
- Attempt all questions.

The actual instructions will vary depending on the subject you are studying for. It is very important you read the instructions on the introductory screen and apply them in the assessment. You don't want to lose marks when you know the correct answer just because you have not entered it in the right format.

In general, the rules set out in the AAT Sample Assessments for the subject you are studying for will apply in the real assessment, but you should carefully read the information on this screen again in the real assessment, just to make sure. This screen may also confirm the VAT rate used if applicable.

A full stop is needed to indicate a decimal point. We would recommend using minus signs to indicate negative numbers and leaving out the comma signs to indicate thousands, as this results in a lower number of key strokes and less margin for error when working under time pressure. Having said that, you can use whatever is easiest for you as long as you operate within the rules set out for your particular assessment.

You have to show competence throughout the assessment and you should therefore complete all of the tasks. Don't leave questions unanswered.

In some assessments, written or complex tasks may be human marked. In this case you are given a blank space or table to enter your answer into. You are told in the assessments which tasks these are (note: there may be none if all answers are marked by the computer).

If these involve calculations, it is a good idea to decide in advance how you are going to lay out your answers to such tasks by practising answering them on a word document, and certainly you should try all such tasks in this Question Bank and in the AAT's environment using the sample assessment.

When asked to fill in tables, or gaps, never leave any blank even if you are unsure of the answer. Fill in your best estimate.

Note that for some assessments where there is a lot of scenario information or tables of data provided (eg tax tables), you may need to access these via 'pop-ups'. Instructions will be provided on how you can bring up the necessary data during the assessment.

Finally, take note of any task specific instructions once you are in the assessment. For example you may be asked to enter a date in a certain format or to enter a number to a certain number of decimal places.

The synoptic assessment for the Advanced Diploma in Accounting will be made up of two component parts. Students will complete component one in the 'locked down' environment of SecureClient in the same way as all other assessments. Component two requires the assessment system to be 'unlocked' to enable students to access spreadsheet software.

Each component has a time allocation has a time allocation of 1 hour 30 minutes. Any time remaining following the completion of competent one cannot be transferred to component two. It will not be possible for students to return to component one once they have completed it and moved onto component two.

Grading

To achieve the qualification and to be awarded a grade, you must pass all the mandatory unit assessments, all optional unit assessments (where applicable) and the synoptic assessment.

The AAT Level 3 Advanced Diploma in Accounting will be awarded a grade. This grade will be based on performance across the qualification. Unit assessments and synoptic assessments are not individually graded. These assessments are given a mark that is used in calculating the overall grade.

How overall grade is determined

You will be awarded an overall qualification grade (Distinction, Merit, and Pass). If you do not achieve the qualification you will not receive a qualification certificate, and the grade will be shown as unclassified.

The marks of each assessment will be converted into a percentage mark and rounded up or down to the nearest whole number. This percentage mark is then weighted according to the weighting of the unit assessment or synoptic assessment within the qualification. The resulting weighted assessment percentages are combined to arrive at a percentage mark for the whole qualification.

Grade definition	Percentage threshold
Distinction	90–100%
Merit	80–89%
Pass	70–79%
Unclassified	0–69% Or failure to pass one or more assessment/s

Re-sits

Some AAT qualifications such as the AAT Advanced Diploma in Accounting have restrictions in place for how many times you are able to re-sit assessments. Please refer to the AAT website for further details.

You should only be entered for an assessment when you are well prepared and you expect to pass the assessment.

AAT qualifications

The material in this book may support the following AAT qualifications:

AAT Advanced Diploma in Accounting Level 3, AAT Advanced Diploma in Accounting at SCQF Level 6 and Further Education and Training Certificate: Accounting Technician (Level 4 AATSA).

Supplements

From time to time we may need to publish supplementary materials to one of our titles. This can be for a variety of reasons. From a small change in the AAT unit guidance to new legislation coming into effect between editions.

You should check our supplements page regularly for anything that may affect your learning materials. All supplements are available free of charge on our supplements page on our website at:

www.bpp.com/learning-media/about/students

Improving material and removing errors

There is a constant need to update and enhance our study materials in line with both regulatory changes and new insights into the assessments.

From our team of authors BPP appoints a subject expert to update and improve these materials for each new edition.

Their updated draft is subsequently technically checked by another author and from time to time non-technically checked by a proof reader.

We are very keen to remove as many numerical errors and narrative typos as we can but given the volume of detailed information being changed in a short space of time we know that a few errors will sometimes get though our net.

We apologise in advance for any inconvenience that an error might cause. We continue to look for new ways to improve these study materials and would welcome your suggestions. If you have any comments about this book, please email nisarahmed@bpp.com or write to Nisar Ahmed, AAT Head of Programme, BPP Learning Media Ltd, BPP House, Aldine Place, London W12 8AA.

Question bank

Section 1 Ethics for Accountants

Task 1.1

Rajesh is a part qualified accounting technician who has recently become employed by RMS Accountancy, a medium sized firm which provides a variety of bookkeeping and accounting services for local businesses.

Rajesh and Jennifer, another accountant at RMS, have been discussing professional ethics and the ways in which the ethical code applies to them. During this discussion Rajesh made the following comments.

(a) **Are these statements true or false?**

Statement	True	False
'I know I act ethically as I have never broken the law and always comply with regulations.'	☐	☐
'The code of professional ethics is legally binding if you are a member of the AAT.'	☐	☐

One of RMS's clients, Carmichael Ltd, has been allocated to Rajesh. Carmichael Ltd is owned by Rajesh's sister, Manju.

(b) **This situation represents which of the following threats to Rajesh's compliance with the fundamental principles?**

	✓
Familiarity	☐
Self-interest	☐
Advocacy	☐

(c) **If Rajesh carries out this work, which fundamental principles would he be most at risk of breaching?**

	✓
Integrity	☐
Objectivity	☐
Confidentiality	☐

(d) Show whether or not Rajesh is required to take each of the following actions in this situation.

Action	Required/not required
Resign from RMS Accountancy	▼
Inform RMS Accountancy of his link with Carmichael Ltd.	▼
Inform the AAT of his link with Carmichael Ltd.	▼

Picklist

Required
Not required

RMS Accountancy prides itself on its strong ethical culture which can, in part, be attributed to the 'tone-at-the-top'.

(e) Which of the below statements best describes what is meant by the tone-at-the-top?

	✓
Leaders of the firm have issued clear policies on the ethical behaviour expected at RMS Accountancy	☐
Leaders of the firm demonstrate the importance of compliance with the fundamental principles	☐
Leaders of the firm require that any potential threat to the fundamental principles is communicated to them in order for the most appropriate action to be taken	☐

The Institute of Business Ethics (IBE) has set out simple ethical tests for business decisions. It claims that an understanding of the transparency, effect and fairness of the decision can help to assess whether or not it is ethical.

(f) Complete the following statement

▼ can be assessed by considering whether or not the decision maker would mind other people knowing the decision that they have taken.

Picklist

Effect
Fairness
Transparency

The Code of Professional Ethics identifies safeguards for members in practice which can be used in the work environment to protect against threats to the fundamental principles.

(g) Are these statements about safeguards true or false?

Statement	True	False
Disciplinary procedures are an example of safeguard.	☐	☐
Safeguards are put in place to eliminate threats from the organisation.	☐	☐

Task 1.2

(a) Are the below statements regarding professional ethics and the ethical responsibilities of accountants true or false?

Statement	True	False
The Code of Professional Ethics provides a set of rules to help accountants determine ethical behaviour	☐	☐
Ethical behaviour is particularly important for AAT members in practice as they work in the public interest	☐	☐

Tony is an AAT member working in practice who provides accounting services to a number of clients. While Tony is on annual leave his colleague, Janis, is carrying out work for one of his clients on his behalf. Janis has found a significant number of errors in the work Tony has carried out for this client.

(b) If Tony is found to have failed to exercise reasonable care and skill, could he be liable to the client for the following?

Action	Required/not required
Breach of contract	▼
Negligence	▼
Fraud	▼

Picklist

Yes
No
Possibly

(c) **The Code of Ethics for Professional Accountants is published by which of the following bodies?**

IFAC	☐
IESBA	☐
AAT	☐

(d) **"The risk of loss resulting from inadequate or failed processes, people and systems or from external events" is a definition of which of the following?**

Operational risk	☐
Business risk	☐
Control risk	☐

Behaving in an ethical manner involves acting appropriately.

(e) **Complete the following statement**

Behaving ethically means acting with integrity, honesty, fairness and [▼] in dealings with clients, suppliers, colleagues and others.to the relevant authority.

Picklists

confidentiality
respect
sensitivity

Janis has a number of documents she needs to pass to a partner to sign off. When she takes the documents to his office she finds there is file regarding the troubled financial state of a client's company. Janis is very familiar with the company as it is her husband's employer.

(f) **Complete the following statement.**

This is a potential [ ] threat on behalf of the junior and looking at the partner's file would be a breach of the [ ] principle.

Picklist 1: advocacy, familiarity, intimidation, self-interest, self-review

Picklist 2: confidentiality, integrity, objectivity, professional behaviour, professional competence and due care

(g) Are the below statements true or false?

Statement	True	False
The principle of confidentiality must always be carefully abided by in all situations	☐	☐
In some situations it is entirely plausible that the principle of integrity could be over-ridden as a result of the circumstances	☐	☐

Task 1.3

(a) Which of the following statements best describes why accountants should comply with a professional code of ethics?

	✓
It is required by law that they do so	☐
To maintain public confidence in the profession	☐
To prevent dishonest individuals from entering the profession	☐

Denys and Maria are student accounting technicians who are employed by a large accounting firm. During a conversation about the relevance of the ethical code, Maria makes the following comments.

(b) Are these statements true or false?

Statement	True	False
'The code of professional ethics does not apply to me yet as I am only a student accounting technician.'	☐	☐
'Ethical codes provide advice as to how to comply with the law.'	☐	☐

(c) **If you have an ethical concern at work, usually the most appropriate first course of action would be to raise this with** [   ] **or** [   ] **?**

Picklist

employee helpline
the AAT
trusted colleague.
your immediate supervisor

The firm is about to take on a new client and Denys is assisting Jane, a more senior accountant, to carry out due diligence producers.

Denys asks Jane the following questions.

(d) **Show whether Jane would be more likely to answer yes or no to each of Denys' questions.**

Action	Yes/No
Are customer due diligence procedures only required for new clients?	▼
Is it acceptable for accountants to pay a referral fee to obtain a new client?	▼
Is it acceptable to offer a commission to employees for bringing in a new client?	▼

Picklist

Yes
No

In order to help prevent and identify money laundering and terrorist financing, financial institutions and non-financial businesses and professions are required to adopt specific measures. One of these measures is to implement customer due diligence.

(e) **How long such customer due diligence information be retained?**

	✓
5 years	☐
7 years	☐
Indefinitely	☐

Whistleblowing is the disclosure by an employee of illegal or unethical practices by his or her employer.

(f) **Are these statements relating to whistleblowing true or false?**

Statement	True	False
Whistleblowing should occur as soon as illegal activity is suspected.	☐	☐
Employees are protected under the Public Information Disclosure Act to ensure they cannot be dismissed for whistleblowing	☐	☐
If the disclosure is in the public interest, then the fundamental principle of confidentiality is not breached	☐	☐
If the employee is bound by a confidentiality clause in their contract, or has signed a non-disclosure agreement, then the employee could still face dismissal	☐	☐

Task 1.4

(a) **Complete the following statement.**

The UK accountancy profession as a whole is regulated by the [   ] and global ethical standards are set by the [   ].

Picklist

AAT
CCAB
FRC
IESBA

All professional accountants have a duty to comply with the five fundamental principles.

(b) **Are these statements true or false?**

Statement	True	False
The duty to comply with the fundamental principles is more relevant to accountants working in practice than accountants working in business	☐	☐
Compliance with the law, as well as the policies and procedures of the organisation for which you work will ensure that you never break the five fundamental principles	☐	☐

Sharon, an AAT member, is preparing the accounts for a client who has employed her services for a number of years. The client has had a difficult year and will struggle to survive if it cannot secure new finance from a potential investor. The client has asked Sharon to omit details of a number of loans they have taken out during the year. Sharon knows that if she does not do as the client asks, it is likely that they will lose the investor and risk going out of business completely.

(c) **This situation is most likely to represent which of the following threats to Sharon's compliance with the fundamental principles?**

	✓
Familiarity	☐
Self-interest	☐
Intimidation	☐

(d) **Which of the fundamental principles is threatened?**

	✓
Integrity	☐
Professional competence and due care	☐
Objectivity	☐

Sharon does not agree to the clients request as she feels this would be a breach of her ethical duty as an accountant.

However, when she presents the accounts to her line manager, Andrew, for review he also suggests that she changes the accounts. Andrew is aware that the firm as a whole is reliant on the client for its own survival and, were this client to go out of business, it is likely that their accountancy business would do. He quietly suggest to Sharon that, if the accounts remain as they are, it is likely that it would not be long before they were both out of a job.

(e) **Show which additional threats to fundamental principles may now also arise.**

Action	Yes/No
Familiarity	▼
Self-interest	▼
Intimidation	▼
Self-review	▼

Picklist

Yes
No

(f) **Which of the following actions would be the most appropriate for Sharon to take next?**

	✓
Change the accounts as requested	☐
Refuse and explain her reasons for doing so with Andrew	☐
Refuse and inform the media as it is in the public interest to disclose the matter	☐

Task 1.5

(a) **Are these statements true or false?**

Statement	True	False
Under the Code of Professional Ethics, as a minimum you are expected to comply with the laws and regulations of the country in which you live and work.	☐	☐
The ethical code exists primarily to enhance the public image of accountancy and increase public confidence in the profession	☐	☐

(b) **Which of the following best describes what is meant by 'independence'?**

	✓
Ensuring all work is carried out in the public interest	☐
Having no previous or current links, financial or otherwise, with a client	☐
Carrying out work objectively and with integrity	☐

(c) **Rotating senior assurance team personnel helps ensure compliance with the five fundamental principles by safeguarding against which of the following threats?**

	✓
Self-review	☐
Self-interest	☐
Familiarity	☐

Marcia is an AAT member who is carrying out an audit of BigBreak Ltd (BB), a holiday company specialising in weekend breaks. During the engagement, Marcia celebrates her

30th birthday and is given an all-inclusive luxury spa-break as a birthday gift from the client.

(d) Which of the below statements best describe the action that Marcia should take.

	✓
She should accept the gift as it is insignificant and will not influence her audit	☐
She should reject the gift as it may appear to others to compromise her objectivity	☐
She should reject the gift as it may appear to others to compromise her integrity	☐

(e) Complete the following statement.

Accountants [   ] accept significant gifts or preferential treatment from a client. This is because it represents [   ] to the fundamental principles.

Picklist

a familiarity threat
a self-interest threat
no threat
should
should not

The fees paid to accountants by a client for undertaking an engagement could be based on a number of factors.

(f) Show which of the below could be taken into account when determining fees.

Action	Yes/No
The skills required to carry out the engagement	▼
The outcome of the engagement	▼
The value of the service to the client	▼

Picklist

Could be taken into account
Must not be taken into account

(g) Are these statements true or false?

Statement	True	False
Tipping off is an offence which can only be carried out by accountants	☐	☐
Accountants can go to jail if they are found guilty of having been involved in money laundering	☐	☐

Task 1.6

(a) Show whether the below statements are true or false?

Statement	True	False
There are no disadvantages to professional accountants of complying with the code of ethics.	☐	☐
Accountants are required under the code of ethics to comply with all relevant laws and regulations	☐	☐
Accountants are required to uphold the reputation of the accounting profession in both their professional and private lives.	☐	☐

The Institute of Business Ethics (IBE) encourages high standards of ethical behaviour in businesses and it sets out simple ethical tests for a business decision.

(b) Putting yourself in the place of the people on the receiving end of the decision you are about to make helps you to assess which of the following?

	✓
Transparency	☐
Effect	☐
Fairness	☐

(c) In which of the following situations would an accountant be required to breach the fundamental principle of objectivity?

	✓
When it is in the public interest to do so	☐
When it is required by law to do so	☐
An accountant should never breach the objectivity principle	☐

Johnson is a trainee accountant who is applying for a job in a new company that will represent a significant step up in his career. He really wants the job and to help his case he exaggerates the extent of his experience to better suit the expectations set out in the job specification.

(d) Which of the below statements best describes this situation?

	✓
Johnson has not compromised his professional ethics; everyone lies a little to get a job.	☐
Johnson has acted irresponsibly and has therefore breached the professional ethic of professional behaviour	☐
Johnson has misled a potential employer and has therefore breached the professional ethic of integrity	☐
Johnson has misled a potential employer and has therefore breached the professional ethic of professional competence and due care	☐

Johnson's new employer is a direct competitor of his former employer. When Johnson starts his new job he uses the skills, knowledge and experience that he gained from working for the competitor.

(e) Show whether the below statements are true or false?

Statement	True	False
It is fine for Johnson to use these skills, knowledge and experience as the new firm would expect a degree of insider knowledge to be obtained as a perk of employing a former employee of the competition.	☐	☐
It is fine for Johnson to use these skills, knowledge and experience provided he does not disclose any confidential information.	☐	☐
It is fine for Johnson to use these skills, knowledge and experience, but only after a reasonable amount of time has elapsed to prevent conflicts of interest arising.	☐	☐

Professional accountants must maintain the confidentiality of information which is obtained in circumstances that give rise to a duty of confidentiality.

(f) Show whether the below statements are true or false in relation to the above?

Statement	True	False
This is an ethical principle	☐	☐
This is a legal obligation	☐	☐

Task 1.7

(a) **Business ethics suggest that businesses have a duty to act in the best interests of which of the following?**

	✓
The shareholders or other key investors	☐
The employees of the organisation	☐
Society as a whole (including shareholders and employees)	☐

(b) **In which of the following situations would an accountant be required to breach confidentiality?**

	✓
When it is in the public interest to do so	☐
When it is required by law to do so	☐
An accountant should never breach confidentiality	☐

(c) **Which of the following statements best describe what is meant by 'tone-at-the-top'?**

	✓
Senior management set clear policies and procedures that are cascaded down through the organisation	☐
Senior management lead by example	☐
Senior management establish a clear disciplinary procedure to ensure ethical breaches are escalated to be dealt with at the top of the organisation	☐

Rita has discovered that she may have been involved in a money laundering operation without her knowledge. She is worried that she may be incriminated if she reports the issue and is fearful of losing her job and damaging her reputation. The money laundering scheme was very small scale and so Rita makes the decision not to disclose the matter. She confronts the perpetrator and informs them that she will have no further dealings with them.

(d) Could Rita be guilty of money laundering?

	✓
No, she was unaware of being involved in money laundering and withdrew from the engagement as soon as she suspected wrong doing	☐
No, the money laundering scheme was very small scale and would therefore be below the threshold for criminal conviction	☐
Yes, if she has been part of the scheme, even unknowingly, she could still be guilty of money laundering	☐

(e) Show whether the below statements are true or false?

Statement	True	False
Rita has tipped off the client	☐	☐
If Rita does fail to disclose her suspicions of money laundering she may face additional charges	☐	☐
If Rita was to make a protected disclosure she may have a defence against any money laundering charges brought against her	☐	☐
If Rita is convicted of money laundering she will have a criminal record	☐	☐

(f) Complete the following sentence.

When unethical or illegal behaviour is uncovered, whistleblowing should be carried out ⬚ . External whistleblowing should take place ⬚ internal discussion with management.

Picklist

as a last resort
following
immediately
prior to
rather than

BPP
LEARNING MEDIA

Task 1.8

(a) Complete the following sentence.

The AAT requires its members to behave in a way that maintains its reputation, maintains [▼] and protects the [▼]

Picklist

best interests of the industry
future of the industry
public confidence
public interest
superior quality of output
users of accounting information

Raffaella is being investigated by the AAT for misconduct as a result of failing to complete the CPD requirements expected of her. She has also failed to reply to an item of correspondence from the AAT.

(b) Do Raffaella's actions represent conclusive proof of misconduct?

Action	Yes/No
Failing to comply with the AAT's CPD requirements	▼
Failing to reply to an item of correspondence from the AAT	▼

Economic, social and environmental responsibilities of finance professionals are interlinked and is sometimes referred to as a 'triple bottom line' approach.

(c) Show whether the following suggestions help to address the economic, social or environmental responsibilities of finance professionals

Action	Economic/Social/Environmental
Carrying out a conference call between various members of regional staff	▼
Holding an away day for members of the finance department	▼
Reducing the future cost of electricity by investing in solar panels	▼

Picklist

Economic
Environmental
Social

Christie is a professional accountant in practice who has had Alpha Ltd as a client for many years. In her professional capacity, Christie has been asked by Alpha Ltd's new landlord to give a written reference confirming that the company is likely to be able to pay rent over the next five years. Alpha Ltd is paying a large fee for supplying the reference.

(d) Show whether the below statements are true or false?

Statement	True	False
Christie should not accept this engagement as the large fee compromises her integrity.	☐	☐
It would be acceptable practice for Christie to include a disclaimer or liability in the written reference.	☐	☐
Christie should not accept this engagement as the length of the relationship with the client compromises her objectivity.	☐	☐
Christie should not accept this engagement as a safeguard against the threat of intimidation presented by this situation	☐	☐

(e) Complete the following sentence

If Christie gives the reference, even though she knows that Alpha limited has no means of paying the rent, she would be committing [▼].

Picklist

fraud by breach of position
fraud by failing to disclose information
fraud by false representation

(f) Are the following statements relating to taxation services true or false?

Statement	True	False
When a member in practice submits a tax return on behalf of a client the responsibilities of the member should be made clear in a letter of engagement.	☐	☐
When a member in practice submits a tax return on behalf of the client, the member assumes all responsibility for the return and computations.	☐	☐

Task 1.9

(a) Complete the following sentence.

Threats to professional competence and due care can be safeguarded by continuing professional development (CPD).

Can CPD also help to safeguard against threats to the following fundamental principles?

Fundamental principle	Yes	No
Confidentiality	☐	☐
Integrity	☐	☐

There are certain services that an accountant cannot legally offer unless they are authorised to do so by the relevant regulatory body in the UK. These services are known as 'reserved areas'.

(b) Show whether or not the following services are considered to be reserved areas

Action	Yes/No
Internal auditing	▼
Insolvency practice	▼
Taxation services	▼

(c) 'Meeting the needs of the present without compromising the ability of future generations to meet their own needs' is the definition of which of the following?

	✓
Corporate Social Reporting (CSR)	☐
Ethical business practices	☐
Sustainability	☐

You are an accountant working in practice and have, for several years, carried out work for two competing hairdressing businesses, Hair By Me and Hair to Infinity. A lease has just become available on the high street in the town in which the two businesses operate. It is in a highly desirable location and both businesses are keen to take on the lease. They have both asked you to act for them in relation to the bid for the lease. On discovery that they were both bidding for the same lease both hairdressing businesses have, independently, offered you an additional £4,000 to act for them exclusively. Neither business is willing for you to act for both parties with respect to the lease.

(d) Show whether or not the following of your fundamental principles are threatened by the above situation

Action	Yes/No
Integrity	▼
Objectivity	▼
Confidentiality	▼
Professional competence and due care	▼
Professional behaviour	▼

The AAT Code provides general principles for ethical issues relating to taxation.

(e) Complete the following statement

The AAT Code says that 'A member providing professional tax services has a duty to put forward the best position in favour of a [▼].'

Picklist

a client or employer
the public
the tax authorities

Rakhee, an AAT member working in the charity sector, has taken on a new member of staff, Mo. Mo is frequently on the phone during normal working hours and sometimes disappears from his desk for long periods of time to make extended personal calls.

(f) What is the most appropriate action for Rakhee to take?

	✓
Escalate the matter to her line manager	☐
Report Mo to the AAT	☐
Discuss the situation with Mo and encourage him to make his phone calls outside normal working hours	☐

Task 1.10

(a) Overall responsibility for ethics in the accountancy profession rests with which of the following organisations?

	✓
IFAC	☐
IESBA	☐
CCAB	☐

A report by the Nolan Committee established **The Seven Principles of Public Life**. These are the principles we would expect holders of public office to take into consideration in their actions in public life.

(b) Which TWO of the following are one of the Seven Principles of Public Life as set out by the Nolan Committee?

	✓
Honesty	☐
Confidentiality	☐
Accountability	☐
Sensitivity	☐

The fundamental principle of professional competence and due care requires accountants to only undertake work in which they have suitable skills and experience in order to be able to complete.

(c) Show whether or not of the following types of legal action could be faced by an accountant who fails to act with sufficient expertise.

Action	Yes/No
Breach of contract	▼
Breach of trust	▼
Professional negligence	▼
Fraud accusations	▼

Lana is a self-employed accountant who specialises in carrying out bookkeeping and accountancy work for other small businesses. She has become aware that one of her clients, a self-employed electrician has been offering clients a lower rate for cash payment. The electrician is not VAT registered, but you suspect that he may be working for cash in order to avoid declaring this income on his tax return.

(d) Which of the following actions would be most appropriate for Lana to take?

	✓
Report the electrician to his trade regulatory body	☐
Cease to work on behalf of the electrician	☐
Disclose the matter publically as the matter is one of public interest	☐

Alfred is a professional accountant working in practice. He has begun to suspect one of his clients, Francois, of money laundering.

(e) Are the following statements true or false?

Statement	True	False
If Alfred does not disclose his suspicions of money laundering, then he himself will have committed a criminal offense	☐	☐
Failure to disclose money laundering suspicions can result in a fine up to £10,000	☐	☐
Alfred must ensure that he makes Francois aware that the relevant disclosures have been made	☐	☐

(f) Which of the following disclosures should Alfred make?

Protected disclosure	☐
Authorised disclosure	☐
Anonymous disclosure	☐

Task 1.11

(a) Are the following statements relating to the threat of advocacy true or false?

Statement	True	False
An accountant who is employed by an organisation is more likely to face an advocacy threat than an accountant working in practice	☐	☐
A dominant individual attempting to influence your decisions is an example of a threat of advocacy	☐	☐
The fundamental principle most likely to be compromised as the result of an advocacy threat is objectivity	☐	☐

Hannah is working on an audit engagement for a client. She is struggling to complete the work in the amount of time available and is finding that she is having to work very long days in an attempt to finish the engagement on time.

BPP
LEARNING MEDIA

(b) Which of Hannah's fundamental principles could this compromise?

	✓
Professional behaviour	☐
Professional competence and due care	☐
Integrity	☐

(c) Show whether the following offences would be prosecuted in a criminal court or heard in a civil court

Action	Criminal/Civil
Misappropriation of assets	▼
Money laundering	▼
Negligence	▼
Fraud	▼

ABC company has recently had their computer system hacked and a number of client records have disappeared from their system.

(d) Which of the following types of operational risk is presented by the above situation?

	✓
Internal fraud	☐
External fraud	☐
Systems failure	☐

Lucy has just finished an audit engagement for an events management company and has issued an unqualified report. She enjoyed the time spent with the client, in particular discussing her shared love of music festivals with some of the key staff.

At the end of the engagement, Lucy finds the following message in her inbox.

Hi Lucy,

Hope that you are well.

Thank you for your hard work in auditing our accounts and issuing an unqualified report. The whole team is really happy with the result and we would like to offer you two tickets to the sold out Magic Fields festival along with backstage passes so you can meet your favourite band.

(e) Which of the following actions should Lucy now take?

	✓
Go to the festival, it is a once in a lifetime opportunity and she knows that she carried out her work in accordance with the ethical code	☐
Inform her manager that the offer has been made to her	☐
Refuse the tickets and report the matter to AAT	☐

Peter is an accountant working in practice. He has just realised that he is caught up in a client's money laundering activities. He panics and shreds the evidence in his client's files.

(f) Which of the following statements are true?

Action	Yes/no
Peter could be found guilty of money laundering	▼
Peter could be found guilty of the offense of tipping off	▼
Peter could be found guilty of prejudicing the investigation	▼

Section 2 VAT

Task 2.1

The following tasks are based on the following workplace scenario of Notes To Go:

You are Arvo, a part-qualified accounting technician. You have recently begun to work for Notes To Go, a VAT-registered business which sells printed music.

Notes To Go is run by Max and Judith in partnership. You handle bookkeeping and VAT compliance under Judith's supervision. Another employee, Lucian, deals with customer service.

(a) Notes To Go wishes to reclaim VAT on its purchases. Are these statements true or false?

Statement	True	False
Notes To Go may reclaim VAT on its purchases through its VAT returns	☐	☐
The VAT on Notes To Go's purchases is known as output tax	☐	☐

(b) Notes To Go has purchased two items:

Standard-rated stationery for total £120
Exempt postage stamps for total £120
What is the net cost of these to Notes To Go?

Item	Net cost
Stationery	▼
Stamps	▼

Picklist

£100
£120

(c) The printed music Notes To Go sells is zero rated. Which of the following are true?

Statement	True	False
Notes To Go is making exempt supplies	☐	☐
The amount of VAT on any sale of printed music will be zero	☐	☐

(d) **Select which are advantages of Notes To Go being registered for VAT.**

	✓
Registration may improve the image of the business	☐
VAT returns need to be prepared on a regular basis	☐
VAT on Notes To Go's purchases may be reclaimed	☐

(e) **Total sales income received by Notes To Go last year was £110,000. Complete the following:**

Turnover last year was [▼] the VAT registration threshold

Picklist

above
below

Notes To Go could apply to HMRC to deregister [▼]

Picklist

because supplies are zero rated
if turnover is low enough

If Notes To Go deregistered, issuing VAT receipts in future would be [▼]

Picklist

optional
prohibited

(f) **You notice that your employer's electricity bill includes standard-rated VAT, but your own home electricity bill includes VAT at the reduced rate. Both bills are for £210 inclusive of VAT.**

Your employer's electricity bill is [▼] net of VAT

Picklist

£168
£175

Your home electricity bill is [▼] net of VAT

Picklist

£210
£200

The VAT on your home electricity bill is borne by [▼]

Picklist

yourself
HMRC

Task 2.2

The following tasks are based on the following workplace scenario of TaxTix LLP:

You are Britt, a part-qualified accounting technician. You are employed by tax accountants TaxTix LLP where you assist with bookkeeping and VAT compliance for various business clients of the firm.

(a) A client has rung TaxTix LLP to ask whether he needs purchase invoices for two items for VAT purposes. Select which he must keep:

	✓
£20 spent at a toll bridge while travelling	☐
Goods costing £35 bought from a vending machine	☐

(b) VAT records [▼] be kept electronically

Picklist

may
must

Records are to be kept for at least [▼] years

Picklist

seven
six
three

(c) Henrik, a new trainee, shows you two purchase invoices addressed to TaxTix LLP. No VAT is shown on these: Henrik asks you the amount of the VAT.

How much will the VAT be on these?	
Standard-rated consultancy services – total price £398.00	
Zero-rated food £120.00	

(d) TaxTix LLP has a few clients who are very late payers. Your manager has asked you to look for any where VAT bad debt relief may be claimed. Which of the following are conditions for this?

	✓
The debt must be more than six years overdue	☐
The input tax must have been paid by the client	☐
The output tax must have been paid to HMRC	☐

(e) **Is this statement true or false regarding VAT bad debt relief?**

Statement	True	False
Relief is claimed through the VAT return as a deduction from output tax.	☐	☐

(f) **Henrik has been asked to make the accounting entries to write off a bad debt. This was a fee of £1,000 plus £200 VAT billed to a former client. Henrik is not sure which accounts to debit and credit and asks you to assist.**

	Debit/Credit	Amount (whole £s)
Bad debts expense account		
VAT account		
Sales ledger control account		

Task 2.3

The tasks are based on the following workplace scenario of D's Doors:

You are Daisuke, a part-qualified accounting technician. You work for D's Doors, a sole trader which sells and fits doors. The business is registered for VAT. It was started by Dee but has now been taken over by her daughter Debbie.

All the supplies D's Doors makes are of standard-rated goods and services. Most of the customers of the business are individual householders but there are also some business clients.

Debbie would like to offer discounts to some customers of D's Doors.

(a) **Debbie would like to offer a 5% discount to Bizyness Ltd if they buy 20 or more doors in a single order.**

If Bizyness Ltd goes ahead and orders 20 doors at one time, the discount would be a

[▼] discount. The discount is [▼] and the value shown on

the invoice will be the [▼] amount.

Picklists

bulk
prompt payment

conditional
unconditional

discounted
undiscounted

(link to www.gov.uk/government/publications/vat-notice-700-the-vat-guide/vat-notice-700-the-vat-guide#output-tax-introduction-and-tax-value)

(b) **Debbie would like to offer a 5% discount to Harold if he buys a back door and pays within 14 days of this being fitted.**

The discount offered would be a [▼] or [▼] discount.

The discount is [▼]. It [▼] be shown on the invoice.

Picklists

bulk
prompt payment

trade
settlement

conditional
unconditional

must
need not

(c) **Harold has ordered the back door. He is not certain yet whether he will pay within 14 days of his door being fitted. Debbie would like to issue a single invoice so that no credit note is needed for early payment.**

Which of the following must the invoice show?

	✓
The deadline for payment for the discount to apply	☐
The amount of the discount	☐
The VAT on the discounted price	☐
A statement that no credit note will be issued	☐

(d) **D's Doors issues a pro forma invoice to Bizyness Ltd while they look at samples of wood before deciding whether to buy.**

Tick which statements about pro forma invoices are correct.

	✓
The pro forma invoice is not a valid VAT invoice	☐
The pro forma invoice must show the price of the goods	☐
The pro forma invoice will enable VAT to be reclaimed by the customer	☐
The pro forma invoice will be worded identically to a normal VAT invoice	☐

Task 2.4

Click on the button below to download the spreadsheet for this task.

Debbie has asked for some illustrations of how discounts affect business figures.

For each standard-rated sale, use the same value before VAT and fill in the amounts you are asked for.

Type only into shaded cells. You may use formulae.

D's Doors

Standard-rated doors offered to a customer for value £2,400.00
Discount of 10% offered for payment within 7 days
Discount of 5% offered for payment within 14 days

	Paid in 5 days' time £	Paid in 10 days' time £	Paid in 20 days' time £
Value	2,400.00	2,400.00	2,400.00
Discount %			
Discounted value			
VAT on standard-rated goods			
	_____	_____	_____
Net amount charged if maximum discount taken up	0.00		

Task 2.5

The following tasks are based on the following workplace scenario of Flora:

You are Fred, a part-qualified accounting technician. Flora is VAT registered and runs a flower shop. You are employed one day per week by Flora to assist with bookkeeping and VAT compliance

Flora decides that joining the flat-rate scheme would mean she needs much less help with her bookkeeping and VAT returns. You currently assist with these tasks. Flora asks you to calculate how much your work hours could be cut from next quarter if flat-rate returns are prepared from then on.

www.aatethics.org.uk/code/members-in-business/conflicts-of-interest/

(a)

This situation creates a conflict of interest which may affect your [▼]

Picklist

objectivity
professional competence and due care

The conflict is between your own interests and those of [▼]

Picklist

Flora
HMRC

The main threat here is a [▼] threat since you are employed and paid by Flora.

Picklist

self-interest
self-review

(b)

This conflict of interest should be disclosed to [▼].

Picklist

Flora
HMRC
The AAT

You may wish to seek advice from [▼], bearing in mind the need for confidentiality to be maintained.

Picklist

the AAT
the VAT helpline

(c)

Exaggerating the likely time needed to carry out the work Flora will want would be a

breach of [▼].

Picklist

integrity
professional competence and due care

Rushing a task to the point that work is not properly checked would be a breach of

[▼].

Picklist

objectivity
professional competence and due care

If you are unable to resolve the conflict your best option is to [▼].

Picklist

report Flora
resign

(d) Flora has realised that because business is increasing, she will need to keep your hours worked the same.

A flat-rate application has been made to HMRC. Flora has asked you to explain what will go into each box on the VAT return once you are operating the flat-rate scheme.

www.gov.uk/government/publications/vat-notice-733-flat-rate-scheme-for-small-businesses/vat-notice-733-flat-rate-scheme-for-small-businesses#keeping-records-and-filling-in-your-vat-return

VAT due in respect of UK sales will go into box [⯆] .

Picklist

1
2
3
4

Total turnover will go into box [⯆] and must [⯆] VAT.

Picklist

4
5
6
7

exclude
include

If there is a purchase of a single capital item for more than £2,000, box [⯆] may be used to show the [⯆] amount. The VAT on the capital item may be shown in box [⯆]

Picklist

VAT-exclusive
VAT-inclusive

1
2
3
4
5
6
7

A claim for bad debt relief may be shown in box [▼]

Picklist

1
2
3
4

Box 2 will show nothing:

[▼]

Picklist

True
False

....

Task 2.6

The following tasks are based on the following workplace scenario of Harpreet:

You are Charlie, a part-qualified accounting technician. You work for an accountancy practice whose clients include Harpreet. Harpreet runs a local sweet shop.

Harpreet has replaced Will with a new junior staff member, Wei. You are explaining some basic concepts of VAT to Wei.

(a)

VAT is initially collected by [▼]

VAT is eventually borne by [▼]

Picklist

HMRC
the final consumer
traders

(b)

VAT is an indirect tax because it is based on [▼]

Picklist

business profits
transactions

(c)

The sweets sold by Harpreet are [▼]

Picklist

goods
services

Which of the following are true?

Statement	True	False
We only need to charge VAT if our customers are also VAT registered	☐	☐
We do not need to charge VAT if our customers pay in cash	☐	☐

(d) Select which are correct about the 'VAT fraction'

	✓
The VAT fraction can be used to find the VAT from the gross sales price	☐
The VAT fraction for reduced-rated supplies is 5%	☐

(e) The shop has purchased two items:

Standard-rated sweets for £240
Exempt postage stamps for £240

What is the net cost of these to Notes To Go?

Item	Net cost
Stationery	▼
Stamps	▼

Picklist

£200
£240

(f)

VAT returns are usually made for [▼] .

Picklist

a year
three months

The deadline for submission is [▼] and [▼] after this.

Picklist

one month
three months

three days
seven days

The deadline for BACS or CHAPS payment is [▼] .

Picklist

one month later
the same as for the return

VAT direct debits are taken [▼] [▼] after the normal
payment deadline.

Picklist

days
seven
three
working days

···

Task 2.7

You have the following information available for Harpreet's next quarterly VAT return:

- All sales and purchases in the quarter were UK supplies
- Income from sales of sweets entered into the till totalled £16,400
- The only other sales were gross cash sales totalling £2,000. This money was not put through the till but other records were kept.
- Standard-rated purchases of sweets inclusive of VAT totalled £2,800
- Zero-rated travel cost £450
- Extra output VAT of £288 needs to be included as a correction from last quarter
- Standard-rated catering exclusive of VAT cost £459. This was spent entertaining local customers.

(a) **Enter the figures for boxes 1 to 5 of the online VAT return for the quarter. Show your working for Box 4**

VAT return for the quarter		£
VAT due in this period on sales and other outputs	Box 1	
VAT due in this period on acquisitions from other EC Member States	Box 2	
Total VAT due (the sum of boxes 1 and 2)	Box 3	
VAT reclaimed in the period on purchases and other inputs, including acquisitions from the EC	Box 4	
Net VAT to be paid to HM Revenue & Customs or reclaimed by you (Difference between boxes 3 and 4)	Box 5	

(b) Because Harpreet has spent time correcting the previous VAT return, this VAT return is being submitted late. This is the first time Harpreet has not submitted a return on time.

Explain what a surcharge liability notice is, and suggest whether the current situation will count as a 'reasonable excuse' for lateness.

Task 2.8

The following tasks are based on the following workplace scenario of Kaykes:

You are Kim, a part-qualified accounting technician. You and your brother Kevin, a professional cook, are setting up a cookery business in your spare time near your home in Manchester. You handle the bookkeeping and VAT compliance.

A possible new client has contacted Kaykes. This is a large business called Sate Ltd. Sate Ltd's financial controller asks Kevin whether you can provide full VAT invoices if they buy large numbers of cakes on repeat order.

Kevin says yes and is now asking you what needs to go onto a full VAT invoice.

Tick the following if they are elements of a full VAT invoice	✓
A sequential invoice number	☐
The time of the supply	☐
Details of the deadline for payment	☐
The date of issue of the document (where different to the time of supply)	☐
Kaykes' address	☐
Kaykes' VAT registration number as supplier	☐
The date from which Kaykes was registered for VAT	☐
A brief description of the type(s) of cake	☐
The number of each type of cake bought	☐
Sate Ltd's address	☐
Sate Ltd's Companies House registration number	☐
Sate Ltd's VAT registration number	☐
A £ sign to show the currency	☐
A note saying that the document is a pro forma	☐
The rate of VAT	☐
The total amount of VAT chargeable	☐

Task 2.9

The following tasks are based on the following workplace scenario of Mo:

You are Mo, a part-qualified accounting technician employed by EeZee plc, which produces and sells electronic equipment.

(a) Calculate the VAT which EeZee plc would pay to HMRC for the quarter based on the following figures (all net of any VAT):

- Standard-rated sales £20,000
- Exempt sales £9,000
- Standard-rated purchases of components £4,000
- Standard-rated services purchased £1,400
- Donation to charity £100
- Applicable flat rate 7.5%

(b)

The VAT payable to HMRC calculated above is shown in box [   ]

of the VAT return.

The figure shown in box 6 will be [   ] which is VAT-inclusive/exclusive.

(c) Jed is currently managing one of EeZee plc's shops.

Jed would like to set up a smaller business in his spare time, selling similar goods to EeZee plc.

He asks you to assist with his accounting.

Explain why working for both Jed and EeZee plc would create an ethical problem.

· ·

Task 2.10

The tasks are based on the following workplace scenario of Switch:

You are Nerys, a part-qualified accounting technician. You work for accountancy firm Neo Bros. At Neo Bros you work on several clients' VAT and bookkeeping, including Switch Cosmetics, a VAT-registered local shop.

Switch has taken on several new full-time staff and you have been asked to check they understand about VAT and pricing of goods for sale.

(a) You notice that Switch's financial records do not show any payments to the new staff. You raise this with Switch's financial controller. She replies:

'You're right, there's nothing in the books for the new joiners. We are paying them but I'm showing the amounts as though they are stock purchases not wages. I know it's wrong, but it means we save on PAYE and national insurance. There's a cash gift for you for keeping this quiet.'

Identify the key ethical and legal issues here and suggest who you should contact about this.

(b) A new financial controller has joined Switch Cosmetics and the business's records are now in order.

You are talking new staff through VAT using an example of typical goods.

A jar of face cream is bought by Switch from a wholesaler. The wholesaler charges

£3.00 plus standard-rated VAT at [▼] . This is [▼] VAT for Switch.

Switch pays the wholesaler a total of [ ] .

Picklists

5%
20%

input
output

Switch offers the face cream for sale for a total advertised price of £7.20. This amount

payable by customers is the [▼] . The VAT on the face cream on sale is

[ ] and this is [▼] VAT for Switch. This VAT is borne by

[▼] .

Picklists

gross price
net value

input
output

HMRC
Switch
the customer

Task 2.11

(a) You have the following information available and are asked to calculate your employer Neo Bros' own VAT payable to HMRC.

Neo Bros uses annual accounting and its VAT year is to 31 December.

- Annual sales of standard-rated services were £201,000 excluding VAT
- Staff wages outside the scope of VAT were £85,000
- Standard-rated stationery purchases inclusive of VAT totalled £2,760
- A new computer was bought for £1,800 inclusive of VAT at 20%
- Exempt travel by employees on business cost £7,100
- A car was purchased for business use costing £10,000 plus £2,000 VAT
- £250 was donated to a local charity

(b) Calculate and explain what VAT payments will be needed for next year's VAT.

(c) What is the threshold for leaving the annual accounting scheme?

Turnover of [   ]

Section 3 Advanced Bookkeeping/Final Accounts Preparation/Management Accounting: Costing

Task 3.1

Liz Turner has been trading for just over 12 months as a dressmaker. She has kept no accounting records at all, and she is worried that she may need professional help to sort out her financial position, and she has approached you.

You meet with Liz and discuss the information that you require her to give you. Sometime later, you receive a letter from Liz providing you with the information that you requested, as follows:

(i)   She started her business on 1 October 20X7. She opened a business bank account and paid in £8,000 of her savings.

(ii) During October she bought the equipment and the inventory of materials that she needed. The equipment cost £3,800 and the inventory of materials cost £2,300. All of this was paid for out of the business bank account.

(iii) A summary of the business bank account for the twelve months ended 30 September 20X8 showed the following.

	£		£
Capital	8,000	Equipment	3,800
Cash banked	32,000	Opening inventory of materials	2,300
		Purchases of materials	18,450
		General expenses	400
		Drawings	14,370
		Balance c/d	680
	40,000		40,000

(iv) All of the sales are on a cash basis. Some of the cash is paid into the bank account while the rest is used for cash expenses. She has no idea what the total value of her sales is for the year, but she knows that she has spent £3,200 on materials and £490 on general expenses. She took the rest of the cash not banked for her private drawings. She also keeps a cash float of £100.

(v)   The gross profit margin on all sales is 50%.

(vi) She estimates that all the equipment should last for five years. You therefore agree to depreciate it using the straight-line method.

(vii) On 30 September 20X8, the payables for materials amounted to £1,600.

(viii) She estimates that the cost of inventory of materials that she had left at the end of the year was £1,200.

You are required to:

(a) Calculate the total purchases for the year ended 30 September 20X8.

£ [ ]

(b) Calculate the total cost of sales for the year ended 30 September 20X8.

£ [ ]

(c) Calculate the sales for the year ended 30 September 20X8.

£ [ ]

(d) Show the entries that would appear in Liz Turner's cash account.

Cash account

Account		£	Account		£
▼			▼		
▼			▼		
▼			▼		
▼			▼		
▼			▼		
▼			▼		
▼			▼		

Picklist

Balance c/d (float)
Bank account
Drawings
General expenses
Materials
Sales

(e) Calculate the total drawings made by Liz Turner throughout the year.

£ [ ]

(f) Calculate the figure for profit for the year ended 30 September 20X8.

£ [ ]

(g) Select which of the attributes below represent the fundamental ethical principles as demonstrated in the Code of Professional Ethics. There may be more than one answer.

	✓
Integrity	☐
Selflessness	☐
Professional behaviour	☐
Objectivity	☐

Task 3.2

Green Bean Limited is a business which makes vegetarian meals for sale to supermarkets. They buy their ingredients locally and their best selling products are as follows.

	Mushroom Risotto	Veggie Paella	Pasta Bake
Sales price per unit	£3.45	£3.30	£3.80
Raw materials per unit	£0.75	£0.60	£1.10
Labour per unit	£0.30	£0.25	£0.50
Annual sales	20,000	15,000	45,000

Fixed costs for the business are £175,000 per annum. Total variable costs are £105,750 per annum.

The factory works for 50 weeks of the year, 35 hours a week.

Green Bean Limited are looking to improve their costing methods. Currently, Green Bean uses a marginal costing methodology

(a) Calculate the contribution per unit for each of the three product lines, writing the amount in the table below.

Product Line	Contribution per unit £
Mushroom Risotto	
Veggie Paella	
Pasta Bake	

Green Bean Limited is considering moving to an absorption based costing system, and they have asked you as their accountant, to explain the key differences between marginal costing and absorption costing.

(b) Write a brief summary outlining the following

(i)   What costs are included in marginal costing
(ii)   What costs are included in absorption costing
(iii) Identify any risks or benefits from using either methodology

Note: calculations are not required.

At the year end, Green Bean invests in a new piece of machinery which costs £45,480. Due to the specialist nature of this machinery, it is planned to be depreciated at a rate of 25% on a reducing balance basis. Company policy is to charge a full year's depreciation charge in the year of acquisition.

(c) Calculate the depreciation charge for the first THREE years based on a reducing balance basis.

Task 3.3

Andrews, Brown and Carter are a partnership who design and install kitchens.

You have the following information about the partnership's business:

- The financial year ends on 31 March.

- Brown and Carter each introduced a further £10,000 capital into the bank account on 1 October 20X6.

- Goodwill was valued at £80,000 on 31 March October 20X7.

- There was no interest on drawings.

	Andrew	Brown	Carter
Profit share, for the period	40%	30%	30%
Capital account balances at 1 April 20X6	£40,000	£30,000	£30,000
Current account balances at 1 April 20X6	£1,160 credit	£420 credit	£5,570 credit
Drawings for the year ended 31 March 20X7	£2,500 each month	£38,000	£45,000

The appropriation account for the year ended 31 March 20X7 has already been prepared by the accountant.

Partnership appropriation account for the year ended 31 March 20X7

	Total £
Profit for appropriation	156,000
Salaries:	
Andrew	15,000
Brown	18,000
Carter	24,000
Interest on capital:	
Andrew	2,860
Brown	1,980
Carter	1,980
Profit available for distribution	92,180

	Total £
Profit shares:	
Andrew	39,536
Brown	27,654
Carter	24,990
Total profit distributed	92,180

(a) **Prepare the current accounts for the partners for the year ended 31 March 20X7. Show clearly the balance carried down. You MUST enter zeros where appropriate in order to obtain full marks. Do NOT use brackets, minus signs or dashes.**

Current accounts

	Andrew £	Brown £	Carter £		Andrew £	Brown £	Carter £
▼				▼			
▼				▼			
▼				▼			
▼				▼			
▼				▼			
▼				▼			

Picklist

Balance b/d
Balance c/d
Capital – Andrew
Capital – Brown
Capital – Carter
Current – Andrew
Current – Brown
Current – Carter
Drawings
Goodwill
Interest on capital
Salaries
Share of profit or loss

(b) Indicate whether the following statements are true or false.

Statement	True	False
An error of commission does not cause an imbalance in the trial balance	☐	☐
The suspense account can appear in the financial statements	☐	☐
An error of principle causes an imbalance in the trial balance	☐	☐
A trial balance is prepared before the financial statements	☐	☐

(c) A manager has control over the costs and revenues but not the assets of their division. What type of responsibility centre is this?

	✓
Cost centre	☐
Investment centre	☐
Profit centre	☐

Task 3.4

You are preparing the year end accounting records for Thomas Brand, who is a sole trader and has a plumbing business.

Thomas' friend, Bill Bailey, did a few months of an accountancy course and decided he would be able to do Thomas' accounts for him. However, Bill has decided that the business is too complex, so Thomas has brought the accounts to Blithe & Co Accountants.

Bill has drafted a trial balance as at 31 December 20XX. However, you discover a number of items which need to be recorded in the accounts.

Account	Debit £	Credit £
Bank	22,450	
Capital		13,200
Purchase ledger control account		4,095
Sales ledger control account	6,725	
Sales		45,200
Purchases	32,570	
Administration costs	750	
	62,495	62,495

A number of items require your attention

- A new vehicle has been acquired for £16,200. It is expected to be sold after five years for £3,800. Vehicles will be depreciated on a straight line basis, with a full year's depreciation in the year of acquisition.

- Sales for December of £1,700 have not yet been recorded. The customer had not paid his invoice at year end.

- A customer paid his outstanding invoice of £800 on 31 December, and this has not yet been recorded.

- Drawings of £1,600 have not yet been recorded in the accounts.

(a) **Calculate the depreciation charge for the year on the new vehicle.**

£ [   ]

(b) **Complete the journal entries using the picklist below, for the acquisition of the new vehicle.**

Details		£	Debit ✓	Credit ✓
	▼			
	▼			

Picklist

Accumulated depreciation
Bank
Depreciation expense
Purchase ledger control account
Sales ledger control account
Vehicle cost

(c) **Complete the journal entry, using the picklist below, for the depreciation charge on the new vehicle.**

Details		£	Debit ✓	Credit ✓
	▼			
	▼			

Picklist

Accumulated depreciation
Bank
Depreciation expense
Purchase ledger control account
Sales ledger control account
Vehicle cost

(d) Complete the extended trial balance below, including your information calculated in parts (b) and (c) and the missing information in the narrative in respect of sales, drawings and trade receivables. Calculate the totals at the bottom of the debit and credit columns in your final trial balance.

	Ledger balance			Trial Balance	
Account	Debit £	Credit £	Adjustments £	Debit £	Credit £
Bank	22,450				
Capital		13,200			
Purchase ledger control account		4,095			
Sales ledger control account	6,725				
Sales		45,200			
Purchases	32,570				
Administration costs	750				
Drawings					
Vehicles – Cost					
Vehicles Accumulated depreciation					
Depreciation expense					
Totals	62,495	62,495			

(e) State THREE reasons for drawing up financial statements, stating TWO possible users of Thomas' sole trader accounts.

```



```

....

Task 3.5

Besta Bikes is a small business which makes bespoke road bikes. The following information is available regarding the cost to make the RX400 road bike.

These are their budgeted costs for year commencing 1 January 20XX

Direct materials	£340 per unit
Direct labour	5 hours @ £14 per hour per unit
Rental of the warehouse	£240,000 per annum

The partnership expects to make and sell 400 bikes in the next year. Each bike retails at £1,700.

(a) Calculate the contribution per road bike. Show your workings.

(b) Calculate the cost per unit on a marginal costing basis. Show your workings.

(c) Calculate the cost per unit if absorption costing method is used. Show your workings.

The partnership is drawing up its year end accounts to 31 December 20XX. They have manufactured 400 bikes as per budget, but sold only 320.

(d) **Calculate the profit or loss for the year based upon the marginal costing basis.**

(e) **Calculate the profit or loss for the year based upon the absorption costing basis.**

(f) **The two fundamental qualitative characteristics of financial information, according to the IASB's *Conceptual Framework* are:**

☐ and ☐

Task 3.6

James Doolittle is a sole trader who has prepared the following trial balance for his business.

	Debit £	Credit £
Bank	11,950	
Capital		74,300
Payables		40,800
Receivables	35,450	
Provision for doubtful debts		3,200
Drawings	19,000	
Fixtures and Fittings	24,500	
Electricity	2,050	
Insurance	2,800	
Miscellaneous expenses	1,500	
Motor expenses	3,100	
Motor vehicles at cost	48,000	
Purchases	245,000	
Accumulated depreciation – fixtures and fittings		8,550
– motor vehicles		29,800
Rent	3,400	
Sales		344,450
Opening inventory	40,200	
Telephone costs	1,950	
VAT		3,050
Wages	54,750	
Closing inventory	43,500	43,500
Depreciation expense – fixtures and fittings	2,450	
Depreciation expense – motor vehicles	7,800	
Accruals		1,000
Prepayments	1,250	
	548,650	548,650

(a) **Prepare the statement of financial position as at 31 March 20YY based on the information in the trial balance.**

	Cost £	Accumulated depreciation £	Carrying amount £
Non-current assets			
Current assets			
Current liabilities			
Net current assets			
Net assets			
Financed by:			

Picklist

Accruals
Capital
Cash and cash equivalents
Closing inventory
Depreciation charges
Drawings
Electricity
Fixtures & Fittings
Insurance
Miscellaneous expenses
Motor expenses
Motor vehicles
Opening inventory
Prepayments
Profit for the year
Purchases
Rent
Sales
Telephone
Trade payables
Trade receivables
VAT
Wages

James is looking to improve the operational information for his business and has been reading lots of business books, however, he is confused about the difference between relevant costs and irrelevant costs.

James is looking to launch a new product, the K57. It will be manufactured on existing machinery, but two new members of staff will need to be employed and trained to do the work as the business is already at capacity. The premises are large enough to take the new machinery, but a new warehouse will be rented to store the new product

He has drawn up a list of his costs, and needs help identifying which costs are relevant and which are irrelevant.

(b) Select the correct box identifying which are relevant or irrelevant costs for James' decision making for the K57 product.

	Relevant cost ✓	Irrelevant cost ✓
Cost of the machinery used to manufacture the K57		
Salaries of the new staff		
Rent on the new storage facility		
Rent on the manufacturing premises		

James has also heard of the term 'Breakeven point' but is not sure what it means.

(c) **Briefly explain what the term means, giving the formula required to calculate the breakeven point in units.**

Task 3.7

Wahleed Mansoor is a sole trader who manufacturers skateboards. The following information has been provided about events on the last day of the year:

- Minor Limited, a customer with a receivable outstanding of £950 has gone into liquidation. It is not expected that this debt will be recoverable.

- A new machine is purchased for £5,000. It will have a useful life of 5 years, and a full year of depreciation is charged in the first year of acquisition. The purchase of the machine has been entered into the trial balance, however, the depreciation has not yet been calculated.

	Debit £	Credit £
Bank	11,950	
Capital		74,300
Payables		40,800
Receivables	35,450	
Discounts allowed	950	
Discounts received		250
Drawings	16,100	
Machinery	24,500	
Electricity	2,050	

	Debit £	Credit £
Insurance	1,800	
Miscellaneous expenses	1,500	
Motor expenses	3,100	
Motor vehicles at cost	48,000	
Purchases	245,000	
Accumulated depreciation – machinery		8,550
– motor vehicles		29,800
Rent	3,400	
Sales		344,450
Opening inventory	40,200	
Telephone costs	1,950	
VAT		3,300
Wages	54,750	
Closing inventory	43,500	43,500
Depreciation expense – machinery	2,450	
Depreciation expense – motor vehicles	7,800	
Accruals		1,000
Prepayments	1,500	
	545,950	545,950

(a) **Prepare the journal for the doubtful debt provision against the debt of Minor Limited.**

Details	Debit £	Credit £

Picklist

Bank
Doubtful debt expense
Doubtful debt provision
Sales ledger control account

(b) **Calculate the depreciation charge for the year ended 31 December 20XX.**

£ [   ]

(c) **Prepare the journal for the depreciation charge as calculated in part (b).**

Details	Debit £	Credit £

Picklist

Accumulated depreciation
Depreciation expense

(d) Prepare Wahleed's statement of profit or loss for the year ended 31 December 20XX.

	£	£
Sales revenue		
Cost of goods sold		
Gross profit		
Add:		
Less:		
Total expenses		
Profit/loss for the year		

Picklist

Accruals
Capital
Cash and cash equivalents
Closing inventory
Depreciation charges
Discounts allowed
Discounts received
Disposal of non-current asset
Drawings
Electricity
Insurance
Miscellaneous expenses
Motor expenses
Opening inventory
Prepayments
Purchases
Rent
Sales
Telephone
Trade payables
Trade receivables
VAT
Wages

The new machine purchased on 31 December 20XX can make the new Trooper skateboard. The following information is available

Sales price per unit	£30
Direct materials	£8.00 per unit
Direct labour	£10.00 per hour. Each unit takes 15 minutes of labour time.
Budgeted sales	250 units

(e) Calculate the total contribution of the Trooper skateboard if the budgeted sales are met in the following year.

£ _____

....

Task 3.8

Joan, Emily and Kate are in partnership sharing profits equally. Emily is allowed a salary of £8,000 per annum and all partners receive interest on their capital balances at 5% per annum.

Given below is the final trial balance of the partnership between Joan, Emily and Kate at 30 June 20X8.

Final trial balance

	Debit £	Credit £
Advertising	3,140	
Bank	4,400	
Capital Joan		25,000
Emily		15,000
Kate		10,000
Payables		33,100
Current accounts Joan		1,000
Emily		540
Kate		230
Receivables	50,000	
Drawings Joan	18,195	
Emily	25,000	
Kate	12,000	
Electricity	4,260	
Furniture and fittings at cost	12,500	
Furniture and fittings – accumulated depreciation		7,025
Insurance	2,600	
Machinery at cost	38,000	
Machinery – accumulated depreciation		23,300
Allowance for doubtful debts		2,500
Cost of goods sold	208,800	
Sales		344,195
Sundry expenses	3,180	

	Debit £	Credit £
Telephone expenses	2,150	
VAT		1,910
Wages	43,200	
Inventory at 30 June 20X8	24,100	
Depreciation expense – machinery	7,600	
Depreciation expense – furniture and fittings	1,825	
Irrecoverable debts expense	2,550	
Accruals		400
Prepayments	700	
	464,200	464,200

(a) **Prepare the statement of profit or loss for the year ended 30 June 20X8.**

Statement of profit or loss for the year ended 30 June 20X8

	£	£
Sales revenue		
Cost of goods sold		
Gross profit		
Less: Expenses		
Total expenses		
Profit for the year		64,890

Picklist

Advertising
Depreciation furniture and fittings
Depreciation machinery
Electricity
Insurance
Irrecoverable debt expense
Sundry expenses
Telephone
Wages

(b) **Write up the profit appropriation account for the partnership as at 30 June 20X8.**

	£
Net profit	
Salaries:	
Emily	
Interest on capital	
Joan	
Emily	
Kate	
Profit available for distribution	
Profit share	
Joan	
Emily	
Kate	

(c) Complete the partners' current accounts showing their share of profits and their drawings. Show the balance b/d on 1 July 20X8. Use the picklist provided.

Current account – Joan

	£		£

Current account – Emily

	£		£

Current account – Kate

	£		£

Picklist

Balance b/f
Balance c/d
Balance b/d
Drawings
Interest on capital
Profit
Salary

(d) The partnership currently operates a FIFO inventory system, select which ONE of the following statements is correct regarding this system.

	✓
FIFO values inventory at the higher values when the market prices are rising	
FIFO values inventory at the lower value when market prices are rising	
FIFO is the most appropriate method of valuation when inventories are mixed when stored.	
FIFO smoothes out price fluctuations making it easier to use the data for decision making	

Task 3.9

Bella Parker is a sole trader who sells wooden toys. She has drawn up her trial balance at the end of the year 31 December 20YY.

	Debit £	Credit £
Sales		265,500
Purchases	143,250	
Opening inventory	10,000	
Closing inventory	13,500	13,500
Office expenses	750	
Insurance	1,400	
Drawings	24,000	
Trade receivable	1,200	
Trade payable		1,350
Accruals		3,200
Prepayments	900	
Capital	70,000	
Cash at bank	16,050	
Suspense	2,500	
	283,550	283,550

The following items were noted:

- Drawings of £2,000 were correctly credited to the bank account, however, no entry was made on the drawings account.

- Cash sales of £500 were banked, however, Bella forgot to include them in the sales account.

- An insurance invoice was posted correctly to the trade payables account, however, the entry was then credited to the insurance account. The invoice was for £500.

- A van was purchased for £8,000 on the last day of the year. It is expected to last 5 years after which it will be sold for scrap for £500. A full year's depreciation will be charged in the year of acquisition.

(a) **Using the information in the narrative above, show the correcting entries in the suspense account below which clear the account.**

Suspense Account

Details	£	Details	£

Picklist

Balance b/f
Balance c/d
Drawings
Insurance
Sales

(b) **Calculate the depreciation charge for the van.**

£ [   ]

(c) Enter the adjustments into the extended trial balance below, showing the revised figures for the draft financial statements.

	Initial trial balance		Adjustments	Revised trial balance	
	Debit £	Credit £			
Sales		265,500			
Purchases	143,250				
Opening inventory	10,000				
Closing inventory	13,500	13,500			
Office expenses	750				
Insurance	1,400				
Drawings	24,000				
Trade receivable	1,200				
Trade payable		1,350			
Accruals		3,200			
Prepayments	900				
Capital	70,000				
Cash at bank	16,050				
Suspense	2,500				
Motor vehicle					
Depreciation expense					
Accumulated depreciation					
	283,550	283,550			

(d) Calculate the gross profit of Bella's business for the year ended 31 December 20YY.

£ [ ]

(e) Identify the point marked 'A' in the graph below.

[ ]

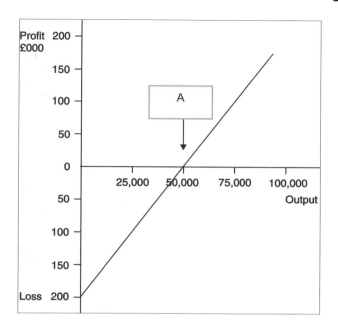

Task 3.10

Bill Barton has a business making clay based paints, which is a high quality product sold to independent decorating stores. He makes the paint in a small factory unit which employs 4 people. He is a sole trader.

The information about the product is supplied below

Claypaint sale price	£48.00 per unit
Direct materials	£18.00 per unit
Direct labour	£6.00 per unit

Each unit takes half an hour of labour throughout the whole process from machine set up to quality control.

Fixed costs are £102,000 per annum. Budgeted sales for the next year are 5,000.

(a) Calculate the breakeven point for the number of units to be sold

	units

(b) Calculate the margin of safety

	%

(c) Calculate the contribution per unit of the claypaint

£	

Bill is looking to attract a new investor, a local businessman, who would be able to launch the product nationwide and to larger stores. However, the businessman will only invest if the profit is at least £73,200.

(d) Calculate the number of units required to be produced to provide the profit required by the investor (assuming all costs remain the same)

	units

Bill's potential investor has asked to see his financial statements for the past two years. The investor has explained that he wants to ensure the business is a 'going concern', but Bill is unsure what that term means.

(e) Select which ONE of the following statements which best explains the term 'going concern'.

	✓
The effect of transactions being recognized when they occur	
That the business will continue in operation for the foreseeable future	
To ensure similar businesses can be compared to allow for investors to assess them	
To ensure the financial statements have been prepared on time	

If Bill goes into business with his new investor, they are going to become a Limited Liability Partnership.

(f) List THREE differences which Bill must be aware of if his business becomes a LLP, compared to his current status as a sole trader.

Section 4 Ethics for Accountants/ Final Accounts Preparation

Task 4.1

Tara is updating an extended trial balance for bank and cash details when she discovers that the petty cash records do not reconcile with the petty cash receipts that have been filed. It appears that over a course of time one person has been over claiming travel expenses.

(a) What is the ethical principle breached here?

(b) What action is required in these circumstances?

(c) Explain the accruals and going-concern concepts.

Task 4.2

While producing a set of accounts for a partnership Tomaz identifies that entertainment expenses have increased by 500% from previous years. On further investigation Tomaz discovers the partnership previously had two people required for expense authorisation. One to raise an expense claim and another to check and authorise the claim but now only one individual raises the claim and authorises payment.

(a) Identify the threats and ethical principle that are most at risk here.

(b) What safeguards can be put in place to reduce the risks that Tomaz faces?

(c) What are the typical contents of a partnership agreement?

Task 4.3

When a partner joins or leaves a partnership there will be a number of procedures to be made to the partnership accounts. These can include adjustments to amounts in the capital accounts and also a new agreements on the profit share ratio. One adjustment that may be needed is to goodwill.

(a) Explain what is meant by goodwill.

(b) What ethical principle is most at risk with goodwill valuations and suggest a safeguard that could help reduce your chosen risk.

(c) Outline the procedures for accounting for goodwill when a new partner joins a partnership.

Task 4.4

Jemima works as an accounts assistant in a mid-sized accountancy firm and her work has so far involved the preparation of financial statements for sole traders. Her supervisor has now requested for Jemima to prepare a set of financial statements for limited company without any additional training.

(a) According to the Code of Professional Ethics identify the ethical principle that Jemima is most at risk if she undertakes this work.

(b) Outline the safeguards that Jemima can follow to reduce the risk of any breach of ethical principles.

There are a number of key differences between the preparation of accounts for sole trader and companies.

(c) Outline the key differences between sole trader and company account preparation.

Task 4.5

(a) What is meant by the term materiality?

A large business has set its materiality level at £5,000 and it has been discovered that two purchase invoices have been fraudulently raised and paid to a member of staff. Each invoice was worth £1,000. A colleague has stated as these amounts are well below the materiality threshold level set there is no need to follow this issue up or investigate further.

(b) How should you respond to your colleague?

Useful financial information will need to possess certain qualitative characteristics.

(c) Outline four qualitative characteristics that help make financial information useful to users.

Task 4.6

Amy is an accounting technician and is in the process of preparing a set of accounts for a sole trader, ABC Supplies. While collecting sales revenue information a customer telephones and asks for Amy to email across other customer details of ABC Supplies. He says he wants this information to be more competitive and without it he may have to take his custom elsewhere.

(a) **What ethical principle and threat are most relevant here?**

(b) **What should Amy do in these circumstance and identify when Amy could disclose customer information.**

The owner of ABC Supplies is considering taking in a partner and operating as a partnership.

(c) **Explain the advantages and disadvantages of operating as a partnership.**

Task 4.7

When preparing a set of final accounts it is important for the preparer to be aware for any potential conflict of interests.

(a) **Explain what is meant by a conflict of interest.**

(b) **What is the appropriate procedure for dealing with potential conflicts of interest?**

Jaz is an accountant in a large accountancy practice and is the process of preparing the final accounts for two separate clients, A and B. After reviewing a member of her staff's working papers Jaz discovers that client A has made a substantial loan (£1m) to B. Jaz is fully aware that B is facing serious financial difficulties and there are doubts whether B will continue to be a going-concern in the foreseeable future.

(c) **What is the threat that Jaz is facing here and suggest safeguards that Jaz can put in place?**

Task 4.8

(a) **When preparing financial statements for a sole trader explain what is meant by the term 'Capital'.**

A sole trader has a capital balance of £56,730 on 1 January 20X6. During the year ended 31 December 20X6 the business made a profit of £38,920 and the owner withdrew cash totalling £24,650 along with inventories taken for personal use amounting to £3,000.

(b) **Calculate the capital balance at 31 December 20X6.**

X and Y are partners in a business selling laptop computers. Both partners have signed a partnership agreement that permits drawings to be made in cash at the end of the financial year. During the most recent reporting period Y has taken a laptop computer for his own personal use and this has not been recorded anywhere in the partnership accounts. X has not informed Y that he has taken this laptop.

(c) **Explain the consequences of Y's actions on the partnership.**

Task 4.9

A business trading as a sole trader or a partnership will be financed by capital invested into the business by its owners and money taken out of the business for the benefit of the owners will be in the form of drawings.

(a) **Looking at capital and drawings explain how this differs from an organisation trading as a limited company?**

An accountant has prepared a limited company set of accounts that has an inflated equity figure effectively overvaluing the company by a considerable amount. This value was used to secure a substantial bank loan. The company has since ceased to trade with the loss of many jobs. After financial press interest in the matter it was found the accountant did not perform the necessary checks to see if his reported equity figure was correct even though equity had increased to £2m from just £25,000 reported in the previous year.

(b) **Identify the two ethical principles that are most at risk here.**

(c) **Explain what is meant by the term professional scepticism.**

Task 4.10

Buildings, machinery, IT equipment and goods purchased for resale are assets which typically have a substantial value in a business. To help reduce the risk of any material misstatement in the final accounts there are two accounting standards that provide guidance on valuation of these types of assets.

Required

(a) Identify the two accounting standards that provide guidance on the accounting treatment of non-current assets such as buildings and current assets of goods purchases for resale.

(b) If an accountant did not keep up to date with changes in accounting standards what ethical principle would be most at risk?

(c) How can an accountant keep up to date with changes in the accountancy profession and identity the consequences when skills are not up to date.

Section 5 Spreadsheets for Accounting

Task 5.1

BetterYou is a company which provides short training courses in mindfulness.

The training courses are delivered in person to small groups of individuals. There are four trainers, Alex, Janine, Simone and Karesh. They are responsible for recruiting individuals to attend their courses.

BetterYou offers four training packages. Level 1, Level 2 and Level 3 are progressive one day courses. Level 2 can only be attended on completion of Level 1, and Level 3 can only be attended on completion of Level 2.

The fourth package 'Complete Mindfulness' incorporates Levels 1-3 and is provided at a reduced cost compared to booking the courses individually. The learner pays for the whole course up front then books on the individual courses as they progress through the levels.

You have been given a spreadsheet **BetterYou.xls** which shows sales figures achieved by each trainer for the April-June quarter in 20X6. It contains two worksheets: 'Sales' and 'Price structure'.

Download this spreadsheet file from www.bpp.com/aatspreadsheets and save in the appropriate location. Rename it using the following format: **'your initial-surname-AAT no –dd.mm.yy-Task5.1'**.

For example: J-Donnovan-123456-12.03xx-Task5.1

A **high degree of accuracy** is required. You **must save your work as an .XLS or .XLSX file** at regular intervals to avoid losing your work.

- Open the renamed spreadsheet and on the 'sales' worksheet insert a column between the columns 'course' and 'units'
  - Give the column the title 'unit price'
  - Use a lookup function to insert the unit price on the sales tab.
- Add a column in column F called 'Total value' and apply a formula to all cells in that column to show the total value of the units sold in each row.
  - Split the screen so that the headings remain visible.
  - Use the autosum function in cell F50 to determine the total values of sales for the quarter.
  - Format the numbers in this column to contain a thousand separator and make the contents of cell F50 bold.
- Create a pivot table and pivot chart showing the total value of sales, broken down by course, made by each of Alex, Janine, Simone and Karesh.
  - Place the pivot table and pivot chart on a new sheet, and rename this sheet 'Total Values'
  - Add a chart title 'Total sales value Apr-Jun'

If any of the trainers manage to recruit 20 or more individuals on to any of the courses in a month, that trainer will receive a bonus of £5 per individual booked on that course.

- Give column G the heading 'Bonus' and use an IF function to show the amount of bonus payments due.
  - Total all bonuses to be paid.
  - Create a pivot table in a new worksheet which shows the total bonus to be paid to each trainer
  - Sort the data in this pivot table to arrange the trainers in ascending order in terms of the bonus payment due to them for the quarter
  - Rename the worksheet 'Bonuses'
- Password protect the entire workbook and using the password Better123

Task 5.2

You have been given a spreadsheet **FinanceTeam.xls** which shows qualification details of members of the finance team at ABC co. It contains two worksheets: 'Finance Team' and 'Subs'.

Download this spreadsheet file from www.bpp.com/aatspreadsheets and save in the appropriate location. Rename it using the following format: **'your initial-surname-AAT no –dd.mm.yy-Task5.2'**.

For example: J-Donnovan-123456-12.03xx-Task5.2

A **high degree of accuracy** is required. You **must save your work as an .XLS or .XLSX file** at regular intervals to avoid losing your work.

- Open the renamed spreadsheet and open the subs worksheet
  - Format the data on this page as a table, include the headings
  - On the finance team worksheet, use a LOOKUP function to complete the subs column
  - Format the subs figures in a red font colour

ABC company offers free health check-ups to all employees aged 40 or older.

- Use conditional formatting to highlight all employees aged 40 and over.
  - Sort the data based on employee number, from lowest to highest.

ABC company employees are given 24 days of holiday per year. When they have served at the company for 5 or more years, they receive an additional 5 days leave per year.

- Rename column J as 'holiday'.
  - Use an IF statement to complete the data in this column to show how many days holiday per year to which each individual is entitled.
- Format the data as a table with light blue shading
  - Use the filter function to display only individuals who are members or students of the AAT who have not yet paid their subs.

Task 5.3

You have been given a spreadsheet **Orders.xls** which shows an extract of a spreadsheet of purchases made by various departments in the organisation. It contains one worksheet: sheet 1.

Download this spreadsheet file from www.bpp.com/aatspreadsheets and save in the appropriate location. Rename it using the following format: **'your initial-surname-AAT no –dd.mm.yy-Task5.3'**.

For example: J-Donnovan-123456-12.03xx-Task5.3

A **high degree of accuracy** is required. You must save your work as an .XLS or .XLSX file at regular intervals to avoid losing your work.

Since this spreadsheet was prepared, the company 'Cater Co' has been rebranded and the name of the company has changed to 'Corporate Catering Company'.

- Open the renamed spreadsheet
    - Use find and replace to update any cells which refer to 'Cater co' to show the new name of the company
    - Rename the worksheet 'order list'
- Create a pivot table and pivot chart in a new worksheet to represented the amount spent with each supplier
    - Rename the chart as 'Spend per supplier'
    - Rename the worksheet 'Supplier spend' and ensure the order of the worksheets is such that the order list worksheet is on the left and the supplier spend worksheet is on the right.
- Return to the Order List worksheet and format the data as a table using data style medium 14
- Select the entire worksheet, copy the contents and paste this into a new worksheet
    - Rename the new worksheet 'Sales team order summary'
    - Apply filters to the data to show only data relating to orders raised by the sales team
- Merge cells A1:E1 and add the text 'Sales Department Order Summary'
    - Change the font size in the merged cell to 16 and centre the text
    - Use the fill function to make the merged cell dark green and change the font colour in this cell to white
    - Remove the gridlines
- Prepare the document for being sent to the sales team. It is important that the sales team can see only their worksheet and none of the workings or data for the other departments
    - Hide the worksheets 'Order list' and 'Supplier Spend'
    - Protect the workbook so that no changes can be made to the source data and the hidden sheets remain hidden (greyed out if attempt to unhide)
    - Use the SaveAs feature to save a copy of this version of the spreadsheet called 'Sales Team Order Summary'

Task 5.4

You have been given a spreadsheet **Inventory.xls** which shows stock held at a distribution centre. It contains four worksheets: 'Inventory list', 'Locations', 'Price List' and 'Order June 20X6'.

Download this spreadsheet file from www.bpp.com/aatspreadsheets and save in the appropriate location. Rename it using the following format: **'your initial-surname-AAT no –dd.mm.yy-Task5.4'**.

For example: J-Donnovan-123456-12.03xx-Task5.4

A **high degree of accuracy** is required. You **must save your work as an .XLS or .XLSX file** at regular intervals to avoid losing your work.

- Open the renamed spreadsheet and go into the location tab

  - Rename column E as location code and format the cell to be the same as the others in this row

  - Create a location code in cell E2 comprising of the aisle, location and bin number, eg 1A3.

  - Apply this formula to all relevant cells in column E.

- Open the inventory list worksheet and use lookup functions to complete

  - The location information in column B
  - The unit price information in column C
  - Insert a formula to calculate the value of each item of inventory in column E

- Insert an function to determine whether or not items are due to be re-ordered in column G.

  - If the item is above the re-order level, this should return the value 0. If the item is on or under the re-order level, this should return the value 1.

- Format the data contained in cells B1:H22 as a table, using Table style medium 14

  - Format cells A1:A22 using the fill function to change the cell colour to blue grey, accent 6, darker 25%, and change the font colour to white to make it more visible.

  - Hide the gridlines to improve the look of the worksheet

  - Sort the data by using the filter on column H to remove all items that have been discontinued

  - Hide column H

- Use the filter function to show only those items that need to be reordered

  - Copy and paste the relevant items on to the Order June 20X6 worksheet to create an order list.

  - Ensure you do not copy over the table format to the new order list

Task 5.5 (10 marks)

You have been given a spreadsheet **Timesheet.xls** which is used by employees of ABC Co. to record the hours they have worked and where they have spent their time. Your spreadsheet currently contains one worksheet: Week 1. This contains details of the time spent by one employee, Harrison, during that week.

Download this spreadsheet file from www.bpp.com/aatspreadsheets and save in the appropriate location. Rename it using the following format: **'your initial-surname-AAT no –dd.mm.yy-Task5.5'**.

For example: J-Donnovan-123456-12.03xx-Task5.5

A **high degree of accuracy** is required. You **must save your work as an .XLS or .XLSX file** at regular intervals to avoid losing your work.

ABC company operates a flexitime system. It counts one working day to be 7.5 hours long. However, employees can work more or fewer hours in any given day, so long as the time is made up elsewhere. If employees accumulate 7.5 hours of flexitime, they can choose to take a 'flexi-day'. A flexi-day is a day off in lieu of the time that has been worked to accumulate these hours and, from the employees point of view, works like an additional day of annual leave.

- Open the renamed spreadsheet

  - Add a formula to cell C30 to calculate the amount of flexi-time earned or used on Monday. Apply this formula to the rest of the days of the week.

  - Add a formula to cell C31 to calculate the current balance of flexitime on Monday. Apply this formula to the rest of the days of the week.

  - Replace the formulas in cells I25 and I28 with more robust formulas to check for errors in the summing of data

As part of the flexi-time system, employees are not allowed to work for less than six hours in any given day.

- Use a data validation function in cells C28:G28 to identify any days where less than six hours are worked.

  - Set the data validation to circle in red any days where fewer than six hours have been worked

Employees are also not allowed to charge more than two hours to the admin account in any given day.

- Use a data validation function to prevent more than two hours of admin being charged on any given day

  - Attempt to change the admin charge on Monday to three hours.

You are given the following information about Harrison's working patterns for the following two weeks:

In week two, Harrison was on annual leave all five days.

In week three, Harrison attended a training course for 8 hours on both Monday and Tuesday. On Wednesday he charged 3 hours to each of projects 1 and 2 and 2 hours to

admin. On Thursday he charged 4 hours to project 1, 3 hours to supervision and 2 hours to admin. On Friday he charged 7 hours to project 3 and one hour to admin.

- Insert two new worksheets

  - Change the name of the new worksheets to 'Week 2' and 'Week 3'

  - Copy the format and formulas used on Week 1 to Week 2 and Week 3 and populate the spreadsheets with the information given above.

  - Link the formula related to flexi-time to ensure the balance from week 1 is carried over to week 2 and so on.

- Insert a new worksheet and rename it 'Summary'

  - Use the data from weeks 1-3 to produce a summary sheet which collates the total number of hours charged to each activity per week.

  - Format the summary sheet in the same style as the weekly worksheets

  - Use the split function to keep the header rows in place

Task 5.6

You have been given a spreadsheet **Sickness.xls** which shows an extract from a record of employee sick leave taken. It contains two worksheets: 'Record' and 'Employee names'.

Download this spreadsheet file from www.bpp.com/aatspreadsheets and save in the appropriate location. Rename it using the following format: **'your initial-surname-AAT no –dd.mm.yy-Task5.2'**.

For example: J-Donnovan-123456-12.03xx-Task5.2

A **high degree of accuracy** is required. You **must save your work as an .XLS or .XLSX file** at regular intervals to avoid losing your work.

- Open the renamed spreadsheet and go into the Record tab

  - Use a lookup function to complete the employee name column

Sickness certificates from a medical professional are required in order to verify any sickness period in excess of 5 days.

- Use an IF statement in column I along with a lookup function in column E to determine whether or not a certificate is required.

  - The IF statement should return the values 0 for no and 1 for yes and the lookup should refer to the table in columns J and K.

  - Hide columns I, J and K

Employees should not take more than 15 sickness days in total per year.

- Insert a pivot table on a new worksheet which summarises the total number of sickness days taken by each employee.

  - Rename this worksheet 'Summary'

Employees are a cause for concern for the organisation if they take frequent short periods of sickness.

- Return to the 'Record' worksheet and sort the data by employee number

  - Use a subtotal function to count the instances of sickness taken by each individual

  - Highlight the entire worksheet and apply conditional formatting to highlight the employee number of any individuals who are at risk of falling into the frequent sickness category

Task 5.7

You have been given a spreadsheet **TestResults.xls** which shows scores achieved by students in four tests and an overall score. It contains one worksheet: 'Test Results'

Download this spreadsheet file from www.bpp.com/aatspreadsheets and save in the appropriate location. Rename it using the following format: **'your initial-surname-AAT no –dd.mm.yy-Task5.7'**.

For example: J-Donnovan-123456-12.03xx-Task5.7

A **high degree of accuracy** is required. You **must save your work as an .XLS or .XLSX file** at regular intervals to avoid losing your work.

- Open the renamed spreadsheet

  - Run a data validation test to remove any duplicate entries

- Prepare a histogram based on the overall scores achieved by the students

  - The bins used should be in intervals of 10, beginning with 100
  - Change the axis to 'No. students' and 'total score'
  - Change the title of the histogram to 'Overall score analysis'

Students who have scored over 140 are considered suitable candidates for a scholarship. The five highest scoring students will automatically gain a place in the scholarship program. There are ten places available. The remaining students who fall into this category will be offered an interview for this program.

- Return to worksheet 'test results' and format the data as a table using table style medium 12

  - Use the filters within the table to identify only those students who will be offered an interview for the scholarship program.

  - Reorder the data using the filter to rank the potential scholarship candidates from highest scoring to lowest scoring

- Add a column called 'outcome' in column H

  - Insert the text 'Scholarship' in this column next to the top 5 students, and Interview against the remaining students

- – Remove the filters, and then refilter to show only students who are below average.
- – Add the text Refer in the outcome box for these students
- – Remove the filters
- – Filter using the outcome filter to identify all students who have passed the tests but who are not contenders for the scholarship program
- Password protect the entire workbook and using the password Test123

Section 6 Spreadsheets for Accounting/Management Accounting: Costing

Task 6.1

You are Ian Chesterton, a part-qualified accounting technician. You work for Hammond Co, which manufactures luxury office furniture.

You cover all aspects of bookkeeping and accounting for the business. You report to Tom Howard, Chief Accountant.

Today's date is 3 January 20X0.

The board of Hammond Co is currently considering an investment in new plant and machinery, which will enable the company to sell a more comfortable make of its office chair. The board will make a decision about this next week. The investment will take place immediately afterwards if the board decides to go ahead.

You have been asked to produce an analysis for the board meeting of this investment, using the net present value (NPV) and payback methods of investment appraisal. In order to fulfil Hammond Co's criteria, the investment must have both a positive NPV and a payback period of less than three years.

You have been given the following details about the investment:

- The investment appraisal should cover a time horizon of four years.

- Hammond Co will need to make an immediate investment in plant and machinery of $240,000.

- Expected sales revenue of the new chair in Year 1 will be $200,000 and expected variable costs will be $100,000.

- Sales revenue and costs are expected to rise by the following percentages in Years 2-4 compared with the previous year.

Year	2	3	4
	10%	5%	3%

- Expected fixed costs will be $20,000 per year and will not change over the four year period.

Download the spreadsheet file from www.bpp.com/aatspreadsheets. Save the spreadsheet file in the appropriate location and rename it in the following format: 'your initial-surname-AAT no-dd.mm.yy-Task1'. For example: H-Darch-123456-12.03.xx-Task1

A **high degree of accuracy** is required. You must **save your work as an .XLS or.XLSX file** at regular intervals to avoid losing your work.

1. Open the renamed file. Calculate the revenues and variable costs for Years 1-4 using the information provided, showing variable costs as a negative figure.

2. Enter the fixed costs for Years 1-4, showing them as a negative figure.

3. In cell A6 enter the narrative Capital expenditure. Enter the amount of capital expenditure in the correct cell and show it as a negative figure.

4. In cell A7 enter the narrative Cash flows and calculate the net cash flows for Years 0-4.

5. In cell A9 enter the narrative Discounted cash flows and calculate the discounted cash flows for Years 0-4, using the cash flows you have calculated and the discount factors given in cells B8-F8.

6. Calculate the NPV and insert it in cell B10. Put an IF statement in cell C10 that will show ACCEPT if the NPV is positive and REJECT if the NPV is negative.

7. Tidy up the NPV calculation by showing all negative figures in brackets and all figures rounded to the nearest $, with commas for 000s.

8. For the payback calculation, copy and paste cells A7-F7 into A12-F12.

9. Show the cumulative cash flows for each year as a running total in cells B13-F13.

10. For the last negative cumulative cash flow, in the cell immediately beneath it in row 14, insert this figure as a positive number. Highlight this figure, the first positive cumulative cash flow and the year number in which the last negative cumulative cash flow occurs by placing a black border around the cells.

11. Use the highlighted figures to carry out a payback calculation in cell B15, expressing your answer as a decimal rounded to two decimal places.

12. Put an IF statement in cell C15 that will show ACCEPT if the payback period is less than three years and REJECT if the payback period is more than three years.

13. Perform a spell check and ensure that the contents of all cells can be seen.

14. Use the proforma email to do the following:

- Comment on the results of your calculations
- Give two advantages of using the payback method of investment appraisal

To:	Tom Howard
From:	Ian Chesterton
Date:	3 January 20X0
Subject:	Investment in plant and machinery

Task 6.2

You are Barbara Wright, a part-qualified accounting technician. You work for Riley Co, which manufactures cups.

You cover all aspects of bookkeeping and accounting for the business. You report to Lynne Dupont, Finance Director.

Today's date is 25 January 20X1.

Lynne Dupont has asked for your assistance in appraising an investment in new machinery, which should enable it to produce cups that are harder-wearing and less likely to break. Lynne Dupont thinks that Riley Co will be able to charge a higher price each year for its new cups, although the variable cost per cup will also increase. Lynne has asked

you to use the net present value (NPV) and payback methods of investment appraisal. In order to fulfil Riley Co's criteria, the investment must have a positive NPV or a payback period of less than four years.

You have been given the following details about the investment:

- The investment appraisal should cover a time horizon of four years.

- Riley Co will need to make an immediate investment in machinery of $300,000.

- Riley Co expects to sell 50,000 new cups a year. The selling price of each cup in Year 1 will be $5 and the expected variable cost per cup will be $3.

- Sales price and variable cost per cup are expected to rise by the following percentages in Years 2-4 compared with the previous year.

Year	2	3	4
Sales price	10%	8%	5%
Variable cost	6%	4%	3%

- Expected fixed costs will be $40,000 per year and will not change over the four year period.

Download the spreadsheet file from www.bpp.com/aatspreadsheets. Save the spreadsheet file in the appropriate location and rename it in the following format: 'your initial-surname-AAT no-dd.mm.yy-Task1'. For example: H-Darch-123456-12.03.xx-Task1

A **high degree of accuracy** is required. You must **save your work as an .XLS or.XLSX file** at regular intervals to avoid losing your work.

1. Open the renamed file. Calculate the revenues and variable costs for Years 1-4 using the information provided, showing variable costs as a negative figure.

2. Enter the fixed costs for Years 1-4, showing them as a negative figure.

3. In cell A6 enter the narrative Capital expenditure. Enter the amount of capital expenditure in the correct cell and show it as a negative figure.

4. In cell A7 enter the narrative Cash flows and calculate the net cash flows for Years 0-4.

5. In cell A9 enter the narrative Discounted cash flows and calculate the discounted cash flows for Years 0-4, using the cash flows you have calculated and the discount factors given in cells B8-F8.

6. Calculate the NPV and insert it in cell B10. Put an IF statement in cell C10 that will show ACCEPT if the NPV is positive and REJECT if the NPV is negative.

7. Tidy up the NPV calculation by showing all negative figures in brackets and all figures rounded to the nearest $, with commas for 000s.

8. For the payback calculation, copy and paste cells A7-F7 into A12-F12.

9. Show the cumulative cash flows for each year as a running total in cells B13-F13.

10. For the last negative cumulative cash flow, in the cell immediately beneath it in row 14, insert this figure as a positive number. Highlight this figure, the first positive cumulative cash flow and the year number in which the last negative cumulative cash flow occurs by placing a black border around the cells.

11. Use the highlighted figures to carry out a payback calculation in cell B15, expressing your answer as a decimal rounded to two decimal places.

12. Put an IF statement in cell C15 that will show ACCEPT if the payback period is less than four years and REJECT if the payback period is more than four years.

13. Perform a spell check and ensure that the contents of all cells can be seen.

14. Use the proforma email to do the following:

    • Comment on the results of your calculations

    • Give two reasons why the NPV method is a better method of investment appraisal than the payback method

To:	Lynne Dupont
From:	Barbara Wright
Date:	25 January 20X1
Subject:	Investment in machinery

Task 6.3

You are Susan Foreman, a part-qualified accounting technician. You work for Kingsley Co, a company that manufactures economy DVD players.

You cover all aspects of bookkeeping and accounting for the business. You report to Charles Frere, Managing Director.

Today's date is 29 February 20X2.

Charles Frere is considering investment in new technology costing $675,000,that will make the production of DVD players more efficient. He has prepared estimates of increases in DVD player sales, based on being able to cut the price as a result of using the new technology. The new technology will lead to increased fixed costs and Charles Frere acknowledges that total variable costs will also increase as a result of increased sales.

Expected total variable costs for Year 1 are $180,000. They are expected to rise by the following percentages in Years 2-4 compared with the previous year.

Year	2	3	4
Variable costs	15%	12%	10%

Fixed costs are expected to be $40,000 in Year 1, and to rise by 5% in each of the following three years.

Charles Frere has asked you to carry out an appraisal of the investment in the new technology, using the net present value (NPV) and internal rate of return (IRR) methods of investment appraisal. In order to fulfil Kingsley Co's criteria, the investment must have a positive NPV or an IRR of more than 11%. Charles Frere has provided you with the results of NPV calculations using discount rates of 10% and 15%, to help in your IRR calculation. For 10% the result is +$27,756, for 15% the result is -$47,539.

Download the spreadsheet file from www.bpp.com/aatspreadsheets. Save the spreadsheet file in the appropriate location and rename it in the following format: 'your initial-surname-AAT no-dd.mm.yy-Task1'. For example: H-Darch-123456-12.03.xx-Task1

A **high degree of accuracy** is required. You must **save your work as an .XLS or.XLSX file** at regular intervals to avoid losing your work.

1. Open the renamed file. Enter the narrative for Variable costs and Fixed costs in cells A4 and A5. Calculate the variable costs and fixed costs for Years 1-4 using the information provided, showing them as negative figures.

2. In cell A6 enter the narrative Capital expenditure. Enter the amount of capital expenditure in the correct cell and show it as a negative figure.

3. In cell A7 enter the narrative Cash flows and calculate the net cash flows for Years 0-4.

4. In cell A9 enter the narrative Discounted cash flows and calculate the discounted cash flows for Years 0-4, using the cash flows you have calculated and the discount factors given in cells B8-F8.

5. Calculate the NPV and insert it in cell B10. Put an IF statement in cell C10 that will show ACCEPT if the NPV is positive and REJECT if the NPV is negative.

6. Tidy up the NPV calculation by showing all negative figures in brackets and all figures rounded to the nearest $, with commas for 000s.

7. Carry out the IRR calculation in cell B11, using the information supplied by Charles Frere. Express your answer to two decimal places. Use conditional format to show an IRR that meets Kingsley Co's criteria in green and an IRR that does not meet Kingsley Co's criteria in red.

8. Perform a spell check and ensure that the contents of all cells can be seen.

9. Use the proforma email to do the following:

    *   Comment on the results of your calculations

    *   Give two reasons why the NPV method is a better method of investment appraisal than the IRR method

To:	Charles Frere
From:	Susan Foreman
Date:	29 February 20X2
Subject:	Investment in new technology

Task 6.4

You are Steven Taylor, a part-qualified accounting technician. You work for Merroney Co, a manufacturer of socks.

You cover all aspects of bookkeeping and accounting for the business. You report to Avril Rolfe, the Chief Finance Officer.

Today's date is 14 March 20X3.

Avril Rolfe is currently contemplating a proposal for Merroney Co to invest in machinery to produce a new range of novelty socks. The machinery will cost $320,000. Fixed costs associated with the machinery are expected to be $60,000 in Year 1 and are not expected to change in subsequent years.

Avril Rolfe has prepared estimates for sales price per unit, variable cost per unit and expected sales for the next four years. Avril however has had to move on to other work and has asked you to complete the investment appraisal.

Avril wants you to use the net present value (NPV) and internal rate of return (IRR) methods of investment appraisal. In order to fulfil Merroney Co's criteria, the investment must have a positive NPV and an IRR of more than 9%. Avril has provided you with the results of NPV calculations using discount rates of 5% and 10%, to help in your NPV calculations. For 5% the result is +$37,191, for 10% the result is -$6,005.

Download the spreadsheet file from www.bpp.com/aatspreadsheets. Save the spreadsheet file in the appropriate location and rename it in the following format: 'your initial-surname-AAT no-dd.mm.yy-Task1'. For example: H-Darch-123456-12.03.xx-Task1

A **high degree of accuracy** is required. You must **save your work as an .XLS or.XLSX file** at regular intervals to avoid losing your work.

1. Open the renamed file. Enter the narrative for Revenues and Variable costs in cells A6 and A7. Calculate the revenues and variable costs for Years 1-4 using the information given in Rows 3-5.

2. Enter the fixed costs for Years 1-4, showing them as a negative figure.

3. In cell A9 enter the narrative Capital expenditure. Enter the amount of capital expenditure in the correct cell and show it as a negative figure.

4. In cell A10 enter the narrative Cash flows and calculate the net cash flows for Years 0-4.

5. In cell A12 enter the narrative Discounted cash flows and calculate the discounted cash flows for Years 0-4, using the cash flows you have calculated and the discount factors given in cells B11-F11.

6. Calculate the NPV and insert it in cell B13. Put an IF statement in cell C13 that will show ACCEPT if the NPV is positive and REJECT if the NPV is negative.

7. Tidy up the NPV calculation, by showing all negative figures in brackets and all figures rounded to the nearest $, with comma for 000s.

8. Carry out the IRR calculation in cell B14, using the information supplied by Avril Rolfe. Express your answer to two decimal places. Use conditional format to show an IRR that meets Merroney Co's criteria in green and an IRR that does not meet Merroney Co's criteria in red.

9. Perform a spell check and ensure that the contents of all cells can be seen.

10. Use the proforma email to do the following:

    • Comment on the results of your calculations.

    • Give two advantages of using the IRR method of investment appraisal

To:	Avril Rolfe
From:	Steven Taylor
Date:	14 March 20X3
Subject:	Investment in machinery

Task 6.5

You are Dodo Chaplet, a part-qualified accounting technician. You work for Maxwell Co, a company that manufactures high quality cosmetic creams.

You cover all aspects of bookkeeping and accounting for the business. You report to Kate Harvey, the Head of Accounts.

Today's date is 11 April 20X4.

Maxwell Co had originally budgeted to make and sell 40,000 units of cosmetic cream in the quarter to 31 March 20X4. However it actually made and sold 45,000 units in the quarter.

Information about the original budget and the actual results are provided.

Download the spreadsheet file from www.bpp.com/aatspreadsheets. Save the spreadsheet file in the appropriate location and rename it in the following format: 'your initial-surname-AAT no-dd.mm.yy-Task1'. For example: H-Darch-123456-12.03.xx-Task1

A **high degree of accuracy** is required. You must **save your work as an .XLS or.XLSX file** at regular intervals to avoid losing your work.

1. Open this renamed file. Calculate the percentage to flex this budget in line with the information about sales and insert this percentage figure into cell D1.

2. In cell D3 enter the title Flexed budget. Calculate the flexed budget for the relevant entries using absolute referencing where appropriate.

3. In cell E3 enter the title Actual results. Use copy and paste to take the actual results from the information you've been given into the correct positions in Column E.

4. In cell F3 insert the title Variances. Calculate the variances for each revenue and each cost. Show these in column F.

5. In cell A15 insert the title Operating profit. Calculate the operating profit for the original budget, flexed budget and actual results.

6. Calculate the overall variance in cell F15.

7. Use conditional formatting in column F to show all favourable variances in green and adverse variances in red.

BPP
LEARNING MEDIA

8. Put an IF statement in cell F17 that will show 'Balanced' if the column totals balance and 'Check' if they do not.

9. Colour cell F17 with a yellow background and black border.

10. Make sure all column headings are in bold.

11. Copy the range A2 to F15 and paste into the new area of the worksheet called Maxwell Co Original budget for the quarter ended 31 March 20X4 (cost summary).

12. Delete the row that contains the Revenue amounts.

13. Produce subtotals for each of: materials, labour, variable overheads and fixed overheads.

14. Show subtotals in original budget, flexed budget, actual results and variances columns.

15. Hide the detail to only show the subtotals and grand total, not the individual components.

16. Return to the original budget, perform a spell check and ensure that all the contents of the cells can be seen.

17. From the variances in cells F5 to F14 identify the most significant favourable variance and the most significant adverse variance. Insert appropriate text in Column G adjacent to each variance, for example 'Most significant favourable variance' and 'Most significant adverse variance'.

18. Use the proforma email to do the following:

    -   Report the flexed budget, actual operating profit and total variance

    -   Explain one possible cause for each of the two variances identified as most favourable and most adverse.

To:	Kate Harvey
From:	Dodo Chaplet
Date:	11 April 20X4
Subject:	Variances in quarter to 31 March 20X4

Task 6.6

You are Ben Jackson, a part-qualified accounting technician. You work for Williams restaurant, a large city centre restaurant.

You cover all aspects of bookkeeping and accounting for the business. You report to Abby Hudson, the Accountant.

Today's date is 1 May 20X5.

In the quarter to 31 March 20X5, the restaurant budgeted to serve 4,500 meals (each budgeted meal consists of an average food and drink cost based on previous customer

behaviour). However the restaurant only served 3,825 meals in the quarter to 31 March 20X5.

Download the spreadsheet file from www.bpp.com/aatspreadsheets. Save the spreadsheet file in the appropriate location and rename it in the following format: 'your initial-surname-AAT no-dd.mm.yy-Task1'. For example: H-Darch-123456-12.03.xx-Task1

A **high degree of accuracy** is required. You must **save your work as an .XLS or.XLSX file** at regular intervals to avoid losing your work.

1. Open this renamed file. Calculate the percentage to flex this budget in line with the information about meals sold and insert this percentage figure into cell D1.

2. In cell D3 enter the title Flexed budget. Calculate the flexed budget for the relevant entries using absolute referencing where appropriate.

3. In cell E3 enter the title Actual results. Use copy and paste to take the actual results from the information you've been given into the correct positions in Column E.

4. In cell F3 insert the title Variances. Calculate the variances for each revenue and each cost. Show these in column F.

5. In cell A16 insert the title Operating profit. Calculate the operating profit for the original budget, flexed budget and actual results.

6. Calculate the overall variance in cell F16.

7. Use conditional formatting in column F to show all favourable variances in green and adverse variances in red.

8. Put an IF statement in cell F18 that will show 'Balanced' if the column totals balance and 'Check if they do not.

9. Colour cell F18 with a yellow background and black border.

10. Make sure all column headings are in bold.

11. Copy the range A2 to F16 and paste into the new area of the worksheet called Williams restaurant Original budget for the quarter ended 31 March 20X5 (cost summary).

12. Delete the row that contains the Revenue amounts.

13. Produce subtotals for each of: consumables, labour, variable overheads and fixed overheads.

14. Show subtotals in original budget, flexed budget, actual results and variances columns.

15. Hide the detail to only show the subtotals and grand total, not the individual components.

16. Return to the original budget, perform a spell check and ensure that all the contents of the cells can be seen.

17. From the variances in cells F5 to F15 identify the most significant favourable variance and the most significant adverse variance. Insert appropriate text in Column G adjacent to each variance, for example 'Most significant favourable variance' and 'Most significant adverse variance'.

18. Use the proforma email to do the following:

- Report the flexed budget, actual operating profit and total variance.

- Explain one possible cause for each of the two variances identified as most favourable and most adverse.

To:	Abby Hudson
From:	Ben Jackson
Date:	1 May 20X5
Subject:	Variances in quarter to 31 March 20X5

Task 6.7

You are Jamie McCrimmon, a part-qualified accounting technician. You work for Westside Hospital.

You cover all aspects of bookkeeping and accounting for the hospital. You report to Laura Wilde, the Finance Director.

Today's date is 11 June 20X6.

The hospital receives $180 per patient day from the government. It has some variable and fixed costs. Some of its staffing costs are stepped fixed costs, which are dependent on patient days. Its staffing costs are as follows:

Patient days per annum	Supervisors	Nurses	Assistants
Up to 20,000	5	8	22
20,000 – 24,000	5	10	26
Over 24,000	5	12	30

The salary for each supervisor is $30,000 each, nurse $23,000, assistant $16,000.

For the year ended 31 May 20X6 the hospital budgeted for 19,000 patient days, but there were actually 21,850 patient days.

Westside Hospital intends to open a new wing in May 20X7, which will allow it to accommodate more patients. For the year ended 31 May 20X8 it plans to budget for 25,000 patient days. However the government has indicated that its total funding will be capped at $4 million.

Download the spreadsheet file from www.bpp.com/aatspreadsheets. Save the spreadsheet file in the appropriate location and rename it in the following format: 'your initial-surname-AAT no-dd.mm.yy-Task1'. For example: H-Darch-123456-12.03.xx-Task1

A **high degree of accuracy** is required. You must **save your work as an .XLS or.XLSX file** at regular intervals to avoid losing your work.

1. Open this renamed file. Calculate the percentage to flex the variable costs in this budget in line with the information about patient days and insert this percentage figure into cell D1.

2. In cell D3 enter the title Flexed budget. Calculate the flexed budget for the relevant entries using absolute referencing where appropriate.

3. In cell E3 enter the title Actual results. Use copy and paste to take the actual results from the information you've been given into the correct positions in Column E on the question worksheet.

4. In cell F3 insert the title Variances. Calculate the variances for each revenue and each cost. Show these in column F.

5. In cell A15 insert the title Surplus/(Deficit). Calculate the operating profit for the original, flexed budget and actual results.

6. Calculate the overall variance in cell F15.

7. Put an IF statement in cell F17 that will show 'Balanced' if the column totals balance and 'Check' if they do not.

8. Colour cell F17 with a yellow background and black border.

9. Make sure all column headings are in bold.

10. Copy the flexed budget figures for staff costs into cells C22-C24 in the area of the spreadsheet labelled Westside Hospital Staffing costs for the year ended 31 May 20X8.

11. Calculate the staffing costs figures for 25,000 patient days and insert them in cells D22-D24.

12. Calculate the difference between the budget figures for staffing costs using 21,850 patient days (current budget) and the budget figures for staffing costs using 25,000 patient days (new budget) figures for staffing costs and insert them in cells E22-E24, showing the total difference in cell E25.

13. Return to the original budget and for each expense category (variable costs, staffing costs and fixed costs), highlight the biggest adverse variance by colouring the cell with a red background and putting a black border round the box.

14. Perform a spell check and ensure that all the contents of the cells can be seen.

15. Use the proforma email to do the following:

    • Report the flexed budget, actual surplus and total variance

    • Report the biggest significant variances in each cost category and explain one possible cause for the biggest variance for a variable cost

    • Briefly discuss whether the hospital needs to be concerned about the cap in government funding, in the light of your calculations of the increases in staffing costs.

To:	Laura Wilde
From:	Jamie McCrimmon
Date:	11 June 20X6
Subject:	Variances for year ended 31 May 20X6 and staff costs

Task 6.8

You are Victoria Waterfield, a part-qualified accounting technician. You work for Farrell Co, a firm of legal and tax consultants.

You cover all aspects of bookkeeping and accounting for the business. You report to Polly Urquhart, one of the partners in the firm.

Today's date is 21 July 20X7.

The figures for the year ended 30 June 20X7 have just become available. Polly wants you to provide an analysis of them. She has supplied you with the original budget, which was based on 15,000 annual chargeable consultant hours. However actual chargeable consultant hours were 16,500. Polly wants the most significant adverse variances in % terms highlighted for her to investigate.

Download the spreadsheet file from www.bpp.com/aatspreadsheets. Save the spreadsheet file in the appropriate location and rename it in the following format: 'your initial-surname-AAT no-dd.mm.yy-Task1'. For example: H-Darch-123456-12.03.xx-Task1

A **high degree of accuracy** is required. You must **save your work as an .XLS or.XLSX file** at regular intervals to avoid losing your work.

1. Open this renamed file. Calculate the percentage to flex this budget in line with the information about and insert this percentage figure into cell D1.

2. In cell D3 enter the title Flexed budget. Calculate the flexed budget for the relevant entries using absolute referencing where appropriate. Show these in column D.

3. In cell E3 enter the title Actual results. Use copy and paste to take the actual results from the information you've been given into the correct positions in column E on the question worksheet.

4. In cell F3 insert the title Variances $. Calculate the variances in $ for revenue and each cost. Show these in column F.

5. In cell A14 insert the title Operating profit. Calculate the operating profit for the original budget, flexed budget and actual results.

6. Calculate the overall variance in $ in cell F14.

7. Put an IF statement in cell F16 that will show 'Balanced' if the column totals balance and 'Check' if they do not.

8. Colour cell F16 with a yellow background and black border.

9. In cell G3 insert the title Variances %. Calculate the variances in % for revenue and each cost. Show these in column G. Note that adverse variances should be shown as negative.

10. Calculate the overall variance in % in cell G14.

11. Make sure all column headings are in bold.

12. Copy the range A5-G13 and paste into the new area of the worksheet called Farrell Co Variance analysis for the year ended 30 June 20X7. Sort the data so that the items with the largest negative % variances are at the top of the list.

13. In the variances % column, highlight the three largest negative variances in red type with a yellow background and black border to their cells.

14. Return to the original budget, perform a spell check and ensure that all the contents of the cells can be seen.

15. Use the proforma email to do the following:

- Report the flexed budget, actual operating profit and total variance

- State the three largest adverse variances in % terms

- Give two reasons why it may be misleading to focus most on the largest adverse variances in % terms

To:	Polly Urquhart
From:	Victoria Waterfield
Date:	21 July 20X7
Subject:	Variances for year ended 30 June 20X7

Task 6.9

You are Zoe Heriot, a part-qualified accounting technician. You work for Carter Co, a company that manufactures chairs for the home.

You cover all aspects of bookkeeping and accounting for the business. You report to Ken Masters, the Chief Executive.

Today's date is 24 July 20X8.

Ken would like the figures for the quarter ended 30 June 20X8 to be analysed. However a problem with the firm's computer system means that sales and production records are currently unavailable. The production department has estimated that Carter Co sold between 11,500 and 12,500 chairs in the quarter to 30 June 20X8. Ken therefore wants you to prepare budgets based on activity levels of 11,500 and 12,500 chairs, to provide yardsticks for measuring performance.

Download the spreadsheet file from www.bpp.com/aatspreadsheets. Save the spreadsheet file in the appropriate location and rename it in the following format: 'your initial-surname-AAT no-dd.mm.yy-Task1'. For example: H-Darch-123456-12.03.xx-Task1

A **high degree of accuracy** is required. You must **save your work as an .XLS or.XLSX file** at regular intervals to avoid losing your work.

1. Open this renamed file. Calculate the percentage to flex the original budget in line with sales being 11,500 and insert this percentage figure into cell D1.

2. In cell D3 enter the title Flexed budget 11,500. Calculate the flexed budget for the relevant entries using absolute referencing where appropriate.

3. In cell F3 enter the title Actual results. Use copy and paste to take the actual results from the information you've been given into the correct positions in Column F on the question worksheet.

4. In cell G3 insert the title Variances 11,500. Calculate the variances for each revenue and each cost. Show these in column G.

5. In cell A15 insert the title Operating profit. Calculate the operating profit for the original budget, flexed budget and actual results.

6. Calculate the overall variance for 11,500 units in cell G15.

7. Use conditional formatting in column G to show all favourable variances in green and adverse variances in red.

8. Put an IF statement in cell G17 that will show 'Balanced' if the column totals balance and 'Check if they do not.

9. Colour cell G17 with a yellow background and black border.

10. Calculate the percentage to flex the original budget in line with sales being 12,500 and insert this percentage figure into cell E1.

11. In cell E3 enter the title Flexed budget 12,500. Calculate the flexed budget for the relevant entries using absolute referencing where appropriate.

12. In cell H3 insert the title Variances 12,500. Calculate the variances for revenue and each cost. Show these in column H.

13. Calculate the operating profit for the flexed budget at 12,500 chairs.

14. Calculate the overall variance for 12,500 units in cell H15.

15. Use conditional formatting in column H to show all favourable variances in green and adverse variances in red.

16. Put an IF statement in cell H17 that will show 'Balanced' if the column totals balance and 'Check' if they do not.

17. Colour cell H17 with a yellow background and black border.

18. Make sure all column headings are in bold.

19. In the section of the worksheet labelled Carter Co Overhead summary for the quarter ended 30 June 20X8, copy and paste the column headers in cells C3-H3 into cells C20-H20.

20. Under each header calculate total figures for each category of costs and total costs at the end.

21. Return to the original budget, perform a spell check and ensure that all the contents of the cells can be seen.

22. Use the proforma email to do the following:

    •   Compare the actual profit figure with the budgeted profit figure for 11,500 and 12,500 chairs

    •   Discuss two concerns that your analysis has raised about the revenues and costs

To:	Ken Masters
From:	Zoe Heriot
Date:	24 July 20X8
Subject:	Analysis of performance for quarter ended 30 June 20X8

Task 6.10

You are Liz Shaw, a part-qualified accounting technician. You work for Tarrant Co, which manufactures small boats.

You cover all aspects of bookkeeping and accounting for the business. You report to Bill Sayers, the Head of Accounts.

Today's date is 19 August 20X9.

The board of Tarrant Co is currently considering an investment in new plant and machinery, that will enable the company to improve the buoyancy of its boats, The board will make a decision about this next week and the investment will take place immediately afterwards if the board decides to go ahead.

You have been asked to produce an analysis for the board meeting of this investment, using the Internal rate of return (IRR) and payback methods of investment appraisal.

You have been given the following details about the investment:

- The investment appraisal should cover a time horizon of five years.

- Tarrant Co will need to make an immediate investment in plant and machinery of $150,000.

- Expected additional sales revenue in Year 1 will be $180,000 and expected variable costs will be $100,000.

- Sales revenue and costs are expected to rise by 5% in Years 2-5 compared with the previous year.

- Expected fixed costs will be $45,000 per year and will not change over the five year period.

Download the spreadsheet file from www.bpp.com/aatspreadsheets. Save the spreadsheet file in the appropriate location and rename it in the following format: 'your initial-surname-AAT no-dd.mm.yy-Task1'. For example: H-Darch-123456-12.03.xx-Task1

A **high degree of accuracy** is required. You must **save your work as an .XLS or.XLSX file** at regular intervals to avoid losing your work.

1. Open the renamed file. Calculate the revenues and variable costs for Years 1-5 using the information provided, showing variable costs as a negative figure.

2. Enter the fixed costs for Years 1-5, showing them as a negative figure.

3. In cell A6 enter the narrative Capital expenditure. Enter the amount of capital expenditure in the correct cell and show it as a negative figure.

4. In cell A7 enter the narrative Cash flows and calculate the net cash flows for Years 0-5.

5. In cell A9 enter the narrative Discounted cash flows and calculate the discounted cash flows for Years 0-5, using the cash flows you have calculated and the discount factors for 10% given in cells B8-G8.

6. Calculate the NPV for 10% and inset it in cell B10.

7. Tidy up the NPV calculation by showing all negative figures in brackets and all figures rounded to the nearest $, with commas for 000s.

8. In cell A12 enter the narrative Discounted cash flows and calculate the discounted cash flows for Years 0-5, using the cash flows you have calculated and the discount factors given for 15% in cells B11-G11.

9. Calculate the NPV for 15% and inset it in cell B13.

10. Tidy up the NPV calculation by showing all negative figures in brackets and all figures rounded to the nearest $, with comma for 000s.

11. Use the NPV figures in cells B10 and B13 to calculate the IRR. Show your answer in cell B14, correct to 2 decimal places.

12. For the payback calculation, copy and paste cells A7-G7 into A16-G16.

13. Show the cumulative cash flows for each year as a running total in cells B17-G17.

14. For the last negative cumulative cash flow, in the cell immediately beneath it in row 18, insert this figure as a positive number. Highlight this figure, the first positive cumulative cash flow and the year number in which the last negative cumulative cash flow occurs by placing a black border around the cells.

15. Use the highlighted figures to carry out a payback calculation in cell B19, expressing your answer as a decimal rounded to two decimal places.

16. Perform a spell check and ensure that the contents of all cells can be seen.

17. Use the proforma email to do the following:

   - Summarise the results of your calculations
   - Explain two problems with the results of the calculations that you have performed

To:	Bill Sayers
From:	Liz Shaw
Date:	19 August 20X9
Subject:	Investment appraisal

Task 6.11

You are Jo Grant, a part-qualified accounting technician. You work for Trent Co, which manufactures garden barbecues.

You cover all aspects of bookkeeping and accounting for the business. You report to Vanessa Andenberg, the Finance Director.

Today's date is 24 September 20X0.

Vanessa has asked you to do some breakeven analysis, based on the budgeted figures for the next 12 months. Forecast sales are 25,000 units and sales price is $60. Cost figures are as follows:

	$
Direct materials	500,000
Direct labour	350,000
Assembly	200,000
Packaging	280,000

40% of assembly costs and 25% of packaging costs are variable.

Vanessa has told you the company's target margin of safety is 20% and its target profit is $180,000.

Download the spreadsheet file from www.bpp.com/aatspreadsheets. Save the spreadsheet file in the appropriate location and rename it in the following format: 'your initial-surname-AAT no-dd.mm.yy-Task1'. For example: H-Darch-123456-12.03.xx-Task1

A **high degree of accuracy** is required. You must **save your work as an .XLS or.XLSX file** at regular intervals to avoid losing your work.

1. Open the renamed file. Calculate total revenue and enter it in cell B2.

2. Enter total direct materials in cell B4 and total direct labour in cell B5.

3. Calculate variable assembly and packaging costs and enter them in cells B6 and B7.

4. Calculate total variable costs and enter them in cell B8.

5. Calculate variable costs per unit, using the budgeted sales volume of 25,000, and enter it in cell B9

6. Calculate contribution per unit, using the budgeted sales price of $60, and enter it in cell B10.

7. Calculate fixed assembly and packaging costs and enter them in cells B12 and B13.

8. Calculate total fixed costs and enter them in cell B14.

9. Calculate the breakeven point in units and enter it in cell B15. Use conditional formatting to show this figure in green if it is less than the budgeted sales volume and red if it is more than the budgeted sales volume.

10. Calculate the breakeven point in revenue terms and enter it in cell B16.

11. Calculate the contribution/sales ratio and enter it in cell B17, showing it to 2 decimal places.

12. Calculate the margin of safety in units and enter it in cell B18.

13. Calculate the margin of safety in % terms and enter it in cell B19, showing it to 2 decimal places. Highlight this figure with a yellow background and black border. Put an IF statement in cell C19 to show HIGHER if it is greater than the target margin of safety of 20%, LOWER if it is less than the target margin of safety.

14. Calculate the volume of sales needed to achieve the target profit of $180,000 and enter it in cell B20. Highlight this figure with a yellow background and black border. Put an IF statement in cell C20 to show LESS if the budgeted sales volume of 25,000 units is lower than the volume of sales needed to achieve the target profit, MORE if the budgeted sales volume Is higher.

15. Perform a spell check and ensure that the contents of all cells can be seen.

16. Use the proforma email to do the following:

    • Comment on the results of your calculations
    • Give two problems with breakeven analysis

To:	Vanessa Andenberg
From:	Jo Grant
Date:	24 September 20X1
Subject:	Breakeven analysis

Section 7 Spreadsheets for Accounting/Final Accounts Preparation

Task 7.1

You are working on a set of accounts for a newspaper publisher that pays its advertising sales employees a bonus dependent on the number of adverts sold during the year.

These employees are expected to sell at least 100 adverts before any bonus is paid. The bonus is paid at a rate of 2.5% based on the individual basic salary for each employee.

The following information is available.

Staff employee number	Basic salary	Adverts sold during the year
123	£20,000	85
124	£22,000	150
125	£28,000	70
126	£25,000	165
127	£20,000	50
128	£18,000	210

Required

Open a spreadsheet and use the IF Function calculate any bonuses payable to each employee.

Your analysis also needs to show each employee's total pay and an overall figure to go into the statement of profit or loss.

Task 7.2

A sole trader wishes to produce a schedule of non-current assets to be capitalised in her statement of financial position. The materiality level has been set at £200 meaning that any expenditure above this level will be capitalised as non-current asset in the statement of financial position and any amounts below £200 will be written-off as an expense in the statement of profit or loss.

The following information is available:

Expenditure	Value
IT Cables	£180
Computer monitor	£210
Desk lamp	£65
Lighting fixture	£340
Filing cabinet (small)	£195
Filing cabinet (large)	£265

Required

Open a spreadsheet and use the data validation function to circle expenditure values that need to be included within non-current assets.

●●

Task 7.3

The Pivotal Partnership has 3 partners; Jeff, Gary and Fran.

The partnership wishes to make use of spreadsheet capabilities to analyse how much the 3 partners have extracted from the partnership.

The following information has been taken from the partnership current accounts.

Item	Jeff	Gary	Fran
Drawings	£3,000	£500	£4,000
Interest on capital	£90	£160	£120
Profit share	£12,750	£12,750	£25,500

Required

Open a spreadsheet and insert a pivot table to analyse the above information.

- **Sort your pivot table on the value of most money taken out of the partnership.**
- **Use light blue infill to show the highest value in each category.**

●●

Task 7.4

A sole trader needs to calculate his closing capital account balance for inclusion in his statement of financial position as at 31 January 20X6. The sole trader started trading on 1 January 20X6.

1.   Capital introduced as at 1 January 20X6 £7,500

2.   Owner purchased fixtures and fittings with a value of £1,678 from his own personal bank account

3.   During the year the owner put £1,500 into the business to help with cash flow

4.   The owner withdrew £500 per month as drawings over the 12 month period

5.   £1,000 was taken out of this account to pay for a laptop for his own personal use

6.   Net profit for the year was £8,600

Required

Open a spreadsheet and construct a capital account for the sole trader showing carried down and brought down amounts. Ignore any VAT implications.

Apply the following formatting to your spreadsheet:

*   **Account heading in bold, italics using size 12 font**
*   **Heading merged and centred over respective columns**
*   **Figures to be presented with thousand separators and no decimals**
*   **Insert currency (£) symbols where relevant**
*   **Use top and double bottom borders on account totals**

Task 7.5

A sole trader needs assistance in the completion of his statement of profit or loss.

He has supplied the following trial balance for the year ended 31 May 20X6.

	£	£
Accruals		350
Bank	23,700	
Capital account		33,200
Closing inventory	9,000	9,000
General expenses	63,800	
Discounts allowed	470	
Drawings	20,000	
Administration costs	3900	
IT Equipment depreciation expense	850	
IT Equipment accumulated depreciation		3,400
IT Equipment at cost	8,500	
Opening inventory	7,800	
Prepayments	530	
Purchases	150,800	
Purchase ledger control account		16,170
Sales		280,480
Sales ledger control account	14,250	
VAT		3,000
Salaries	42,000	
	345,000	345,000

Required

(a) **Open a spreadsheet and prepare a statement of profit or loss for the year ended 31 May 20X6.**

   Your statement must use appropriate formulas where relevant and be formatted in a style suitable to meet your client's needs

(b) Your client has requested for security purposes he would like add security to the numeric cells of the statement of profit or loss.

   Use cell protection to lock the numeric data on your prepared statement.

....

Task 7.6

Karen, Jake and Saffron are in partnership. You have the following information about the business.

The financial year ends on 31 August 20X6.

Partners' annual salaries:
Karen – £11,400
Jake – £14,400
Saffron – £9,600

Partners' interest on capital:
Karen – £1,000 per full year
Jake – £1,200 per full year
Saffron – £600 per full year

Profit share:
Karen – 20%
Jake – 65%
Saffron – 15%

Profit during the year ended 31 August 20X6 was £180,000.

The partners have requested your assistance in calculating the profit available for distribution between the partners.

Required

(a) **Open a spreadsheet and prepare the appropriation account for the partnership for the year ended 31 August 20X6.**

   Your statement must use appropriate formulas where relevant and be formatted in a style suitable to meet the partnership's needs.

   Apply the following formatting to your spreadsheet:

   - **Headings to be formatted in bold**
   - **Figures to be presented with thousand separators and no decimals**
   - **Insert currency (£) symbols where relevant**
   - **Use top and double bottom borders totals**
   - **Interest paid formatted in red font**

(b) **As an accuracy check use an IF Function to test whether profit for distribution equals total profit distributed. Your function should be able to indicate whether the entries are "Correct" or "Incorrect".**

Task 7.7

A trader has lost his sales records in a flood. You have been asked to reconstruct the sales figures along with a gross profit figure for his statement of profit or loss.

The following information is available:

- Inventory at the start of the year £1,500
- Inventory at the end of the year £1,800
- Purchases during the year £7,600
- The business operates on a profit margin of 20%

Required

(a) **Open a spreadsheet and using appropriate formulas calculate the missing sales and gross profit information.**

(b) **A company adds a 60% mark-up to cost of sales to arrive at a sales figure and intends to use a spreadsheet function to quickly calculate how much cost of sales will be.**

Open a spreadsheet and enter the following information and formula in cell B3.

	A	B
1	Mark-up factor	1.60
2	Cost of sales	100
3	Sales	=B1*B2

(c) **Using the Goal Seek function calculate how much the cost of sales will be if sales are £3,200.**

....

Task 7.8

You have been allocated the task of calculating the depreciation charge and carrying values of a company's non-current assets for the year ended 31 December 20X6.

You have been given the following information.

Property - depreciated on a straight-line basis over a 50 year period
Motor vehicles - depreciated on a reducing balance method – at a rate of 30%
Fixtures and fittings – depreciated on a reducing balance – at a rate of 10%

Details as at 31 December 20X5:

	Cost £	Accumulated depreciation £
Property	650,000	195,000
Motor vehicles	45,000	22,950
Fixtures and fittings	27,000	5,130

Required

Open a spreadsheet and using appropriate formulas calculate the following for the year ended 31 December 20X6.

- **Individual depreciation charges to be entered in the statement of profit or loss**
- **Individual carrying amounts**
- **A total carrying amount to be entered into the statement of financial position**

Task 7.9

The following information relates to the statement of financial position of an extended trial balance.

Trial Balance – SOFP
Accruals		500
Prepayments	450	
Depn		2500
Capl		10000
Receivables	675	
Payables		1125
Non-current assets	10000	
Bank	3000	

Required

Open a spreadsheet and enter the above information.

- Use the Find and Replace function to change 'Depn' to 'Depreciation' and 'Capl' to 'Capital'

- Use the Sort function to sort names and data into A to Z order

- Heading merged and centred over respective columns

- Figures to be presented to two decimal places, with thousand separators

- Total columns using AutoSum

- Use top and double bottom borders on column totals

Task 7.10

The following table relates to a business's regional operations. The business trades in four areas and each area uses three types of non-current assets.

To complete the business's statement of financial position it will be necessary to total each category of non-current asset.

Non-current asset at cost	Area	£000
Property	1	265
Property	2	380
Property	3	420
Property	4	165
Motor vehicles	1	36
Motor vehicles	2	40
Motor vehicles	3	37
Motor vehicles	4	43
Furniture	1	6
Furniture	2	10
Furniture	3	15
Furniture	4	5

Required

Open a spreadsheet and enter the information the table above.

Using the Subtotal function to calculate sub-totals for each category of non-current asset along with a grand total for all non-current assets.

Answer bank

Answer bank

Section 1 Ethics for Accountants

Task 1.1

(a)

Statement	True	False
'I know I act ethically as I have never broken the law and always comply with regulations.'	☐	✓
'The code of professional ethics is legally binding if you are a member of the AAT.'	☐	✓

(b)

Familiarity	✓
Self-interest	☐
Advocacy	☐

(c)

Integrity	☐
Objectivity	✓
Confidentiality	☐

(d)

Action	Required/not required
Resign from RMS Accountancy	Not required
Inform RMS Accountancy of his link with Carmichael Ltd.	Required
Inform the AAT of his link with Carmichael Ltd.	Not required

(e)

Leaders of the firm have issued clear policies on the ethical behaviour expected at RMS Accountancy	☐
Leaders of the firm demonstrate the importance of compliance with the fundamental principles	☑
Leaders of the firm require that any potential threat to the fundamental principles is communicated to them in order for the most appropriate action to be taken	☐

(f)

| Transparency | can be assessed by considering whether or not the decision maker would mind other people knowing the decision that they have taken.

(g)

Statement	True	False
Disciplinary procedures are an example of safeguard.	☑	☐
Safeguards are put in place to eliminate threats from the organisation.	☐	☑

Task 1.2

(a)

Statement	True	False
The Code of Professional Ethics provides a set of rules to help accountants determine ethical behaviour	☐	☑
Ethical behaviour is particularly important for AAT members in practice as they work in the public interest	☐	☑

(b)

Action	Required/not required
Breach of contract	Yes
Negligence	Yes
Fraud	Possibly

(c)

IFAC	☐
IESBA	☑
AAT	☐

(d)

Operational risk	☑
Business risk	☐
Control risk	☐

(e)

Behaving ethically means acting with integrity, honesty, fairness and [sensitivity] in dealings with clients, suppliers, colleagues and others.to the relevant authority.

(f)

This is a potential [self-interest] threat on behalf of the junior and looking at the partner's file would be a breach of the [confidentiality] principle.

(g)

Statement	True	False
The principle of confidentiality must always be carefully abided by in all situations	☐	☑
In some situations it is entirely plausible that the principle of integrity could be over-ridden as a result of the circumstances	☐	☑

Task 1.3

(a)

It is required by law that they do so	☐
To maintain public confidence in the profession	☑
To prevent dishonest individuals from entering the profession	☐

(b)

Statement	True	False
'The code of professional ethics does not apply to me yet as I am only a student accounting technician.'	☐	☑
'Ethical codes provide advice as to how to comply with the law.'	☑	☐

(c) If you have an ethical concern at work, usually the most appropriate first course of action would be to raise this with [your immediate supervisor] or [employee helpline] ?

(d)

Action	Yes/No
Are customer due diligence procedures only required for new clients?	No
Is it acceptable for accountants to pay a referral fee to obtain a new client?	Yes
Is it acceptable to offer a commission to employees for bringing in a new client?	Yes

(e)

5 years	☑
7 years	☐
Indefinitely	☐

(f)

Statement	True	False
Whistleblowing should occur as soon as illegal activity is suspected.	☐	☑
Employees are protected under the Public Information Disclosure Act to ensure they cannot be dismissed for whistleblowing	☑	☐
If the disclosure is in the public interest, then the fundamental principle of confidentiality is not breached	☑	☐
If the employee is bound by a confidentiality clause in their contract, or has signed a non-disclosure agreement, then the employee could still face dismissal	☐	☑

Task 1.4

(a)

The UK accountancy profession as a whole is regulated by the $\boxed{\text{FRC}}$ and global ethical standards are set by the $\boxed{\text{IESBA}}$.

(b)

Statement	True	False
The duty to comply with the fundamental principles is more relevant to accountants working in practice than accountants working in business	☐	☑
Compliance with the law, as well as the policies and procedures of the organisation for which you work will ensure that you never break the five fundamental principles	☐	☑

(c)

Familiarity	☑
Self-interest	☐
Intimidation	☐

(d)

Integrity	☑
Professional competence and due care	☐
Objectivity	☐

(e)

Action	Yes/No
Familiarity	No
Self-interest	Yes
Intimidation	Yes
Self-review	No

(f)

Change the accounts as requested	☐
Refuse and explain her reasons for doing so with Andrew	☑
Refuse and inform the media as it is in the public interest to disclose the matter	☐

Task 1.5

(a)

Statement	True	False
Under the Code of Professional Ethics, as a minimum you are expected to comply with the laws and regulations of the country in which you live and work.	☑	☐
The ethical code exists primarily to enhance the public image of accountancy and increase public confidence in the profession	☐	☑

(b)

Ensuring all work is carried out in the public interest	☐
Having no previous or current links, financial or otherwise, with a client	☐
Carrying out work objectively and with integrity	☑

(c)

Self-review	☐
Self-interest	☐
Familiarity	☑

(d)

She should accept the gift as it is insignificant and will not influence her audit	☐
She should reject the gift as it may appear to others to compromise her objectivity	☑
She should reject the gift as it may appear to others to compromise her integrity	☐

(e)

Accountants ┌ should not ┐ accept significant gifts or preferential treatment from a client. This is because it represents │ a self-interest threat │ to the fundamental principles.

(f)

Action	Yes/No
The skills required to carry out the engagement	Could be taken into account
The outcome of the engagement	Must not be taken into account
The value of the service to the client	Could be taken into account

(g)

Statement	True	False
Tipping off is an offence which can only be carried out by accountants	☑	☐
Accountants can go to jail if they are found guilty of having been involved in money laundering	☑	☐

Task 1.6

(a)

Statement	True	False
There are no disadvantages to professional accountants of complying with the code of ethics.	☐	☑
Accountants are required under the code of ethics to comply with all relevant laws and regulations	☑	☐
Accountants are required to uphold the reputation of the accounting profession in both their professional and private lives.	☑	☐

(b)

Transparency	☐
Effect	☐
Fairness	☑

(c)

When it is in the public interest to do so	☐
When it is required by law to do so	☐
An accountant should never breach the objectivity principle	☑

(d)

Johnson has not compromised his professional ethics; everyone lies a little to get a job.	☐
Johnson has acted irresponsibly and has therefore breached the professional ethic of professional behaviour	☐
Johnson has misled a potential employer and has therefore breached the professional ethic of integrity	☐
Johnson has misled a potential employer and has therefore breached the professional ethic of professional competence and due care	☑

(e)

Statement	True	False
It is fine for Johnson to use these skills, knowledge and experience as the new firm would expect a degree of insider knowledge to be obtained as a perk of employing a former employee of the competition.	☐	☑
It is fine for Johnson to use these skills, knowledge and experience provided he does not disclose any confidential information.	☑	☐
It is fine for Johnson to use these skills, knowledge and experience, but only after a reasonable amount of time has elapsed to prevent conflicts of interest arising.	☐	☑

(f)

Statement	True	False
This is an ethical principle	☑	☐
This is a legal obligation	☑	☐

Task 1.7

(a)

The shareholders or other key investors	☐
The employees of the organisation	☐
Society as a whole	☑

(b)

When it is in the public interest to do so	☐
When it is required by law to do so	☑
An accountant should never breach confidentiality	☐

(c)

Senior management set clear policies and procedures that are cascaded down through the organisation	☐
Senior management lead by example	☑
Senior management establish a clear disciplinary procedure to ensure ethical breaches are escalated to be dealt with at the top of the organisation	☐

(d)

No, she was unaware of being involved in money laundering and withdrew from the engagement as soon as she suspected wrong doing	☐
No, the money laundering scheme was very small scale and would therefore be below the threshold for criminal conviction	☐
Yes, if she has been part of the scheme, even unknowingly, she could still be guilty of money laundering	☑

(e)

Statement	True	False
Rita has tipped off the client	☐	☑
If Rita does fail to disclose her suspicions of money laundering she may face additional charges	☑	☐
If Rita was to make a protected disclosure she may have a defence against any money laundering charges brought against her	☐	☑
If Rita is convicted of money laundering she will have a criminal record	☑	☐

(f)

When unethical or illegal behaviour is uncovered, whistleblowing should be carried out ⬚ as a last resort ⬚. External whistleblowing should take place ⬚ following ⬚ internal discussion with management.

··

Task 1.8

(a)

The AAT requires its members to behave in a way that maintains its reputation, maintains ⬚ public confidence ⬚ and protects the ⬚ public interest ⬚

(b)

Action	Yes/No
Failing to comply with the AAT's CPD requirements	Yes
Failing to reply to an item of correspondence from the AAT	No

(c)

Action	Economic/Social/Environmental
Carrying out a conference call between various members of regional staff	Economic OR Environmental
Holding an away day for members of the finance department	Social
Reducing the future cost of electricity by investing in solar panels	Economic OR Environmental

Note: Both Economic and Environmental are valid answers for the first and third requirements of this question. Marks would be awarded for either of these choices.

(d)

Statement	True	False
Christie should not accept this engagement as the large fee compromises her integrity.	☐	☑
It would be acceptable practice for Christie to include a disclaimer or liability in the written reference.	☑	☐
Christie should not accept this engagement as the length of the relationship with the client compromises her objectivity.	☐	☑
Christie should not accept this engagement as a safeguard against the threat of intimidation presented by this situation	☐	☑

(e)

If Christie gives the reference, even though she knows that Alpha limited has no means of paying the rent, she would be committing | fraud by false representation |.

(f)

Statement	True	False
When a member in practice submits a tax return on behalf of a client the responsibilities of the member should be made clear in a letter of engagement.	☑	☐
When a member in practice submits a tax return on behalf of the client, the member assumes all responsibility for the return and computations.	☐	☑

Task 1.9

(a)

Fundamental principle	Yes	No
Confidentiality	✓	☐
Integrity	✓	☐

(b)

Action	Economic/Social/Environmental
Internal auditing	No
Insolvency practice	Yes
Taxation services	No

(c)

Corporate Social Reporting (CSR)	☐
Ethical business practices	☐
Sustainability	☑

(d)

Action	Yes/No
Integrity	No
Objectivity	Yes
Confidentiality	Yes
Professional competence and due care	No
Professional behaviour	No

(e)

The AAT Code says that 'A member providing professional tax services has a duty to put forward the best position in favour of a ⟨client or employer⟩.'

(f)

Escalate the matter to her line manager	☐
Report Mo to the AAT	☐
Discuss the situation with Mo and encourage him to make his phone calls outside normal working hours	☑

Task 1.10

(a)

IFAC	☑
IESBA	☐
CCAB	☐

(b)

Honesty	☑
Confidentiality	☐
Accountability	☑
Sensitivity	☐

(c)

Action	Yes/No
Breach of contract	Yes
Breach of trust	Yes
Professional negligence	Yes
Fraud accusations	Yes

(d)

Report the electrician to his trade regulatory body	☐
Cease to work on behalf of the electrician	☑
Disclose the matter publically as the matter is one of public interest	☐

(e)

Statement	True	False
If Alfred does not disclose his suspicions of money laundering, then he himself will have committed a criminal offense.	✓	☐
Failure to disclose money laundering suspicions can result in a fine up to £10,000	☐	✓
Alfred must ensure that he makes Francois aware that the relevant disclosures have been made	☐	✓

(f)

Protected disclosure	✓
Authorised disclosure	☐
Anonymous disclosure	☐

Task 1.11

(a)

Statement	True	False
An accountant who is employed by an organisation is more likely to face an advocacy threat than an accountant working in practice	☐	✓
A dominant individual attempting to influence your decisions is an example of a threat of advocacy	☐	✓
The fundamental principle most likely to be compromised as the result of an advocacy threat is objectivity.	✓	☐

(b)

Professional behaviour	☐
Professional competence and due care	✓
Integrity	☐

(c)

Action	Criminal/Civil
Misappropriation of assets	Criminal
Money laundering	Criminal
Negligence	Civil
Fraud	Criminal

(d)

Internal fraud	☐
External fraud	☑
Systems failure	☐

(e)

Go to the festival, it is a once in a lifetime opportunity and she knows that she carried out her work in accordance with the ethical code	☐
Inform her manager that the offer has been made to her	☑
Refuse the tickets and report the matter to AAT	☐

(f)

Action	Yes/no
Peter could be found guilty of money laundering	Yes
Peter could be found guilty of the offense of tipping off	No
Peter could be found guilty of prejudicing the investigation	Yes

Section 2 VAT

Task 2.1

(a)

Statement	True	False
Notes To Go may reclaim VAT on its purchases through its VAT returns	✓	☐
The VAT on Notes To Go's purchases is known as output tax	☐	✓

(b)

Item	Net cost
Notes To Go may reclaim VAT on its purchases through its VAT returns	£100
The VAT on Notes To Go's purchases is known as output tax	£120

(c)

Statement	True	False
Notes To Go is making exempt supplies	☐	✓
The amount of VAT on any sale of printed music will be zero	✓	☐

(d)

Registration may improve the image of the business	✓
VAT returns need to be prepared on a regular basis	☐
VAT on Notes To Go's purchases may be reclaimed	✓

(e)

Turnover last year was [above] the VAT registration threshold

Notes To Go could apply to HMRC to deregister [because supplies are zero rated]

If Notes To Go deregistered, issuing VAT receipts in future would be [prohibited]

(f)

Your employer's electricity bill is [£175] net of VAT

Your home electricity bill is [£200] net of VAT

The VAT on your home electricity bill is borne by [above]

Task 2.2

(a)

£20 spent at a toll bridge while travelling	☐
Goods costing £35 bought from a vending machine	☑

(b)

VAT records [may] be kept electronically

Records are to be kept for at least [six] years

(c)

How much will the VAT be on these?	
Standard-rated consultancy services – total price £398.00	£66.33
Zero-rated food £120.00	£0

(d)

The debt must be more than six years overdue	☐
The input tax must have been paid by the client	☐
The output tax must have been paid to HMRC	☑

(e)

Statement	True	False
Relief is claimed through the VAT return as a deduction from output tax.	☐	☑

(f)

	Debit/Credit	Amount (whole £s)
Bad debts expense account	DR	£1,000
VAT account	DR	£200
Sales ledger control account	CR	£1,200

Task 2.3

(a)

If Bizyness Ltd goes ahead and orders 20 doors at one time, the discount would be a [bulk] discount. The discount is [unconditional] and the value shown on the invoice will be the [discounted] amount.

(b)

The discount offered would be a [prompt payment] or [settlement] discount. The discount is [conditional]. It [need not] be shown on the invoice.

(c)

The deadline for payment for the discount to apply	✓
The amount of the discount	✓
The VAT on the discounted price	✓
A statement that no credit note will be issued	☐

(d)

The pro forma invoice is not a valid VAT invoice	☑
The pro forma invoice must show the price of the goods	☑
The pro forma invoice will enable VAT to be reclaimed by the customer	☐
The pro forma invoice will be worded identically to a normal VAT invoice	☐

Task 2.4

	Paid in 5 days' time £	Paid in 10 days' time £	Paid in 20 days' time £
Value	2,400.00	2,400.00	2,400.00
Discount %	10%	5%	0%
Discounted value	2,160.00	2,280.00	2,400.00
VAT on standard-rated goods	432.00	456.00	480.00
	2,592.00	2,736.00	2,880.00
Net amount charged if maximum discount taken up	2,160.00		

Task 2.5

(a)

This situation creates a conflict of interest which may affect your [objectivity]

The conflict is between your own interests and those of [Flora]

The main threat here is a [self-interest] threat since you are employed and paid by Flora.

(b)

This conflict of interest should be disclosed to [Flora].

You may wish to seek advice from [the AAT], bearing in mind the need for confidentiality to be maintained.

(c)

Exaggerating the likely time needed to carry out the work Flora will want would be a breach of [integrity].

Rushing a task to the point that work is not properly checked would be a breach of professional competence and due care .

If you are unable to resolve the conflict your best option is to resign .

(d)

VAT due in respect of UK sales will go into box 1 .

Total turnover will go into box 6 and must include VAT.

If there is a purchase of a single capital item for more than £2,000, box may be used to show the VAT-exclusive amount. The VAT on the capital item may be shown in box 4

A claim for bad debt relief may be shown in box 4

Box 2 will show nothing: True

Task 2.6

(a)

VAT is initially collected by traders

VAT is eventually borne by the final consumer

(b)

VAT is an indirect tax because it is based on transactions

(c)

The sweets sold by Harpreet are goods

Statement	True	False
We only need to charge VAT if our customers are also VAT registered	☐	✓
We do not need to charge VAT if our customers pay in cash	☐	✓

(d)

The VAT fraction can be used to find the VAT from the gross sales price	✓
The VAT fraction for reduced-rated supplies is 5%	☐

(e)

Item	Net cost
Stationery	£200
Stamps	£240

(f)

VAT returns are usually made for [three months] .

The deadline for submission is [one month] and [seven days] after this.

The deadline for BACS or CHAPS payment is [the same as the for the return] .

VAT direct debits are taken [three] [working days] after the normal payment deadline.

....

Task 2.7

(a)

VAT return for the quarter		£
VAT due in this period on sales and other outputs (16,400 + 2,000)/6 + 288 =	Box 1	3,354.67
VAT due in this period on acquisitions from other EC Member States	Box 2	0.00
Total VAT due (the sum of boxes 1 and 2)	Box 3	3,354.67
VAT reclaimed in the period on purchases and other inputs, including acquisitions from the EC **Working:** Sweets 2,800/6 = 466.66 Travel 0 Catering 0 Total	Box 4	 466.67
Net VAT to be paid to HM Revenue & Customs or reclaimed by you (Difference between boxes 3 and 4)	Box 5	2,888.00

(b)

There will be a surcharge liability notice in place for 12 months following the default this quarter. A further default would lead to a penalty, but only if it involves VAT paid late.

Being busy with the corrections to the previous return is not likely to be an acceptable excuse to HMRC.

Task 2.8

	✓
A sequential invoice number	☑
The time of the supply	☑
Details of the deadline for payment	☐
The date of issue of the document (where different to the time of supply)	☑
Kaykes' address	☑
Kaykes' VAT registration number as supplier	☑
The date from which Kaykes was registered for VAT	☐
A brief description of the type(s) of cake	☑
The number of each type of cake bought	☑
Sate Ltd's address	☑
Sate Ltd's Companies House registration number	☐
Sate Ltd's VAT registration number	☑
A £ sign to show the currency	☑
A note saying that the document is a pro forma	☐
The rate of VAT	☑
The total amount of VAT chargeable	☑

Task 2.9

(a)

Turnover

$20{,}000 \times 1.2 = 24{,}000$

$\underline{+ 9{,}000}$

$33{,}000$

$\times 7.5\%$

$= \pounds2{,}475$ VAT payable for the quarter

(b)

The VAT payable to HMRC calculated above is shown in box | 1 |

of the VAT return.

The figure shown in box 6 will be | £33,000 | which is VAT-inclusive/exclusive.

(c)

There is a conflict of interest.

I, or my firm, may wish to take on Jed as an extra client. However we would then be acting for two rival businesses.

This could threaten both objectivity and also confidentiality.

It might be possible to reduce threats to an acceptable level, if EeZee were informed and safeguards were put in place. However this seems unlikely on the information given.

Task 2.10

(a)

The treatment is deliberately incorrect. If Switch are paying too little tax as a result, it amounts to evasion which is a criminal offence.

The offer of a financial incentive to say nothing presents a self-interest threat to objectivity. Integrity is also threatened by the suggestion of concealing the truth, and withholding tax, from HMRC.

I would speak first to the financial controller to ask her to correct the treatment. If she refuses I would then speak to my manager at Neo Bros.

(b)

A jar of face cream is bought by Switch from a wholesaler. The wholesaler charges

£3.00 plus standard-rated VAT at | 20% | . This is | input | VAT for Switch.

Switch pays the wholesaler a total of | £3.60 | .

Switch offers the face cream for sale for a total advertised price of £7.20. This amount payable by customers is the [gross price]. The VAT on the face cream on sale is

[£1.20] and this is [output] VAT for Switch. This VAT is borne by [the customer].

Task 2.11

(a)

Output VAT		
201,000 x 20%		40,200
Input VAT		
Wages –		
Stationery 2,760/6	460	
Computer 1,800/6	300	
Travel –		
Car –		
Charity –		
		(760)
VAT payable		£39,440

(b)

Nine payments on account must be made. Each is 10% of the VAT payable in the last return, ie 10% × £39,440 = £3,944

The first is due at the end of April, then every month up to December.

Any balance is then due two months after the end of the VAT year.

(c)

Turnover of [£1,600,000]

Section 3 Advanced Bookkeeping/Final Accounts Preparation/Management Accounting: Costing

Task 3.1

(a)

£	25,550

Workings

	£
Opening inventory	2,300
Payments: bank	18,450
cash	3,200
Payables	1,600
Total purchases	25,550

(b)

£	24,350

Workings

	£
Purchases (from (a))	25,550
Closing inventory	(1,200)
Total cost of sales	24,350

(c)

£	48,700

Workings

	£
Cost of sales (from (b))	24,350
Total sales (× 2) (gross profit margin 50%)	48,700

(d)

Cash account

Account	£	Account	£
Sales (from (c))	48,700	Bank account	40,000
		Materials	3,200
		General expenses	490
		Drawings	4,910
		(balancing figure)	
		Bal c/d (float)	100
	48,700		48,700

(e)

£	19,280

Workings

	£
Bank account	14,370
Cash account (from (d))	4,910
Total drawings	19,280

(f)

£	21,090

Workings

	£	£
Sales (from (c))		48,700
Cost of sales (from (b))		(24,350)
Gross profit		24,350
General expenses (400 + 490)	890	
Depreciation (3,800/5)	760	
		(1,650)
Profit for the year		22,700

(g)

	✓
Integrity	☑
Selflessness	☐
Professional behaviour	☑
Objectivity	☑

Selflessness is one of the Nolan principles not one of the fundamental ethical principles from the Code of Professional Ethics

Task 3.2

(a)

Product Line	Workings (for information only)	Contribution per unit £
Mushroom Risotto	3.45-0.75-0.30	2.40
Veggie Paella	3.30-0.60-0.25	2.45
Pasta Bake	3.80-1.10-0.50	2.20

(b)

> Marginal costing
>
> - Variable costs are included in the marginal costing calculation.
>
> - In line with IAS 2, and therefore closer to financial reporting requirements, and suitable for a business with a closely integrated management and financial reporting system
>
> - If inventory levels are falling, marginal costing profit will be higher as less fixed overheads are carried forward under absorption costing.
>
> Absorption costing
>
> - Both variable costs and fixed costs are included in absorption costing.
>
> - This allows management to see whether all of the costs associated with the business have been covered by the proposed sales target for the year.
>
> - The value of remaining stock at year end is higher under absorption costing as a result of including fixed costs within their value.
>
> - If inventory levels are increasing, profit will be higher as more fixed overheads are carried forward to the following period in closing inventory.
>
> - Recommended for cost plus pricing (as ensuring all costs covered)
>
> - It is therefore possible to manipulate the year-end profit figure by ensuring a higher level of stock at year end. This is a risk especially if there is incentive for management (such as bonuses) to manipulate the inventory figure at year end.

(c)

> Year 1: 45,480 × 25% = 11,370
>
> Year 2: (45,480-11,370) × 25% = 8,527.50
>
> Year 3: (45,480-11,370-8,527.50) × 25% = 6,395.62

Task 3.3

(a)

Current accounts

	Andrew £	Brown £	Carter £		Andrew £	Brown £	Carter £
Drawings W1 ▼	30,000	38,000	45,000	Balance b/d ▼	1,160	420	5,570
Balance c/d ▼	25, 892	10,054	14,204	Salaries ▼	15,000	18,000	24,000
▼				Interest on capital ▼	2,860	1,980	1,980
▼				Share of profit or loss ▼	36,872	27,654	27,654
▼				Balance c/d ▼	0	0	
▼				▼			
	55,892	48,054	59,204		58,892	48,054	59,204

W1 Drawings:

Andrew: £2,500 × 12 months = £30,000

Drawings for Brown and Carter taken from question

(b)

Statement	True	False
An error of commission does not cause an imbalance in the trial balance	✓	☐
The suspense account can appear in the financial statements	☐	✓
An error of principle causes an imbalance in the trial balance	☐	✓
A trial balance is prepared before the financial statements	✓	☐

An error of commission would not cause an imbalance in the trial balance because debits=credits (it is an error because the figures have been posted to the wrong account).

The suspense account is a temporary differences account and should be cleared prior to completion of the final trial balance. It should never be shown in the financial statements.

An error of principle does not cause an imbalance because debits=credits (it is an error because the figures have been posted to the wrong type of account).

A trial balance is always prepared prior to completion of the financial statements.

(c)

	✓
Cost centre	☐
Investment centre	☐
Profit centre	☑

A manager of an investment centre has control over the costs, revenues and assets of the division.

A manager of a profit centre has control over costs and revenues but not assets.

A manager of a cost centre has control over the costs but not the revenues or the assets.

....

Task 3.4

(a)

£	2,480

(b)

Details		£	Debit ✓	Credit ✓
Vehicle cost	▼	16,200	✓	
Bank	▼	16,200		✓

(c)

Details		£	Debit ✓	Credit ✓
Depreciation expense	▼	2,480	✓	
Accumulated depreciation	▼	2,480		✓

(d)

Account	Ledger Balance £	Adjustments £	Trial Balance Debit £	Credit £
Bank	22,450	(17,800)	5,450	
Capital	13,200			13,200
Purchase ledger control account	4,095			4,095
Sales ledger control account	6,725	1,700	7,625	
Sales	45,200	(1,700)		46,900
Purchases	32,570		32,570	
Administration costs	750		750	
Drawings		1,600	1,600	
Vehicles – Cost		16,200	16,200	
Vehicles Accumulated depreciation		2,480		(2,480)
Depreciation expense		2,480	2,480	
Totals			66,675	66,675

(e)

(1) To assess the FINANCIAL POSITION of a business (assets and liabilities, in the form of a statement of financial position)

(2) To monitor the FINANCIAL PERFORMANCE of a business (whether it is making a profit or loss, in the form of the statement of profit or loss)

(3) To understand the CHANGES IN FINANCIAL POSITION (through a cash flow statement)

Key users of a sole traders accounts may be: the owner of the business (Thomas himself), suppliers (if credit is to be extended to the business), lenders (such as a bank if Thomas decided to expand his business).

Task 3.5

(a)

> Contribution per road bike is calculated as sale price less variable costs:
>
> | Sale price per bike | 1,700 |
> |---|---|
> | Direct materials | (340) |
> | Direct labour | (70) |
> | **Contribution** | 1,290 |

(b)

> Marginal cost per unit is calculated by adding together the variable costs per unit.
>
> Therefore
>
> | Direct labour | £14 × 5 hours | = £70 |
> |---|---|---|
> | Direct material | | = £340 |
> | **Total marginal cost per unit £410** | | |

(c)

> Absorption cost per unit is calculated using this formula
>
> $$\frac{\text{Total fixed overheads} + \text{total variable costs}}{\text{Total budgeted units}}$$
>
> Therefore,
>
> $$\frac{£240,000 + (£340 \times 400 \text{ units}) + (5 \times £14 \times 400 \text{ units})}{400 \text{ units}}$$
>
> $$= \frac{£240,000 + £28,000 + £136,000}{400}$$
>
> $$= £1,010 \text{ per unit}$$

(d)

	£
Sales revenue 320 × £1700	544,000
Less:	
Cost of production	
400 × £410	164,000
Less: closing inventory	
80 × £410	(32,800)
	(131,200)
Contribution	412,800
Less: fixed costs	(240,000)
Profit	172,800

(e)

	£
Sales revenue 320 x £1700	544,000
Less:	
Cost of production	
400 × £1,010	404,000
Less: closing inventory	
80 × £1,010	(80,800)
	(323,200)
Profit	220,800

(f)

Relevance and Faithful representation

Task 3.6

(a)

	Cost £	Accumulated depreciation £	Carrying amount £
Non-current assets			
Fixtures & Fittings	24,500	8,550	15,950
Motor vehicles	48,000	29,800	18,200
Current assets			
Cash and cash equivalents	11,950		
Trade receivables (W1)	32,250		
Prepayments	1,250		
Inventory	43,500		
		88,950	
Current liabilities			
Trade payables	40,800		
VAT	3,050		
Accruals	1,000		
		44,850	
Net current assets			44,100
Net assets			**78,250**
Financed by:			
Capital			74,300
Profit for the year			22,950
Less:			
Drawings			(19,000)
			78,250

Workings

W1: 35,450-3,200 = 32,250

(b)

	Relevant cost ✓	Irrelevant cost ✓
Cost of the machinery used to manufacture the K57		✓
Salaries of the new staff	✓	
Rent on the new storage facility	✓	
Rent on the manufacturing premises		✓

As the K57 will be manufactured on existing machinery and in existing premises, these are already costs to the business, and does not affect the decision making. The costs will be incurred regardless of whether James decides to manufacture the new product.

The costs of the new staff (salaries, training costs, recruitment costs) would be relevant costs, as would the cost of renting a new storage facility. If the K57 did not go ahead, these costs would not be incurred.

(c)

The break-even point for a company is the sales volume which will give the company a profit of £nil.

If sales exceed the breakeven point, the company will make a profit. Breakeven analysis is also referred to as cost-volume-profit analysis

Formula:

Breakeven point = Number of units of sale required to breakeven

$$= \frac{\text{Fixed costs}}{\text{Unit contribution}} \times 100$$

Task 3.7

(a)

Details	Debit £	Credit £
Doubtful debt expense	950	
Doubtful debt provision		950

(b)

£	£1,000

Workings

£5,000/5 years = £1,000 per annum, full year's charge in the year of acquisition.

(c)

Details	Debit £	Credit £
Depreciation expense	1,000	
Accumulated depreciation		1,000

(d)

	£	£
Sales revenue		**344,450**
Less:		
Opening inventory	40,200	
Purchases	245,000	
Less: Closing inventory	(43,500)	
	241,700	
Cost of goods sold		**(241,700)**
Gross profit		**102,750**
Add:		
Discounts received		250
Less:		**103,000**

	£	£
Discounts allowed	950	
Depreciation expense (W2)	11,250	
Doubtful debt expense (W1)	950	
Electricity	2,050	
Insurance	1,800	
Motor expenses	3,100	
Miscellaneous expense	1,500	
Rent	3,400	
Telephone	1,950	
Wages	54,750	
Total expenses		**81,700**
Profit/loss for the year		**21,300**

(e)

£	£4,875

Workings

Contribution per unit:

Sales price	£30.00
Direct materials	£8.00
Direct labour	£2.50
	£19.50

Budgeted sales of 250 × £19.50 = £4,875

Task 3.8

(a)

	£	£
Sales revenue		344,195
Cost of goods sold		(208,800)
Gross profit		**135,395**
Less: Expenses		
Advertising	3,140	
Electricity	4,260	
Insurance	2,600	
Sundry expenses	3,180	
Telephone expenses	2,150	
Wages	43,200	
Depreciation machinery	7,600	
furniture and fittings	1,825	
Irrecoverable debt expense	2,550	
Total expenses		(70,505)
Profit for the year		**64,890**

(b)

	£
Net profit	**64,890**
Salaries:	
Emily	(8,000)
Interest on capital	
Joan (25,000 × 5%)	(1,250)
Emily (15,000 × 5%)	(750)
Kate (10,000 × 5%)	(500)
Profit available for distribution	**54,390**
Profit share (54,390/3)	
Joan	18,130
Emily	18,130
Kate	18,130
	54,390

(c)

Current account – Joan

	£		£
Drawings	18,195	Balance b/d	1,000
Balance c/d	2,185	Interest on capital	1,250
		Profit	18,130
	20,380		**20,380**
		Balance b/d	2,185

Current account – Emily

	£		£
Drawings	25,000	Balance b/f	540
Balance c/d	2,420	Salary	8,000
		Interest on capital	750
		Profit	18,130
	27,420		**27,420**
		Balance b/d	2,420

Current account – Kate

	£		£
Drawings	12,000	Balance b/f	230
Balance c/d	6,860	Interest on capital	500
		Profit	18,130
	18,860		**18,860**
		Balance b/d	6,860

(d)

	✓
FIFO values inventory at the higher values when the market prices are rising	✓
FIFO values inventory at the lower value when market prices are rising	
FIFO is the most appropriate method of valuation when inventories are mixed when stored.	
FIFO smoothes out price fluctuations making it easier to use the data for decision making	

Task 3.9

(a)

Suspense Account

Details	£	Details	£
Balance b/f	2,500	Drawings	2,000
Sales	500	Insurance	1,000
		Balance c/d	0
	3,000		**3,000**

(b)

£	£1,500

Workings

(£8,000 – £500)/ 5 years

(c)

	Initial trial balance		Adjustments	Revised trial balance	
	Debit £	Credit £			
Sales		265,500	(500)		266,000
Purchases	143,250			143,250	
Opening inventory	10,000			10,000	
Closing inventory	13,500	13,500		13,500	13,500
Office expenses	750			750	
Insurance	1,400		1,000	2,400	
Drawings	24,000		2,000	26,000	
Trade receivable	1,200			1,200	
Trade payable		1,350			1,350
Accruals		3,200			3,200
Prepayments	900			900	
Capital	70,000			70,000	
Cash at bank	16,050		(8,000)	8,050	
Suspense	2,500		(2,500)		
Motor vehicle			8,000	8,000	
Depreciation expense			1,875	1,875	
Accumulated depreciation			(1,875)		1,875
	283,550	283,550	0	285,925	285,925

(d)

£	126,250

Workings

Sales	266,000
Less	
Opening Inventory	10,000
Purchases	143,250
Less: Closing inventory	(13,500)
	(139,750)
Gross profit	126,250

(e)

> The point at which costs = revenue, therefore making nil profit

Task 3.10

(a)

4,250	units

Workings

$$\frac{102,000}{(£48.00 - £24.00)} = 4,250 \text{ units}$$

(b)

15%	%

Workings

$$\frac{5000 - 4,250}{5000} = 15\%$$

(c)

£	24 per unit

Workings

£48 - £18 - £6 = £24 per unit

(d)

7,300	units

Workings

$$\frac{£102,000 + £73,200}{£24 \text{ per unit}} = 7,300 \text{ units}$$

(e)

	✓
The effect of transactions being recognized when they occur	
That the business will continue in operation for the foreseeable future	✓
To ensure similar businesses can be compared to allow for investors to assess them	
To ensure the financial statements have been prepared on time	

(f) **Any THREE of the following reasons**

1. The LLP must be registered with the Registrar of Companies. A sole trader does not need to be registered.

2. Formation documents must be signed by at least two members. A sole trader requires no formal documentation in terms of its formation.

3. The partnership must file annual returns and financial statements. A sole trader prepares financial statements, however, these are not filed with the Registrar of Companies.

4. The partnership may require an audit. Sole traders do not require audits.

5. The LLP is a separate legal entity. This is not the case with sole traders.

6. Members liability is limited to an amount stated in the partnership agreement. A sole trader has unlimited liability for any debts incurred in the business.

7. As the financial statements are filed with the Registrar of Companies, the business is now open to scrutiny and the figures can be viewed by any interested party. As a sole trader, the financial statements of a business are private (unless specifically requested by an interested party such as a bank or investor). The accounts of an LLP are in the public domain, whereas this is not the case for a sole trader.

8. The preparation of the financial statements must be completed in line with Generally Accepted Accounting Principles and Accounting Standards. Accounting Standards are not required to be followed in the preparation of sole trader financial statements.

Section 4 Ethics for Accountants/Final Accounts Preparation

Task 4.1

(a) The ethical principle breached is integrity as travel claims have been made dishonestly. This can be viewed as fraud and is a criminal offence. In addition the inflated travel expenses would have decreased reported profits and also taxable profits resulting in an underpayment of tax.

(b) This issue should be reported to a supervisor or line manager. If this is not reported or disclosed then Tara will be implicating herself in the fraud.

(c) The accruals concept accounts for transactions when they occur in a reporting period instead of when cash is received or paid. An example can be when a sale that is made just before the year-end and where payment is received in the next reporting period. In this situation the accruals concept requires the sale to be reported in the period when the sale was actually made and a corresponding trade receivable posted to reflect that the sale was outstanding at the year-end. Other examples of the accruals concept can include; prepayments, adjustments for opening and closing inventories and depreciation.

The going-concern concept requires preparation of the financial statements on the assumption that the business will continue to trade for the foreseeable future.

This will mean that non-current assets will be carried in the statement of financial position at their original cost less accumulated depreciation. If a business is not a going-concern then the non-current assets will be carried at a value closer to their actual realisable value if sold on the open market. This is especially relevant to businesses that use specialised machinery that have little use outside that specific business or industry.

Task 4.2

(a) The threats most involved here are self-interest and self-review. This is because there can be a self-interest in making claims for non-existent expenses and a self-review threat as the same person is effectively reviewing his or her expense claim. The ethical principle most at risk here is the integrity principle as it may be possible that expenses claims have been made dishonestly.

(b) A simple safeguard would be to reintroduce two members to staff to raise and review expense claims. There is less risk when two individuals have to be in collusion to facilitate a fraud. Another safeguard can be to rotate staff who are responsible for accounting for expense claims. This can reduce the risk of one person to have total control over a function and can help to identify any discrepancies when new staff take over responsibility.

(c) The contents of a partnership agreement can include the following:

The capital that each partner is required to initially invest into the business. This may include a minimum balance to be retained in the business.

If any interest is payable on balances on the partners' capital accounts. The agreement will also state the rate of interest and when to be received.

How profits are to be shared among partners. This profit share ratio will need to be updated when there is a change of partners or if it is agreed that the profit share should be amended.

Agreement on whether drawings can be made from the partnership. If drawings can be made then there may also be agreement on the date when drawings can be made.

Whether interest is chargeable on any drawings made by the partners. The agreement will also state the rate of interest and when to be charged.

The agreement will need to specify the salaries to be paid to partners. There can be differences in the amount of salaries paid to partners due to experience, qualifications or the amount of work put into the partnership business.

Task 4.3

(a) Goodwill is an intangible non-current asset that is an asset delivers a profit over and above the profit from the tangible assets of a business. Goodwill can arise from having a valuable brand name, customer loyalty or through special expertise of staff. As goodwill is intangible it can be very difficult to value and therefore is normally excluded from assets in the statement of financial position.

(b) The objectivity principle is most at risk when valuing goodwill as there can be a temptation for the valuer to be biased and place a too high figure for the goodwill figure. A possible safeguard here can be to have an independent valuer who should not be influenced when arriving at a valuation.

(c) The accounting procedure will be:

(i) Create and debit a goodwill account with the value of goodwill.

(ii) Credit the present partners using the current profit sharing ratio.

(iii) When the new partner joins debit capital accounts for goodwill using the new profit sharing ratio and credit the goodwill account.

In this way goodwill is recognised in the partner's capital accounts and then subsequently eliminated. Once this procedure has been completed the balance on the goodwill account will be nil.

Task 4.4

(a) The ethical principle most at risk in these circumstances is professional competence and due care. The professional competence and due care principle states that members require the required level of knowledge and skills to complete tasks in hand.

(b) The most robust and immediate safeguard Jemima can put in place here is not to complete this task until she has developed the necessary skills and knowledge to complete it to the standard expected.

The skills and knowledge can be obtained by a combination of the following examples of continuing professional development methods:

(i)   College and online courses
(ii)   Internal training
(iii)   Professional body seminars
(iv)   Professional journals
(v)   Peer learning
(vi)   Internet research

(c) The key differences between companies and sole traders can be outlined as follows:

There are specific accounting standards that apply to companies and not to sole traders.

Formats of the statement of profit or loss and statement of financial position are standardised with required headings and terminology. Sole traders have some flexibility on layouts that can be used.

Companies are obliged to produce additional statements. An example is the cash flow statement.

There are strict public filing rules and deadlines for companies to adhere to.

Tax on profit is included in a company's financial statements but does not appear in a sole traders financial statements.

Non-current assets are shown net of depreciation on the face of a company's financial statements. This is not normally the case for sole traders.

Companies are required to prepare notes to the accounts so that accounting policies and other information can be disclosed to users. Sole traders do not have a requirement for this additional disclosure.

Task 4.5

(a) Materiality is a concept that provides a cut-off value on how transactions are to be treated in the financial statements. An example can be when identifying whether an expenditure should be capitalised as a non-current asset in the statement of financial position or written-off as an expense in the statement of profit or loss. A materiality policy may set the materiality level at £500 so office expenditure under this amount would be an expense and anything over this threshold treated as a non-current asset. Different businesses will have a different level of materiality. What is material for a small business may not be for a larger business. A useful rule to keep in mind is if a misstatement or omission of an item changes a user's view of results then this item is likely to be material.

(b) The colleagues' statement is incorrect as materiality levels do not apply to criminal acts of money laundering. The Latin term for this is that there is no de minimis rule to exempt **from** the law. In this instance this matter should be reported to the business's Money Laundering Reporting Officer. The colleague appears to have an interest in not pursuing this issue further so may be involved in the fraud in some way. In which case care needs to be taken not to tip-off that this being reported.

(c) The four qualitative characteristics for financial information are:

Relevance

Financial information needs to be relevant to the use it is intended for. A test for relevance is if the information would economic decisions of users. Another aspect of relevance is timeliness as out of date information will be misleading for users.

Reliability

Financial information needs to represent the economic substance of transactions and be free from bias. When information is reliable users will have confidence in using the information to base their decision making on.

Comparability

This characteristic requires information to be complied and prepared on a consistent basis so that users can make useful comparisons between different businesses or time periods.

Ease of understanding

Information needs to be presented in such a way that a reasonably informed person would be able to interpret and make use of the information. Over complex information can make understanding difficult and will result in loss of value to users.

Task 4.6

(a) The ethical principle most at risk here is confidentiality as any information must not be disclosed without proper authority. Not only does Amy have a professional responsibility to keep information confidential but also there is a legal requirement under the Data Protection Act to keep individual information secure.

The threat most evident is intimidation as the customer is threatening to withdraw his custom if Amy does not comply with his request.

(b) Amy must refuse this request and to maintain complete confidentiality regarding customer details.

If Amy was to contact each customer and ask for specific authorisation to release information about them in this way then it can be acceptable. Other times when information can be disclosed is when it is in the public interest and if there is a legal requirement to do so.

(c) Advantages of operating as a partnership is the opportunity of ABC Supplies to bring additional capital and expertise into the business. Having a partnership arrangement can also help to expand the business by taking on new clients or customers or by perhaps diversifying into new areas of business.

Disadvantages can include disagreements between partners over business strategy, decision making, and how profits are to be shared. Potential disagreements can be minimised by having a formal partnership agreement before the partnership commences trading.

A partnership also has the same status as a sole trader with unlimited liability and this can be seen as disadvantage for the partners as they can become liable for the activities of the other partner or partners.

There has been a trend towards limited liability partnerships that have the basic features of a partnership set-up along with limited liability status.

Task 4.7

(a) A conflict of interest is where an individual's objectivity may become threatened due to the circumstances of an assignment or relationship. An example can be where an accountant is acting on behalf of two clients whose business interests overlap.

(b) The accountant will need to identify if any conflict of interest threats exist. If threats do exist and are considered to be significant then safeguards need to be put in place to reduce those threats to an acceptable level.

(c) There is a clear conflict of interest here as Jaz is preparing the accounts for both parties and is aware of sensitive information that is relevant to the loan A has made to B. In these circumstances Jaz must remain independent and complete any work with objectivity and without bias. A principle at threat here is confidentiality and Jaz needs to be very careful in not disclosing confidential information to either party.

The safeguards that Jaz can put in place may include:

- Inform both clients that she is acting for both clients

- Obtain written consent to act on behalf of both clients. This may include confidentiality agreements.

- Investigate whether a colleague may be able to handle the work of one of the clients

- Have a senior partner to independently review Jaz's work to ensure independence and confidentiality is being observed

- Ensure that any information is kept confidential within Jaz's office by having a 'Chinese Wall' to keep information secure or a code of conduct on access.

- In the last resort if all other safeguards are still not adequate resign from one of the assignments.

Task 4.8

(a) Capital represents the long-term investment into the business by its owner. When a business is started the owner may inject cash into business and this can be used to purchase non-current assets such as motor vehicles and current assets, for example inventories.

Over a period of time the amount of capital that is owed to the owner by the business will fluctuate due to profits and losses made by the business and drawings taken out of the business by the owner.

The capital of the business will be shown in the capital section of the statement of financial position.

(b) Answer: £68,000

Workings

Opening capital	56,730
Profit for the year	38,920
	95,650
Less drawings (24,650 + 3,000)	27,650
Closing capital	68,000

(c) The laptop Y has taken should be recorded as drawings and needs to reduce the balance of Y's partnership current account accordingly to the value of the laptop. Withdrawals of capital from a business are treated as drawings whether taken as cash or in other assets.

Y has been dishonest in not disclosing his actions to X and is in breach of the ethical principle of integrity.

The appropriate double entry will be:

Dr: Y's Current account £x

Cr: Purchases in the journal entry £x

£x = the value of the laptop

Task 4.9

(a) A limited company is financed by equity and this can be made up of share capital where shares have been issued and also accumulated profits that have been added to the reserves of the company.

Normally the owners of the business, the shareholders, will extract money from the company in the form of dividends paid from accumulated profits made by the company.

This is different to a sole trader or partnership arrangement where the owner or owners invest capital into the business and subsequently withdraw capital in the form of drawings.

(b) The two ethical principles most affected here are professional competence and due care and professional behaviour. The accountant did not take due care when not checking the equity figure was correct. Professional behaviour is also threatened as reports in the financial press and other media will bring disrepute to the accountancy profession.

Observing that equity had increased by 80 times from the previous year the accountant may have had some doubts over the accuracy of this increase.

(c) Professional scepticism is where a professional person may question the accuracy or validity of any information or evidence that is made available to them in the completion of their work. As the equity figure is a material amount in the financial statements the accountant should have initially questioned whether the £2m figure was correct and plan his work to obtain evidence to substantiate this figure.

Task 4.10

(a) The two relevant accounting standards here are:

IAS 2 Inventories

IAS 16 Property, plant and equipment

(b) The ethical principle most at risk when being out of date in knowledge and skills is professional competence and due care.

(c) An accountant can keep their skills and knowledge up to date by completing regular continuing professional development (CPD). Evidence of complying with the professional competence and due care can be achieved by keeping a CPD Log to record and explain any CPD activities completed. It is important to note that professional bodies do require completing of CPD and if a member is found to be in non-compliance then it is likely the body will take disciplinary action against the member.

If it is found that a member's work has been completed without all the necessary skills required this may also result in breach of contract with the risk of being sued for negligence by an injured party who may have suffered a loss due to sub-standard work.

Section 5 Spreadsheets for Accounting

Task 5.1

- Open the renamed spreadsheet and on the 'sales' worksheet insert a column between the columns 'course' and 'units'

  - Give the column the title 'unit price'
  - Use a lookup function to insert the unit price on the sales tab.

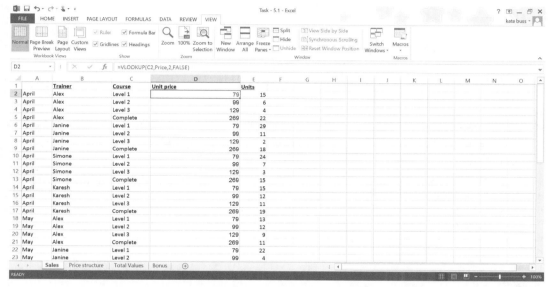

- Add a column in column F called 'Total value' and apply a formula to all cells in that column to show the total value of the units sold in each row.

  - Split the screen so that the headings remain visible.

  - Use the autosum function in cell F50 to determine the total values of sales for the quarter.

  - Format the numbers in this column to contain a thousand separator and make the contents of cell F50 bold.

Answer bank

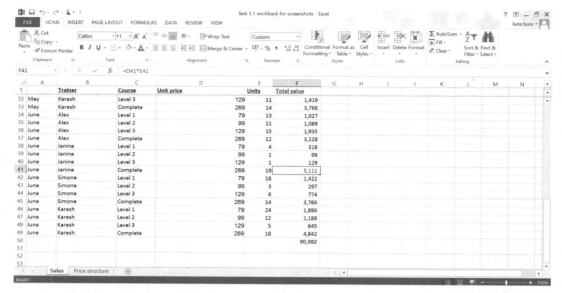

- Create a pivot table and pivot chart showing the total value of sales, broken down by course, made by each of Alex, Janine, Simone and Karesh.

  - Place the pivot table and pivot chart on a new sheet, and rename this sheet 'Total Values'

  - Add a chart title 'Total sales value Apr-Jun'

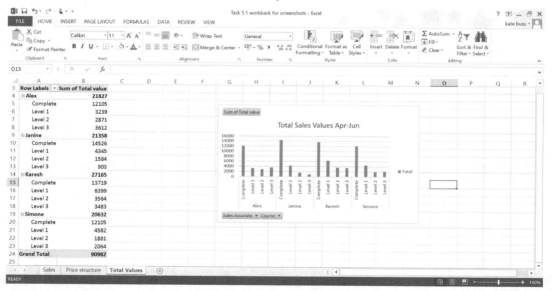

If any of the trainers manage to recruit 20 or more individuals on to any of the courses in a month, that trainer will receive a bonus of £5 per individual booked on that course.

- Give column G the heading 'Bonus' and use an IF function to show the amount of bonus payments due.

  - Total all bonuses to be paid.

BPP
LEARNING MEDIA

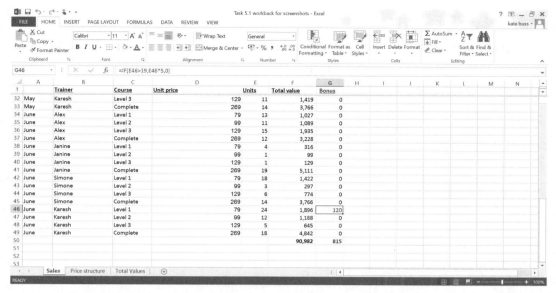

- Create a pivot table in a new tab which shows the total bonus to be paid to each trainer

- Sort the data in this pivot table to arrange the trainers in ascending order in terms of the bonus payment due to them for the quarter

- Rename the tab 'Bonuses'

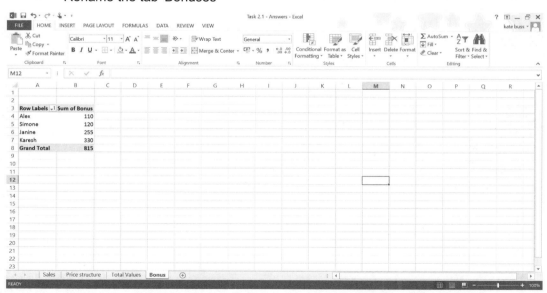

- Password protect the entire workbook and using the password Better123

Task 5.2

- Open the renamed spreadsheet and open the subs worksheet

  - Format the data on this page as a table, include the headings

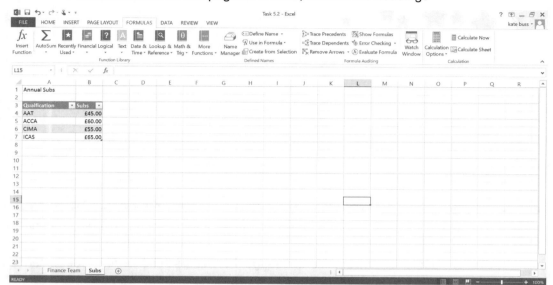

  - On the finance team worksheet, use a VLOOKUP function to complete the subs column

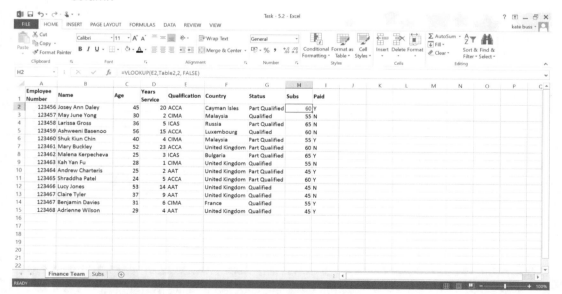

  - Format the subs figures in a red font colour

- Use conditional formatting to highlight all employees aged 40 and over

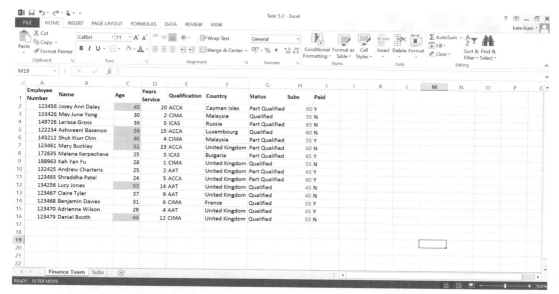

— Sort the data based on employee number, from lowest to highest.

• Rename column J as 'holiday'.

   — Use an IF statement to complete the data in this column to show how many days holiday per year to which each individual is entitled.

Answer bank

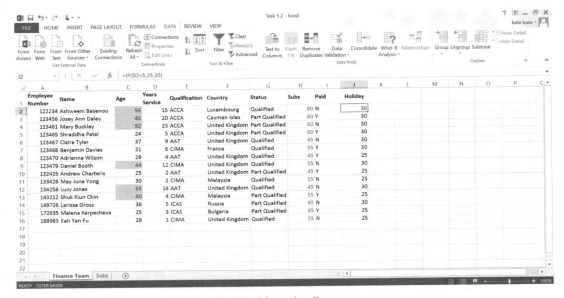

- Format the data as a table with light blue shading
  - Use the filter function to display only individuals who are members or students of the AAT who have not yet paid their subs.

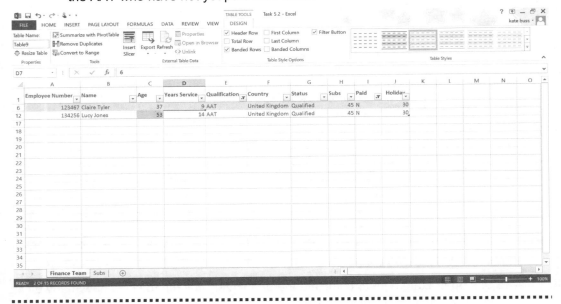

Task 5.3

- Open the renamed spreadsheet
  - Use find and replace to update any cells which refer to 'Cater co' to show the name of the new company

BPP
LEARNING MEDIA

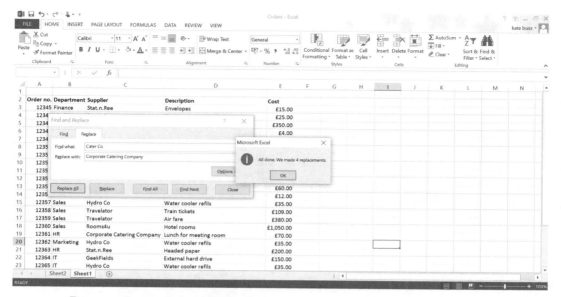

- Rename the worksheet 'order list'

- Create a pivot table and pivot chart in a new worksheet to represented the amount spent with each supplier

  - Rename the chart as 'Spend per supplier'

  - Rename the worksheet 'Supplier spend' and ensure the order of the worksheets is such that the order list worksheet is on the left and the supplier spend worksheet is on the right.

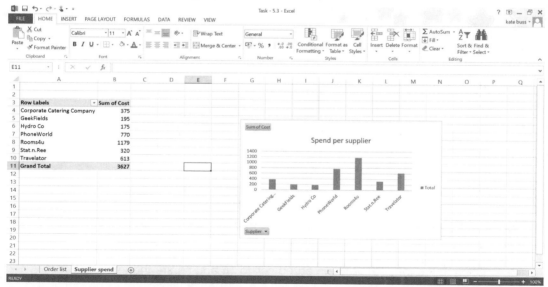

- Return to the Order List worksheet and format the data as a table using data style medium 14

Answer bank

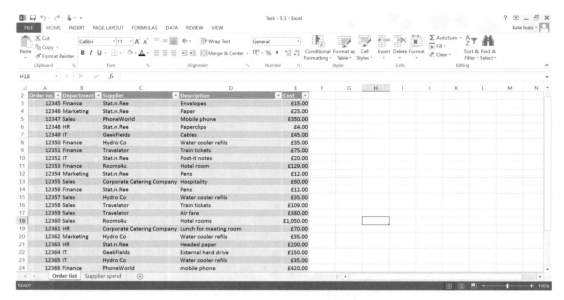

- Select the entire worksheet, copy the contents and paste this into a new worksheet

  - Rename the new worksheet 'Sales team order summary'

  - Apply filters to the data to show only data relating to orders raised by the sales team

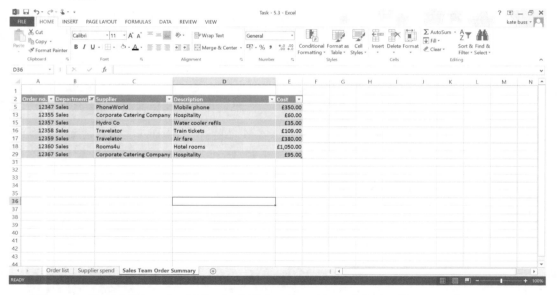

- Merge cells A1:E1 and add the text 'Sales Department Order Summary'

  - Change the font size in the merged cell to 16 and centre the text

  - Use the fill function to make the merged cell dark green and change the font colour in this cell to white

  - Remove the gridlines

- Prepare the document for being sent to the sales team. It is important that the sales team can see only their worksheet and none of the workings or data for the other departments

    – Hide the worksheets 'Order list' and 'Supplier Spend'

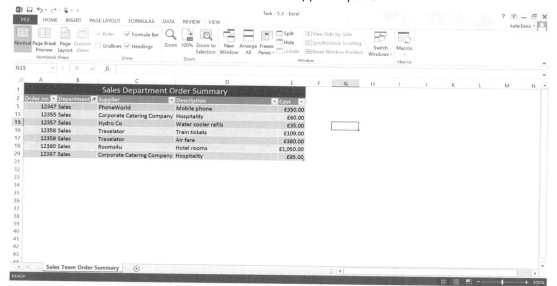

    – Protect the workbook so that no changes can be made to the source data and the hidden sheets remain hidden (greyed out if attempt to unhide)

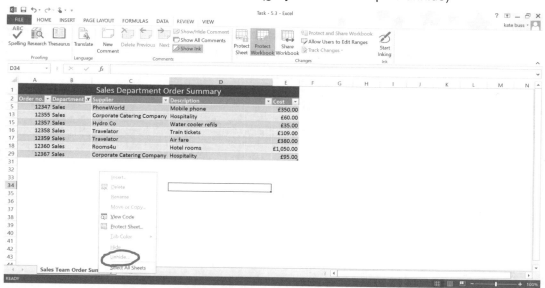

    – Use the SaveAs feature to save a copy of this version of the spreadsheet called 'Sales Team Order Summary'

Task 5.4

- Open the renamed spreadsheet and go into the location tab

  - Add the header 'location code' to column E and format the cell to be the same as the others in this row

  - Create a location code in cell E2 comprising of the aisle, location and bin number, eg 1A3.

  - Apply this formula to all relevant cells in column E.

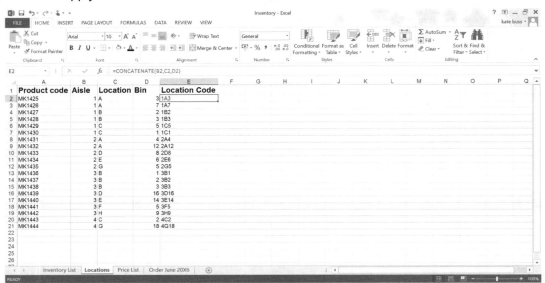

- Open the inventory list worksheet and use lookup functions to complete

  - The location information in column B

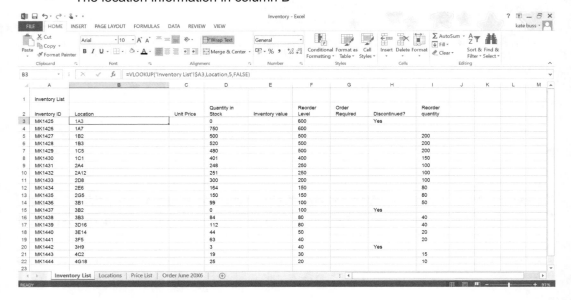

BPP
LEARNING MEDIA

- The unit price information in column C

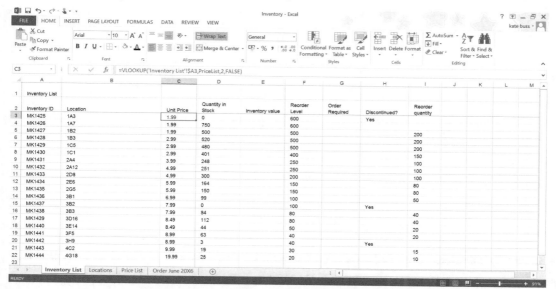

- Insert a formula to calculate the value of each item of inventory in column E

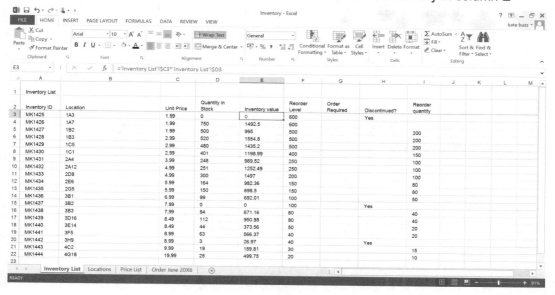

-

- Insert an IF function to determine whether or not items are due to be re-ordered in column G.

  - If the item is above the re-order level, this should return the value 0. If the item is on or under the re-order level, this should return the value 1.

Answer bank

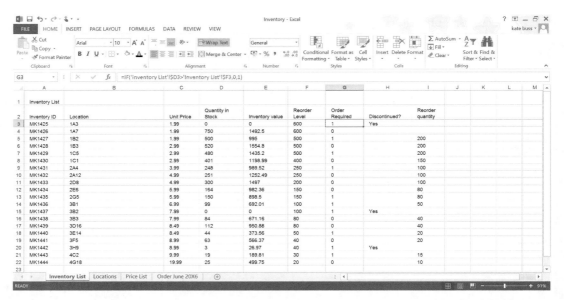

- Format the data contained in cells B1:H22 as a table, using Table style medium 14

    - Format cells A1:A22 using the fill function to change the cell colour to blue grey, accent 6, darker 25% and change the font colour to white to make it more visible

    - Hide the gridlines to improve the look of the worksheet

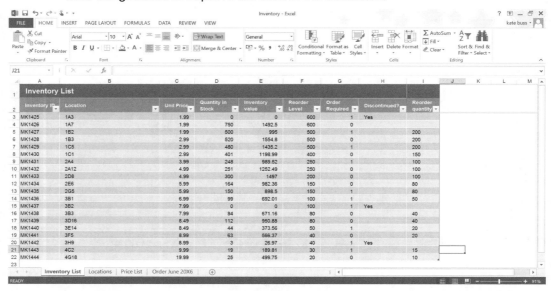

    - Sort the data by using the filter on column H to remove all items that have been discontinued

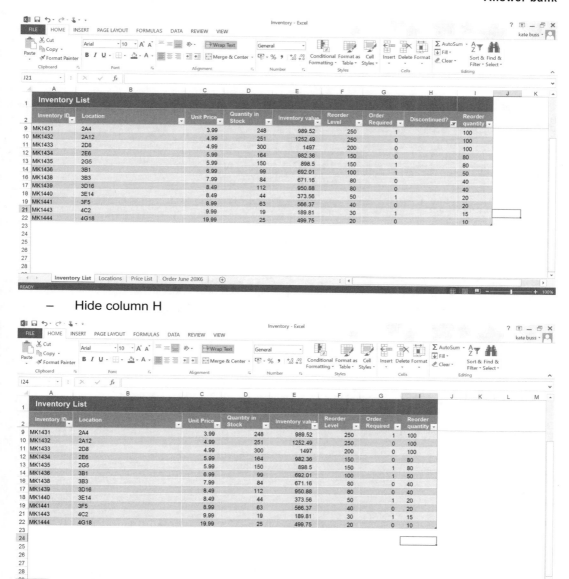

– Hide column H

- Use the filter function to show only those items that need to be reordered

Answer bank

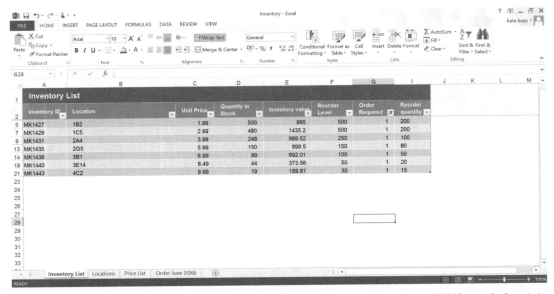

- Copy and paste the relevant items on to the Order June 20X6 worksheet to create an order list.

- Ensure you do not copy over the table format to the new order list

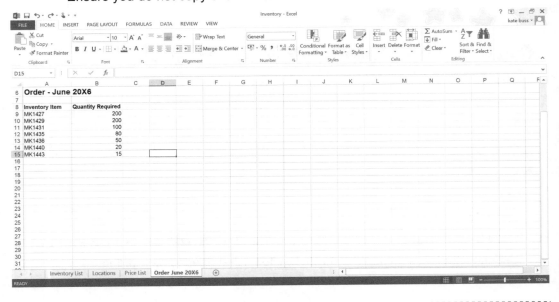

Task 5.5

- Open the renamed spreadsheet
  - Add a formula to cell C31 to calculate the amount of flexi-time earned or used on Monday. Apply this formula to the rest of the days of the week.

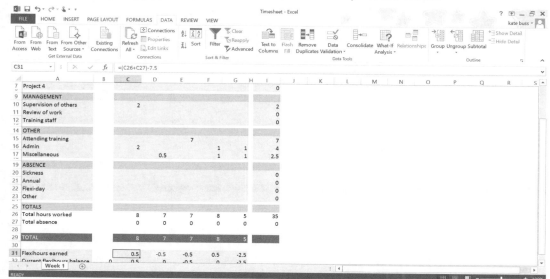

  - Add a formula to cell C32 to calculate the current balance of flexitime on Monday. Apply this formula to the rest of the days of the week.

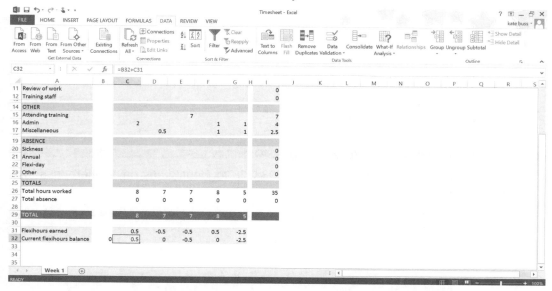

  - Replace the formulas in cells I25 and I28 with more robust formulas to check for errors in the summing of data

Answer bank

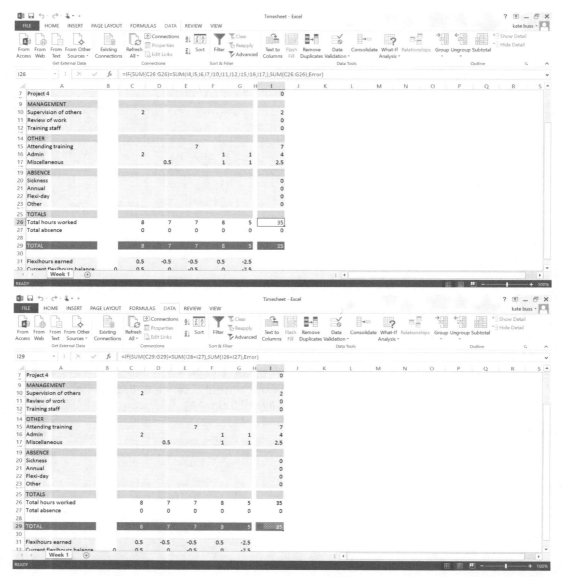

- Use a data validation function in cells C28:G28 to identify any days where less than six hours are worked.

  - Set the data validation to circle in red any days where fewer than six hours have been worked

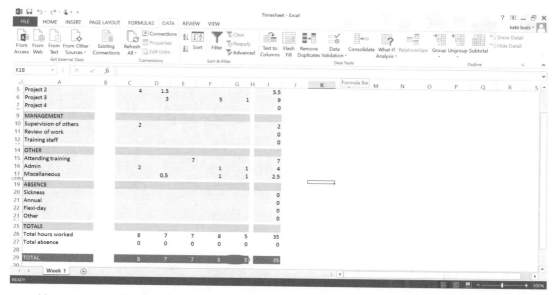

- Use a data validation function to prevent more than two hours of admin being charged on any given day

  - Attempt to change the admin charge on Monday to three hours.

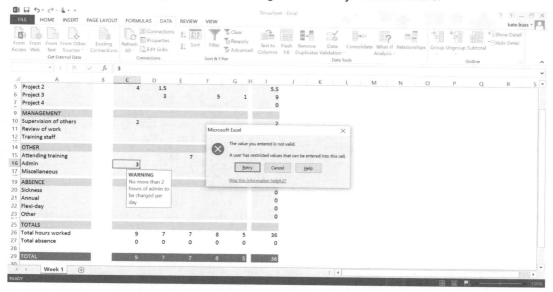

- Insert two new worksheets

  - Change the name of the new worksheets to 'Week 2' and 'Week 3'

  - Copy the format and formulas used on Week 1 to Week 2 and Week 3 and populate the spreadsheets with the information given above.

  - Link the formula related to flexi-time to ensure the balance from week 1 is carried over to week 2 and so on.

Answer bank

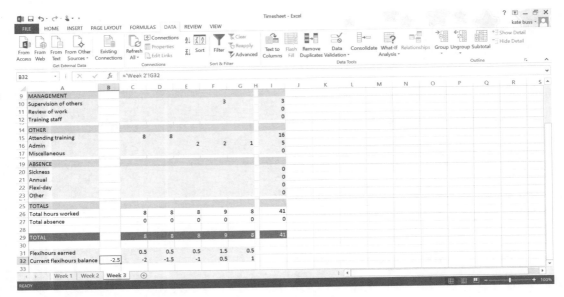

- Insert a new worksheet and rename it 'Summary'

  - Use the data from weeks 1-3 to produce a summary sheet which collates the total number of hours charged to each activity per week.

  - Format the summary sheet in the same style as the weekly worksheets

  - Use the split function to keep the header rows in place

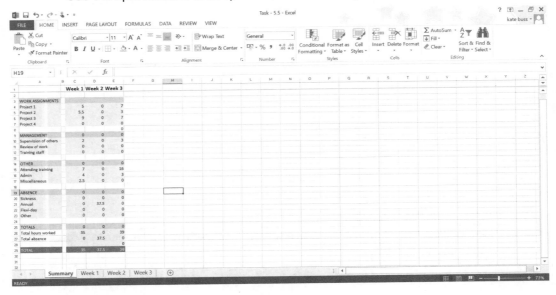

Task 5.6

- Open the renamed spreadsheet and go into the Record tab

  - Use a lookup function to complete the employee name column

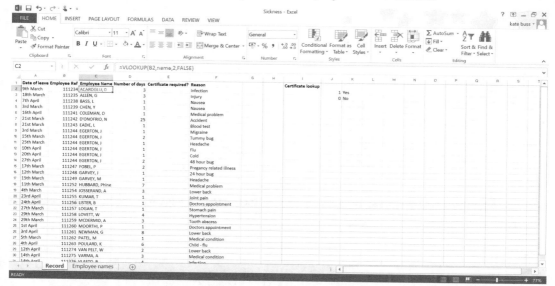

- Use an IF statement in column I along with a lookup function in column E to determine whether or not a certificate is required.

  - The IF statement should return the values 0 for no and 1 for yes and the lookup should refer to the table in columns J and K.

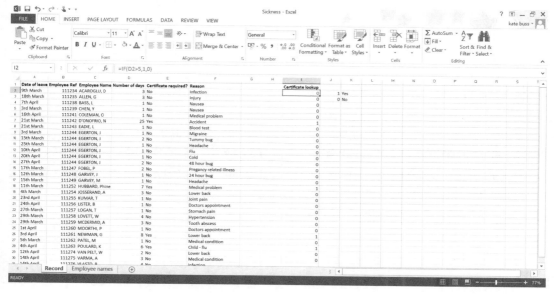

Answer bank

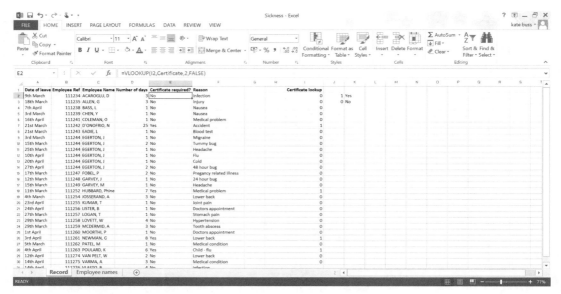

- Hide columns I, J and K

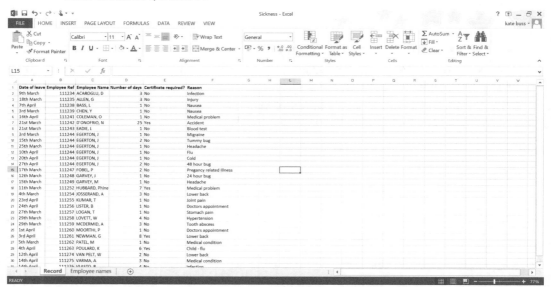

- Insert a pivot table on a new worksheet which summarises the total number of sickness days taken by each employee.

  - Rename this worksheet 'Summary'

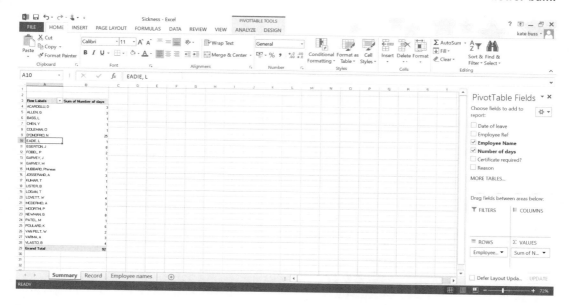

- Return to the 'Record' worksheet and sort the data by employee number

  - Use a subtotal function to count the instances of sickness taken by each individual

  - Highlight the entire worksheet and apply conditional formatting to highlight the employee number of any individuals who are at risk of falling into the frequent sickness category

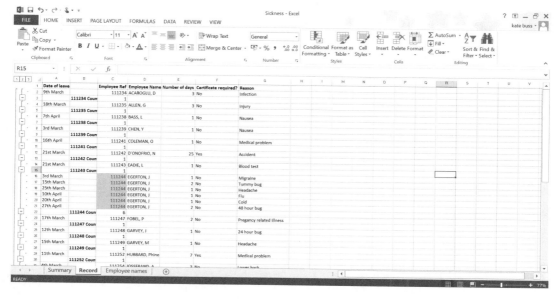

Task 5.7

- Open the renamed spreadsheet
    - Run a data validation test to remove any duplicate entries

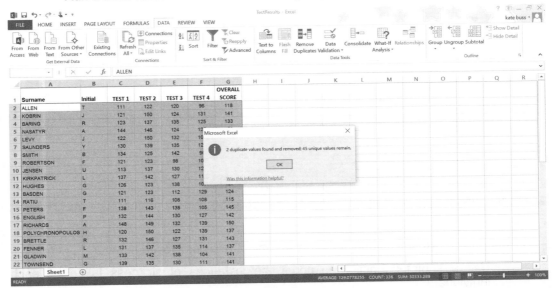

- Prepare a histogram based on the overall scores achieved by the students
    - The bins used should be in intervals of 10, beginning with 100
    - Change the axis to 'No. students' and 'total score'
    - Change the title of the histogram to 'Overall score analysis'

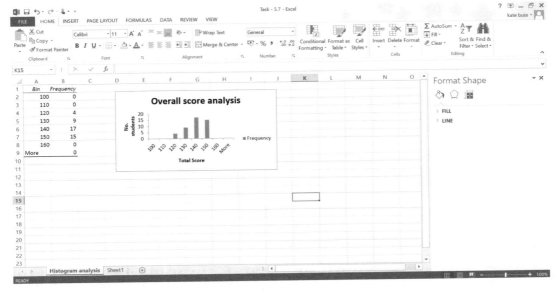

- Return to worksheet 'test results' and format the data as a table using table style medium 12

  - Use the filters within the table to identify only those students who will be offered an interview for the scholarship program.

  - Reorder the data using the filter to rank the potential scholarship candidates from highest scoring to lowest scoring

Answer bank

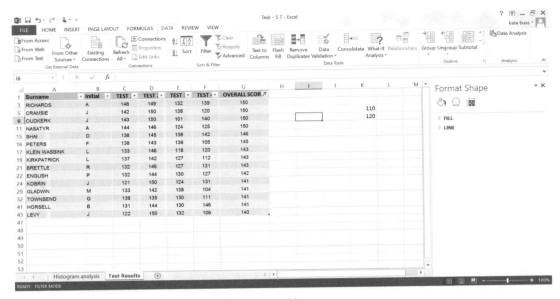

- Add a column called 'outcome' in column H

  - Insert the text 'Scholarship' in this column next to the top 5 students, and Interview against the remaining students

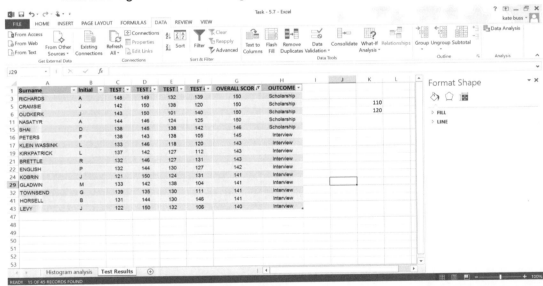

  - Remove the filters, and then refilter to show only students who are below average.

BPP
LEARNING MEDIA

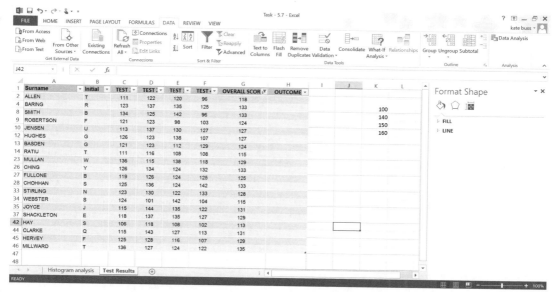

    –   **Add the text Refer in the outcome box for these students**

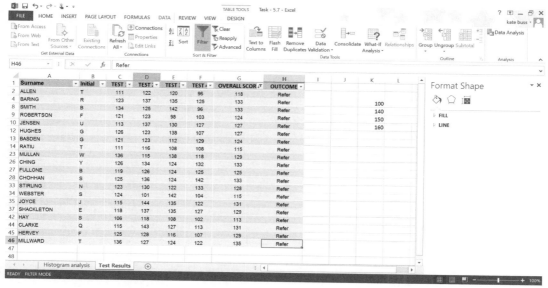

    –   Remove the filters

    –   Filter using the outcome filter to identify all students who have passed the tests but who are not contenders for the scholarship program

Answer bank

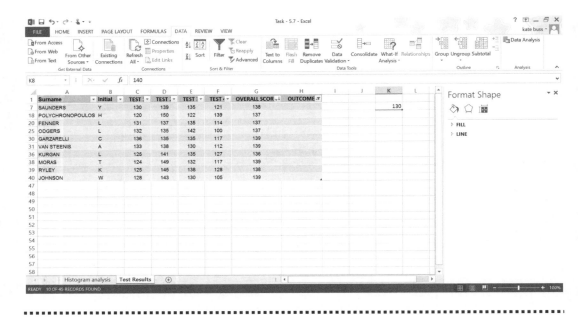

Section 6 Spreadsheets for Accounting/Management Accounting: Costing

Task 6.1

To:	Tom Howard
From:	Ian Chesterton
Date:	3 January 20X0
Subject:	Investment in plant and machinery

Hi Tom

The results of the calculations that you asked me to carry out are as follows:

- NPV $52,997

- Payback period 2.73 years

On both criteria we should proceed with the investment, as it has a positive NPV and a payback period of less than 3 years.

Two advantages of using the payback method are:

- It is a relatively simple calculation

- It takes into account cash flow and when we will recover our initial investment

	A	B	C	D	E	F
1	NPV					
2	Year	0	1	2	3	4
3	Revenues		200,000	220,000	231,000	237,930
4	Variable costs		(100,000)	(110,000)	(115,500)	(118,965)
5	Fixed costs		(20,000)	(20,000)	(20,000)	(20,000)
6	Capital expenditure	(240,000)				
7	Cash flows	(240,000)	80,000	90,000	95,500	98,965
8	Present value factor 9%	1.0000	0.9174	0.8417	0.7722	0.7084
9	Discounted cash flows	(240,000)	73,392	75,753	73,745	70,107
10	Net present value	52,997	ACCEPT			
11	Payback					
12	Cash flows	(240,000)	80,000	90,000	95,500	98,965
13	Cumulative cash flows	(240,000)	(160,000)	(70,000)	25,500	124,465
14				70,000		
15	Payback calculation	2.73	ACCEPT			

Task 6.2

To:	Lynne Dupont
From:	Barbara Wright
Date:	25 January 20X1
Subject:	Investment in machinery

Hi Lynne

The results of the calculations that you asked me to carry out are as follows:

- NPV -$50,380

- Payback period 3.71 years

The NPV is negative, so on that criteria we should not proceed with the investment. The payback period is however less than our maximum period, so according to the payback criteria we should proceed with the investment.

It would be better to use the NPV result to determine our decision, as NPV is a better method than payback for the following reasons:

- It takes into account the time value of money

- It considers all the cash flows related to the investment, not just those occurring within the payback period

	A	B	C	D	E	F
1	NPV					
2	Year	0	1	2	3	4
3	Revenues		250,000	275,000	297,000	311,850
4	Variable costs		(150,000)	(159,000)	(165,360)	(170,321)
5	Fixed costs		(40,000)	(40,000)	(40,000)	(40,000)
6	Capital expenditure	(300,000)				
7	Cash flows	(300,000)	60,000	76,000	91,640	101,529
8	Present value factor 11'	1.0000	0.9009	0.8116	0.7312	0.6587
9	Discounted cash flows	(300,000)	54,054	61,682	67,007	66,877
10	Net present value	(50,380)	REJECT			
11	Payback					
12	Cash flows	(300,000)	60,000	76,000	91,640	101,529
13	Cumulative cash flows	(300,000)	(240,000)	(164,000)	(72,360)	29,169
14					72,360	
15	Payback calculation	3.71	ACCEPT			

Task 6.3

To:	Charles Frere
From:	Susan Foreman
Date:	29 February 20X2
Subject:	Investment in new technology

Hi Charles

The results of the calculations that you asked me to carry out are as follows:

- NPV -$33,522
- IRR 11.84%

The NPV is negative, so on that criteria we should not proceed with the investment. The IRR is however more than our target IRR, so according to the IRR criteria we should proceed with the investment.

It would be better to use the NPV result to determine our decision, as NPV is a better method than IRR for the following reasons:

- It takes into account the absolute value of the investment
- It is not distorted by unusual patterns of cash flows

	A	B	C	D	E	F
1	NPV					
2	Year	0	1	2	3	4
3	Revenues		400,000	450,000	510,000	590,000
4	Variable costs		(180,000)	(207,000)	(231,840)	(255,024)
5	Fixed costs		(40,000)	(42,000)	(44,100)	(46,305)
6	Capital expenditure	(675,000)				
7	Cash flows	(675,000)	180,000	201,000	234,060	288,671
8	Present value factor 14'	1.0000	0.8772	0.7695	0.6750	0.5921
9	Discounted cash flows	(675,000)	157,896	154,670	157,991	170,922
10	Net present value	(33,522)	REJECT			
11	IRR	11.84				

Task 6.4

To:	Avril Rolfe
From:	Steven Taylor
Date:	14 March 20X3
Subject:	Investment in machinery

Hi Avril

The results of the calculations that you asked me to carry out are as follows:

- NPV $10,265
- IRR 9.30%

On both criteria we should proceed with the investment, as it has a positive NPV and an IRR that is more than our target IRR of 9%.

Two advantages of using the IRR method are:

- It takes into account the time value of money
- It gives a clear % answer

	A	B	C	D	E	F
1	NPV					
2	Year	0	1	2	3	4
3	Sales units		60,000	70,000	80,000	90,000
4	Sales price per unit		5.00	5.50	6.00	6.60
5	Variable cost per unit		(3.00)	(3.40)	(3.80)	(4.30)
6	Revenues		300,000	385,000	480,000	594,000
7	Variable costs		(180,000)	(238,000)	(304,000)	(387,000)
8	Fixed costs		(60,000)	(60,000)	(60,000)	(60,000)
9	Capital expenditure	(320,000)				
10	Cash flows	(320,000)	60,000	87,000	116,000	147,000
11	Present value factor 8%	1	0.9259	0.8573	0.7938	0.7350
12	Discounted cash flows	(320,000)	55,554	74,585	92,081	108,045
13	Net present value	10,265	ACCEPT			
14	IRR	9.30				

Task 6.5

To:	Kate Harvey
From:	Dodo Chaplet
Date:	11 April 20X4
Subject:	Variances in quarter to 31 March 20X4

Hi Kate

The operating profit variance from the flexed budget was $9,800 favourable. This arose because the budgeted profit when flexed to the actual volume of 45,000 units was $311,500, whereas we made an actual profit of $321,300.

The single most significant variance was aloe vera, which was $27,000 favourable. This could have been achieved by changing suppliers.

The single most significant adverse variance was quality control expenses, which was $6,975 adverse. This could have been due to problems with the materials being supplied – possibly linked to the favourable variance for aloe vera.

	A	B	C	D	E	F	G	H	I	J
1				12.50%						
2	Maxwell Co Original budget for the quarter ended 31 March 20X4									
3			Original budget	Flexed budget	Actual results	Variances				
4										
5	Revenue		920,000	1,035,000	1,040,000	5,000				
6	Materials	Silk powder	264,000	297,000	300,000	-3,000				
7	Materials	Silk amino acids	32,000	36,000	37,500	-1,500				
8	Materials	Aloe vera	224,000	252,000	225,000	27,000	Most significant favourable variance			
9	Direct labour	Skilled	30,000	33,750	37,100	-3,350				
10	Direct labour	Unskilled	15,000	16,875	17,500	-625				
11	Variable overheads	Supervision	30,000	33,750	36,200	-2,450				
12	Variable overheads	Quality control	25,000	28,125	35,100	-6,975	Most significant adverse variance			
13	Fixed overheads	Sales and distribution	18,000	18,000	22,400	-4,400				
14	Fixed overheads	Administration	8,000	8,000	7,900	100				
15	Operating profit		274,000	311,500	321,300	9,800				
16										
17						Balanced				
18										
19	Maxwell Co Original budget for the quarter ended 31 March 20X4 (cost summary)									
20			Original budget	Flexed budget	Actual results	Variances				
21										
25	Materials total		520,000	585,000	562,500	22,500				
28	Direct labour total		45,000	50,625	54,600	-3,975				
31	Variable overheads total		55,000	61,875	71,300	-9,425				
34	Fixed overheads totals		26,000	26,000	30,300	-4,300				
35	Costs		646,000	723,500	718,700	4,800				
36										

Task 6.6

To:	Abby Hudson
From:	Ben Jackson
Date:	1 May 20X5
Subject:	Variances in quarter to 31 March 20X5

Hi Abby

The operating profit variance from the flexed budget was $115 adverse. This arose because the budgeted profit when flexed to the actual volume of 3,825 meals sold was $82,195, whereas we made an actual profit of $82,080.

The biggest single favourable variance was revenue, which was $7,000 favourable. This could have arisen because customers chose a more expensive mix of food and drink than we budgeted for in an average meal.

The biggest single adverse variance was kitchen staff wages, which was 2,750 adverse. The adverse variance for waiters' wages was almost as high, suggesting that that we employed staff for more hours than the business needed them.

	A	B	C	D	E	F	G	H	I	J
1				-15%						
2	Williams restaurant Original budget for the quarter ended 31 March 20X5									
3			Original budget	Flexed budget	Actual results	Variances				
4										
5	Revenue		220,000	187,000	194,000	7,000	Most significant favourable variance			
6	Consumables	Food	18,000	15,300	16,100	-800				
7	Consumables	Drink	7,800	6,630	6,850	-220				
8	Labour	Waiter wages	13,000	11,050	13,650	-2,600				
9	Labour	Kitchen staff wages	14,000	11,900	14,650	-2,750	Most significant unfavourable variance			
10	Variable overheads	Energy	9,500	8,075	7,770	305				
11	Variable overheads	Administration	1,000	850	900	-50				
12	Fixed overheads	Manager's salary	13,500	13,500	13,500	0				
13	Fixed overheads	Chef's salary	12,000	12,000	12,900	-900				
14	Fixed overheads	Rent, rates and depreciation	13,000	13,000	12,700	300				
15	Fixed overheads	Financial and administration	12,500	12,500	12,900	-400				
16	Operating profit		105,700	82,195	82,080	-115				
17										
18						Balanced				
19	Williams restaurant Original budget for the quarter ended 31 March 20X5 (Cost summary)									
20			Original budget	Flexed budget	Actual results	Variances				
21										
24	Consumables total		25,800	21,930	22,950	-1,020				
27	Labour total		27,000	22,950	28,300	-5,350				
30	Variable overheads total		10,500	8,925	8,670	255				
35	Fixed overheads total		51,000	51,000	52,000	-1,000				
36	Total costs		114,300	104,805	111,920	-7,115				

Task 6.7

To:	Laura Wilde
From:	Jamie McCrimmon
Date:	11 June 20X6
Subject:	Variances for year ended 31 May 20X6 and staff costs

Hi Laura

The operating profit variance from the flexed budget was $94,000 adverse. This arose because the budgeted profit when flexed to the actual number of 21,850 patient days was $239,000, whereas we made an actual surplus of $145,000.

The most significant adverse overhead variances in each cost category were a variance of $5,000 in catering costs (variable costs), a variance of $14,000 for nurse costs (staff costs) and a variance of $40,000 in administration costs (fixed costs). The catering costs could have been higher than expected due to a general increase in food prices.

The increase of $110,000 in costs for staff needed to cope with 25,000 patient days will be a concern to our hospital. The maximum amount of funding that the hospital will receive when it is able to take 25,000 patient days is $4 million, which is an increase of only $67,000 on current funding, leaving a shortfall of $43,000. The $4 million will also need to cover an increase in variable costs, increasing the risks that the hospital will run a deficit.

	A	B	C	D	E	F	G
1				15%			
2	Westside Hospital Original budget for the year ended 31 May 20X6						
3			Original budget	Flexed budget	Actual results	Variances	
4							
5	Revenue		3,420,000	3,933,000	3,933,000	0	
6	Variable costs	Catering	440,000	506,000	511,000	(5,000)	
7	Variable costs	Laundry	120,000	138,000	142,000	(4,000)	
8	Variable costs	Pharmacy	560,000	644,000	638,000	6,000	
9	Staff costs	Supervisors	150,000	150,000	160,000	(10,000)	
10	Staff costs	Nurses	184,000	230,000	244,000	(14,000)	
11	Staff costs	Assistants	352,000	416,000	421,000	(5,000)	
12	Fixed costs	Administration	750,000	750,000	790,000	(40,000)	
13	Fixed costs	Security	80,000	80,000	82,000	(2,000)	
14	Fixed costs	Rent and property	780,000	780,000	800,000	(20,000)	
15	Surplus/(Deficit)		4,000	239,000	145,000	(94,000)	
16							
17						Balanced	
18							
19	Westside Hospital Staffing costs for the year ended 31 May 20X8						
20			Current budget	New budget	Increase		
21							
22	Staff costs	Supervisors	150,000	150,000	-		
23	Staff costs	Nurses	230,000	276,000	46,000		
24	Staff costs	Assistants	416,000	480,000	64,000		
25	Increase				110,000		

Task 6.8

To:	Polly Urquhart
From:	Victoria Waterfield
Date:	21 July 20X7
Subject:	Variances for year ended 30 June 20X7

Hi Polly

The operating profit variance from the flexed budget was $145,700 adverse. This arose because the budgeted profit when flexed to the actual volume of 16,500 chargeable consultant hours was $980,200, whereas we made an actual surplus of $834,500.

In % terms the three largest adverse variances were the casual wages (13.64%), printing, postage and stationery (12.50%) and telephone (8.59%). Whilst we might be concerned that these are adverse variances, the three highest adverse cost variances in $ terms are completely different and we may be more worried about these.

The largest adverse variance of all in $ terms was for revenue and we may wish to examine the reasons for this separately.

	A	B	C	D	E	F	G
1					10%		
2	Farrell Co Original budget for the year ended 30 June 20X7						
3			Original budget	Flexed budget	Actual results	Variances $	Variances %
4							
5	Revenue		2,000,000	2,200,000	2,100,000	(100,000)	(4.55)
6	Fixed overheads	Administration staff salaries	100,000	100,000	105,000	(5,000)	(5.00)
7	Fixed overheads	Consultants' salaries	960,000	960,000	990,000	(30,000)	(3.13)
8	Variable overheads	Casual wages	14,000	15,400	17,500	(2,100)	(13.64)
9	Fixed overheads	Motor and travel costs	75,000	75,000	80,000	(5,000)	(6.67)
10	Fixed overheads	Telephone	8,000	8,000	8,200	(200)	(2.50)
11	Variable overheads	Telephone	18,000	19,800	21,500	(1,700)	(8.59)
12	Variable overheads	Printing, postage and stationery	16,000	17,600	19,800	(2,200)	(12.50)
13	Fixed overheads	Premises and equipment	24,000	24,000	23,500	500	2.08
14	Operating profit		785,000	980,200	834,500	(145,700)	(14.86)
15							
16						Balanced	
17							
18	Farrell Co Variance analysis for the year ended 30 June 20X7						
19			Original budget	Flexed budget	Actual results	Variances $	Variances %
20							
21	Variable overheads	Casual wages	14,000	15,400	17,500	(2,100)	(13.64)
22	Variable overheads	Printing, postage and stationery	16,000	17,600	19,800	(2,200)	(12.50)
23	Variable overheads	Telephone	18,000	19,800	21,500	(1,700)	(8.59)
24	Fixed overheads	Motor and travel costs	75,000	75,000	80,000	(5,000)	(6.67)
25	Fixed overheads	Administration staff salaries	100,000	100,000	105,000	(5,000)	(5.00)
26	Revenue		2,000,000	2,200,000	2,100,000	(100,000)	(4.55)
27	Fixed overheads	Consultants' salaries	960,000	960,000	990,000	(30,000)	(3.13)
28	Fixed overheads	Telephone	8,000	8,000	8,200	(200)	(2.50)
29	Fixed overheads	Premises and equipment	24,000	24,000	23,500	500	2.08

Task 6.9

To:	Ken Masters
From:	Zoe Heriot
Date:	24 July 20X8
Subject:	Analysis of performance for quarter ended 30 June 20X8

Hi Ken

I have compared the actual results with what the budget would have been for 11,500 units and 12,500 units. Rather worryingly, the actual profit of $297,900 is less than both of the budgeted profits. At 11,500 units the actual profit is $13,900 less than the budgeted profit of $311,800 and at 12,500 units the actual profit is $45,100 less than the budgeted profit of $343,000.

It is clear from the figures that the fixed costs and costs of Material B were over-budget whatever the level of sales.

The other figures show conflicting pictures about what the level of production and sales was. The actual revenue is much closer to the budgeted revenue for 11,500 units, but the other cost figures are closer to the budgeted figures for 12,500 units. This suggests either that we did not achieve the level of revenue we expected on what we sold, or that there was a general problem controlling costs.

	A	B	C	D	E	F	G	H
1				15%	25%			
2	Carter Co Original budget for the quarter ended 30 June 20X8							
3			Original budget	Flexed budget 11,500	Flexed budget 12,500	Actual results	Variances 11,500	Variances 12,500
4								
5	Revenue		600,000	690,000	750,000	700,000	10,000	-50,000
6	Materials	A	40,000	46,000	50,000	49,000	-3,000	1,000
7	Materials	B	44,000	50,600	55,000	56,000	-5,400	-1,000
8	Materials	C	32,000	36,800	40,000	39,200	-2,400	800
9	Direct labour	Skilled	72,000	82,800	90,000	87,000	-4,200	3,000
10	Direct labour	Unskilled	36,000	41,400	45,000	44,000	-2,600	1,000
11	Variable overheads	Supervision	42,000	48,300	52,500	51,000	-2,700	1,500
12	Variable overheads	Production planning	22,000	25,300	27,500	26,700	-1,400	800
13	Fixed overheads	Sales and distribution	25,000	25,000	25,000	26,500	-1,500	-1,500
14	Fixed overheads	Finance and administration	22,000	22,000	22,000	22,700	-700	-700
15	Operating profit		265,000	311,800	343,000	297,900	-13,900	-45,100
16								
17							Balanced	Balanced
18								
19	Carter Co Overhead summary for the quarter ended 30 June 20X8							
20			Original budget	Flexed budget 11,500	Flexed budget 12,500	Actual results	Variances 11,500	Variances 12,500
21								
22	Materials	summary	116,000	133,400	145,000	144,200	-10,800	800
23	Direct labour	summary	108,000	124,200	135,000	131,000	-6,800	4,000
24	Variable overheads	summary	64,000	73,600	80,000	77,700	-4,100	2,300
25	Fixed overheads	summary	47,000	47,000	47,000	49,200	-2,200	-2,200
26	Cost summary		335,000	378,200	407,000	402,100	-23,900	4,900

Task 6.10

To:	Bill Sayers
From:	Liz Shaw
Date:	19 August 20X9
Subject:	Investment appraisal

Hi Bill

I've carried out the investment appraisal that you wanted. The results are that the payback period on in the investment is 3.69 years and the IRR is 12.87%.

Two problems with the results of the calculations are:

- I have not been given any benchmarks against which to assess whether the figures for payback period and IRR are satisfactory

- Net present value is considered to be a better method of investment appraisal than payback or IRR, as it uses discounted cash flows (which payback period does not) and provides a clear measure in absolute terms of whether a project is acceptable (which IRR does not)

	A	B	C	D	E	F	G
1	IRR						
2	Year	0	1	2	3	4	5
3	Revenues		180,000	189,000	198,450	208,373	218,791
4	Variable costs		(100,000)	(105,000)	(110,250)	(115,763)	(121,551)
5	Fixed costs		(45,000)	(45,000)	(45,000)	(45,000)	(45,000)
6	Capital expenditure	(150,000)					
7	Cash flows	(150,000)	35,000	39,000	43,200	47,610	52,241
8	Present value factor 10%	1.0000	0.9091	0.8264	0.7513	0.6830	0.6209
9	Discounted cash flows	(150,000)	31,819	32,230	32,456	32,518	32,436
10	Net present value	11,458					
11	Present value factor 15%	1.0000	0.8696	0.7561	0.6575	0.5718	0.4972
12	Discounted cash flows	(150,000)	30,436	29,488	28,404	27,223	25,974
13	Net present value	(8,475)					
14	IRR	12.87					
15	Payback						
16	Cash flows	(150,000)	35,000	39,000	43,200	47,610	52,241
17	Cumulative cash flows	(150,000)	(115,000)	(76,000)	(32,800)	14,810	67,051
18					32,800		
19	Payback calculation	3.69					

Task 6.11

To:	Vanessa Andenberg
From:	Jo Grant
Date:	24 September 20X1
Subject:	Breakeven analysis

Hi Vanessa

I've carried out the breakeven calculations that you asked me to carry out. They show that the breakeven sales volume is 16,500 units and the breakeven sales revenue is $990,000. We should achieve a contribution/sales ratio of 0.33. The margin of safety in units is 8,500, in % terms 34%, which is greater than our target of 20%. However our budgeted sales are 500 units short of the sales needed to achieve our target profit of $180,000.

Two problems with breakeven analysis are:

- It assumes fixed costs are constant
- It assumes variable costs per unit are constant

	A	B	C
1		**Breakeven calculations**	
2	**Revenue**	1,500,000	
3	**Variable costs**		
4	Direct materials	500,000	
5	Direct labour	350,000	
6	Assembly	80,000	
7	Packaging	70,000	
8	Total variable costs	1,000,000	
9	Variable costs per unit	40	
10	Contribution per unit	20	
11	**Fixed costs**		
12	Assembly	120,000	
13	Packaging	210,000	
14	Total fixed costs	330,000	
15	Breakeven point in units	16,500	
16	Breakeven point in revenue	990,000	
17	Contribution/Sales ratio	0.33	
18	Margin of safety in units	8,500	
19	Margin of safety in %	34.00	HIGHER
20	Target profit volume	25,500	LESS

Section 7 Spreadsheets for Accounting/Final Accounts Preparation

Task 7.1

	A	B	C	D	E	F
1	Adverts	100				
2	Bonus rate	2.5%				
3						
4	Staff employee number	Basic salary	Adverts sold during the year	Bonus	Total pay	
5	123	£20,000	85	£0	£20,000	
6	124	£22,000	150	£550	£22,550	
7	125	£28,000	70	£0	£28,000	
8	126	£25,000	165	£625	£25,625	
9	127	£20,000	50	£0	£20,000	
10	128	£18,000	210	£450	£18,450	
11	Total pay for all employees				£134,625	
12						

Suggested formulas

	A	B	C	D	E
1	Adverts	100			
2	Bonus rate	0.025			
3					
4	Staff employee number	Basic salary	Adverts sold during the year	Bonus	Total pay
5	123	20000	85	=IF(C5>B$1,B5*B$2, 0)	=(B5+D5)
6	124	22000	150	=IF(C6>B$1,B6*B$2, 0)	=(B6+D6)
7	125	28000	70	=IF(C7>B$1,B7*B$2, 0)	=(B7+D7)
8	126	25000	165	=IF(C8>B$1,B8*B$2, 0)	=(B8+D8)
9	127	20000	50	=IF(C9>B$1,B9*B$2, 0)	=(B9+D9)
10	128	18000	210	=IF(C10>B$1,B10*B$2, 0)	=(B10+D10)
11	Total pay for all employees				=SUM(E5:E10)
12					

Task 7.2

	A	B
1	**Expenditure**	**Value**
2	IT Cables	£180
3	Computer monitor	£210
4	Desk lamp	£65
5	Lighting fixture	£340
6	Filing cabinet (small)	£195
7	Filing cabinet (large)	£265
8		
9		

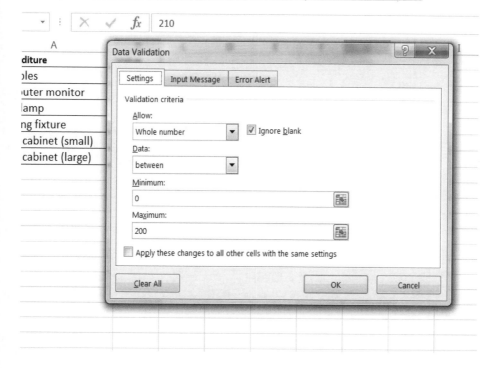

Task 7.3

	A	B	C	D	E	F
1	Item	Jeff	Gary	Fran		
2	Drawings	3,000	500	£4,000		
3	Interest on capital	90	£160	120		
4	Profit share	£12,750	£12,750	£25,500		
5						
6						
7		Column Labels ▾				
8	Values	Drawings	Interest on capital	Profit share	Grand Total	
9	Sum of Fran	4000	120	25500	29620	
10	Sum of Jeff	3000	90	12750	15840	
11	Sum of Gary	500	160	12750	13410	
12						
13						
14						

PivotTable Fields ▾ ×

Choose fields to add to report: ⚙ ▾

☑ **Item**
☑ **Jeff**
☑ **Gary**
☑ **Fran**

MORE TABLES...

Drag fields between areas below:

▼ FILTERS	▥ COLUMNS
	Item ▼

≡ ROWS	Σ VALUES
Σ Values ▼	Sum of... ▼
	Sum of... ▼

☐ Defer Layout Upda...   UPDATE

Task 7.4

	A	B	C	D	E	F	G
1			*Capital account*				
2			£			£	
3		Drawings	6,000	01/01/X6	Capital introduced	7,500	
4		Laptop	1,000		Fixtures and fitings	1,678	
5					Cash	1,500	
6	31/01/X6	Balance c/d	12,278		Profit	8,600	
7			19,278			19,278	
8				01/01/X7	Balance b/d	12,278	
9							
10							

Suggested formulas

	B	C	D	E	F	G
1		*Capital account*				
2		£			£	
3	Drawings	6000	01/01/X6	Capital introduced	7500	
4	Laptop	1000		Fixtures and fitings	1678	
5				Cash	1500	
6	Balance c/d	=SUM((F7-(C3+C4)))		Profit	8600	
7		=F7			=SUM(F3:F6)	
8			01/01/X7	Balance b/d	=C6	
9						
10						
11						

Task 7.5

(a)

	A	B	C	D	E	F	G	H
1				Mr A Client				
2				Statement of Profit or Loss				
3				For the year ended 31 May 20X6				
4								
5					£		£	
6	Sales revenue						280,480	
7	Opening inventory				7,800			
8	Purchases				150,800			
9	Closing inventory				9,000			
10	Cost of sales						149,600	
11	Gross profit						130,880	
12								
13	Less expenses							
14	General expenses				63,800			
15	Discounts allowed				470			
16	Administration costs				3,900			
17	IT Equipment depreciation				850			
18	Salaries				42,000			
19							111,020	
20	Net profit						19,860	
21								

Suggested formulas

	A	B	C	D	E	F	G	H
1					Mr A Client			
2					Statement of Profit or Loss			
3					For the year ended 31 May 20X6			
4								
5					£		£	
6	Sales revenue						280480	
7	Opening inventory				7800			
8	Purchases				150800			
9	Closing inventory				9000			
10	Cost of sales						=SUM(E7+E8-E9)	
11	Gross profit						=G6-G10	
12								
13	Less expenses							
14	General expenses				63800			
15	Discounts allowed				470			
16	Administration cos				3900			
17	IT Equipment depr				850			
18	Salaries				42000			
19							=SUM(E14:E18)	
20	Net profit						=G11-G19	
21								

Answer bank

(b)

Task 7.6

(a) & (b)

	A	B	C	D
1	**Partnership appropriation account**			
2	**For the year ended 31 August 20X6**			
3			£	
4	**Profit for the year**		180,000	
5	**Salaries:**			
6	Karen		11,400	
7	Jake		14,400	
8	Saffron		9,600	
9	**Interest on capital**			
10	Karen		1,000	
11	Jake		1,200	
12	Saffron		600	
13	Totals		38,200	
14	**Profit available for distrubution**		141,800	
15	Profit share			
16	Karen	20%	28,360	
17	Jake	65%	92,170	
18	Saffron	15%	21,270	
19	**Total profit distributed**	100%	141,800	
20				
21		**Accuracy check**	Correct	
22				

Suggested formulas

	A	B	C	D
1	**Partnership appropriation account**			
2	**For the year ended 31 August 20X6**			
3			£	
4	**Profit for the year**		180000	
5	**Salaries:**			
6	Karen		11400	
7	Jake		14400	
8	Saffron		9600	
9	**Interest on capital**			
10	Karen		1000	
11	Jake		1200	
12	Saffron		600	
13	Totals		=SUM(C6:C12)	
14	**Profit available for distrubution**		=(C4-C13)	
15	Profit share			
16	Karen	0.2	=C14*B16	
17	Jake	0.65	=C14*B17	
18	Saffron	0.15	=C14*B18	
19	**Total profit distributed**	=SUM(B16:B18)	=SUM(C16:C18)	
20				
21		**Accuracy check**	=IF(C14=C19,"Correct","Incorrect")	
22				

Task 7.7

(a)

	A	B	C	D	E
1		£		£	
2	**Sales**			**9,125**	
3	Opening inventory	1,500			
4	Add purchases	7,600			
5	Less closing inventory	-1,800			
6	Cost of sales			7,300	
7	**Gross proft**			**1,825**	
8					
9	**Alternative G.P. calculation**			**1,825**	
10					
11					
12					
13	**Profit profile**	%			
14	Sales	100			
15	Cost of sales	80			
16	Profit	20			
17					
18					

Suggested formulas

	A	B	C	D	E
1		£		£	
2	Sales			=D6*100/80	
3	Opening inventory	1500			
4	Add purchases	7600			
5	Less closing inventory	-1800			
6	Cost of sales			=SUM(B2:B5)	
7	**Gross proft**			=D2-D6	
8					
9	**Alternative G.P. calculation**			=D6*20/80	
10					
11					
12					
13	**Profit profile**	%			
14	Sales	100			
15	Cost of sales	80			
16	Profit	20			
17					
18					

(b)

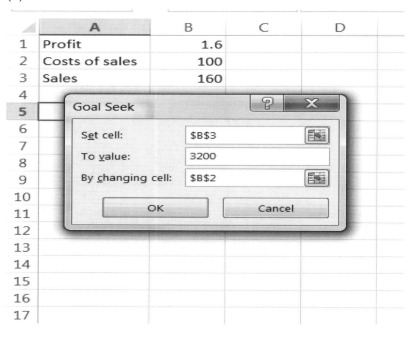

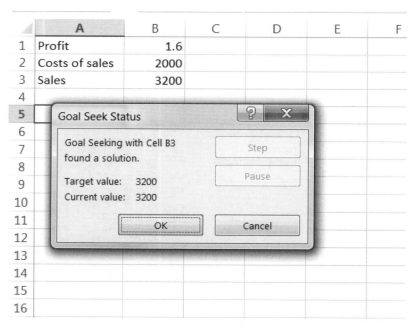

Task 7.8

	A	B	C	D	E	F
1	Property	50				
2	Motor vehicles	30%				
3	Fixtures and fittings	10%				
4						
5			20X5		20X6	
6		Cost	Accumulated depreciation	Depreciation charge	Accumulated depreciation	Carrying amount
7		£	£	£	£	£
8	Property	650,000	195,000	13,000	208,000	442,000
9	Motor vehicles	45,000	22,950	6,615	29,565	15,435
10	Fixtures and fitings	27,000	5,130	2,187	7,317	19,683
11						**477,118**
12						
13						

Suggested formulas

	A	B	C	D	E	F
1	Property	50				
2	Motor vehicles	0.3				
3	Fixtures and fittings	0.1				
4						
5			20X5		20X6	
6		Cost	Accumulated depreciation	Depreciation charge	Accumulated depreciation	Carrying amount
7		£	£	£	£	£
8	Property	650000	195000	=B8/B1	=C8+D8	=B8-E8
9	Motor vehicles	45000	22950	=(B9-C9)*B2	=C9+D9	=B9-E9
10	Fixtures and fitings	27000	5130	=(B10-C10)*B3	=C10+D10	=B10-E10
11						=SUM(F8:F10)
12						
13						
14						
15						

Task 7.9

	A	B	C	D
1	**Trial Balance - SOFP**			
2	Accruals		500.00	
3	Bank	3,000.00		
4	Capital		10,000.00	
5	Depreciation		2,500.00	
6	Non-current assets	10,000.00		
7	Payables		1,125.00	
8	Prepayments	450.00		
9	Receivables	675.00		
10		14125	14125	
11				
12				

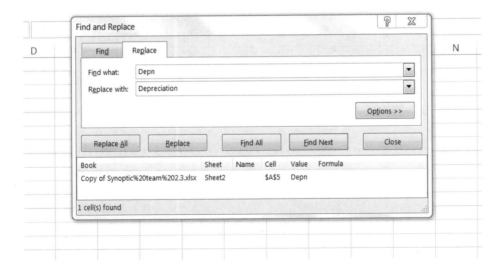

BPP
LEARNING MEDIA

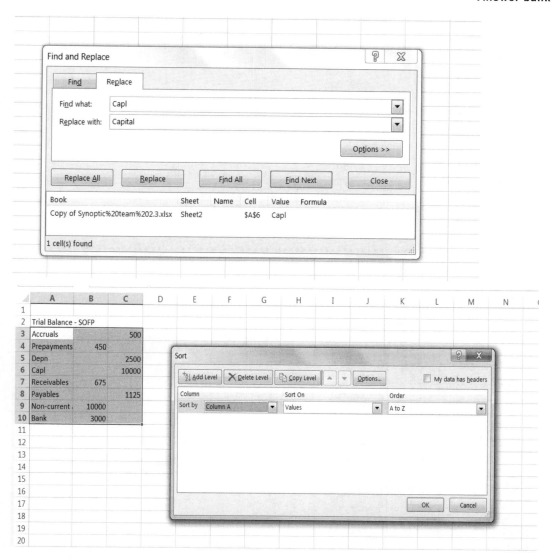

Suggested formulas

Answer bank

	A	B	C	D
1		**Trial Balance - SOFP**		
2	Accruals		500	
3	Bank	3000		
4	Capital		10000	
5	Depreciation		2500	
6	Non-current assets	10000		
7	Payables		1125	
8	Prepayments	450		
9	Receivables	675		
10		=SUM(B2:B9)	=SUM(C2:C9)	
11				

Task 7.10

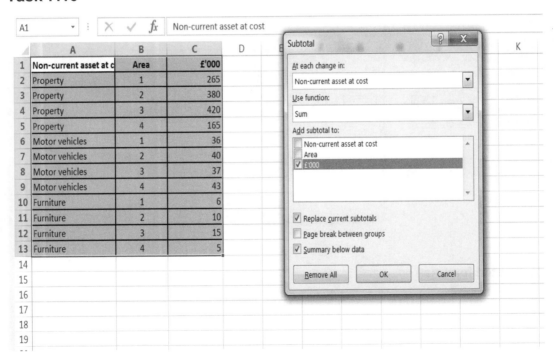

BPP
LEARNING MEDIA

	A	B	C	D
1	**Non-current asset at c**	**Area**	**£'000**	
2	Property	1	265	
3	Property	2	380	
4	Property	3	420	
5	Property	4	165	
6	**Property Total**		1230	
7	Motor vehicles	1	36	
8	Motor vehicles	2	40	
9	Motor vehicles	3	37	
10	Motor vehicles	4	43	
11	**Motor vehicles Total**		156	
12	Furniture	1	6	
13	Furniture	2	10	
14	Furniture	3	15	
15	Furniture	4	5	
16	**Furniture Total**		36	
17	**Grand Total**		1422	
18				

Answer bank

AAT AQ2016 SAMPLE ASSESSMENT
Level 3 Synoptic Assessment

Time allowed: 3 hours

AAT AQ2016 SAMPLE ASSESSMENT

Level 3 Synoptic Assessment
AAT sample assessment

Scenario context data – BLM & Co

You are Sam Jones, a part-qualified accounting technician. You work for BLM & Co, a business which manufactures and sells sinks.

BLM & Co is owned and run by Brian and Lakmani Moore in partnership. You cover all aspects of bookkeeping and accounting for the business.

Task 1.1 (15 marks)

In the exam you will be able to access relevant extracts from the Code of Ethics via a pop-up window. This information is available in the Appendix which can be found at the back of this book.

This task is based on a workplace scenario separate to the rest of the assessment.

Wajid is an accountant who works for Laleham Ltd, a large organisation with many employees. Tara, a new accountant with Laleham Ltd, has made two statements to Wajid about how she believes the ethical code applies to her.

(a) Are these statements true or false?

Statement	True	False
'I have no duty to act in the public interest provided that I act in the interests of Laleham Ltd and the accountancy profession.'	☐	☐
'The ethical code provides detailed rules on how I should act in every possible situation that I might encounter at work'	☐	☐

(b) Show whether or not the ethical code specifically requires Tara to take each of the following actions in order to act in line with the principle of professional behaviour.

Action	Required/not required
Comply with all regulations that affect Laleham Ltd.	▼
Promote the reputation of the profession at every opportunity.	▼

Drop-down list:

Required
Not required

Wajid has noticed that Tara does not conduct her work thoroughly and she often completes it late. He believes that, as a result of Tara's lack of diligence, she is in breach of one of the fundamental principles.

(c) Which fundamental principles has Tara breached?

Integrity ☐

Professional competence and due care ☐

Objectivity ☐

Tara has been told that she is facing disciplinary procedures because she has behaved unethically.

(d) Show whether or not each organisation below may bring disciplinary procedures against Tara for her unethical behaviour.

AAT [▼] bring disciplinary procedures against Tara.

The National Crime Agency (NCA) [▼] bring disciplinary procedures against Tara.

Laleham Ltd (Tara's employer) [▼] bring disciplinary procedures against Tara.

Drop-down list:

May
May not

Employment regulations require employers to pay workers at least at the National Minimum Wage (NMW).

Laleham Ltd makes high levels of profits. The Chief Executive insists that managers should be paid at a very high rate with regular bonuses, but workers should receive only the NNW, with no entitlement to bonuses.

(e) Show whether the following statements are true or false.   (2 marks)

Statement	True	False
The Chief Executive's policy on employee pay raises doubts about the ethical nature of the leadership and culture of Laleham Ltd.	☐	☐
Because Laleham Ltd complies with the NMW regulations, it is automatically considered to be behaving ethically in relation to its employees.	☐	☐

Ian is an accountant who has just started working for Penton Ltd, reporting to Hettie, who is also an accountant. Ian has discovered a material error in Penton Ltd's last corporation tax return.

(f) What action must Ian now take?   **(2 marks)**

Resign.   ☐

Advise HMRC of the error without disclosing any information   ☐
to Hettie or Penton Ltd.

Tell Hettie about the error and recommend that Penton Ltd   ☐
disclose the error to HMRC.

Hettie realises that she has inadvertently become involved in Penton Ltd's money laundering operation.

(g) Complete the following statement

Hettie may have a defence against a money laundering charge if she makes
[▼] to the relevant authority.

Picklists:

A protected disclosure
An authorised disclosure
A prompt disclosure

••

Task 1.2 (16 marks)

In the exam you will be able to access relevant extracts from the Code of Ethics and Rates of VAT and tax points via pop-up windows. This information is available in the Appendix which can be found at the back of this book.

This task is based on the workplace scenario of BLM & Co.

Today's date is 15 April 20X7.

You are checking an invoice. that was issued to a customer yesterday, for standard rated goods. The invoice is incomplete. so does not currently comply with what is required on a VAT invoice.

From: BLM & Co 200-210 Farm Road Endsleigh EN61 7DS	To: Emporium Ltd 178 Judd Road Endsleigh EN62 8SP	Invoice date: 14 April 20X7	Invoice number: CJL69840
Purchase Order: 3214	Delivery date : 25/03/X7		
Description	Quantity	Per unit	
		£	£
Jade 1.5 bowl and drainer	15 units	145.00	2,175.00
	VAT at standard rate		362.50
	Total		2,537.50

(a) **What should be shown on the invoice as the tax point of this supply?**

25 March 20X7 ☐

14 April 20X7 ☐

(b) **What other piece of information must be inserted to make this a valid VAT invoice?**

Emporium Ltd's VAT registration number. ☐

BLM & Co's VAT registration number. ☐

(c) **What is the correct amount of VAT that should be included on the invoice?**

£ [ ]

BLM & Co's VAT account at 31 March, the end of its last VAT period, is as follows:

VAT account

		£			£
06/02	Cash book	60,880.98	01/01	Balance b/d	60,880.98
31/03	Purchases day book	99,120.25	31/03	Sales day book	161,728.27
31/03	Sales returns day book	3,529.57	31/03	Purchases returns day book	2,403.68
31/03	Balance c/d	61,482.13			
		225,012.93			225,012.93

(d) **What figure will be inserted in Box 1 of the VAT return for the VAT period ended 31 March 20X7?**

£ [ ]

On reviewing BLM & Co's day books. you have found two errors:

- output VAT of £2.983.50 on a sales invoice was wrongly recorded as sales on 29 March

- a supplier had overstated input VAT by £50 on an invoice received and posted by BLM on 27 March.

You prepare journals to correct these errors.

(e) **Once the journals have been processed, what will be the revised balance carried down on the VAT account?**

£ [   ]

You discover that BLM & Co has been supplying sinks to Malone Ltd, a company owned and run by the brother of your fully-qualified colleague, Jed Malone. When you look at the relevant invoices you realise that Jed has been misrecording VAT so that BLM & Co's sales to Malone Ltd are overstated. As a result, Malone Ltd qualifies for a 15% trade discount on its future purchases from BLM & Co.

(f) **Applying the conceptual framework from the ethical code, which of the following describes the situation faced by Jed Malone when recording sales to his brothers company? Choose ONE option.**

A self-review threat to professional competence and due care. ☐

A familiarity threat to objectivity. ☐

An intimidation threat to professional behaviour. ☐

You conclude that the deliberate misrecording of VAT is unethical behaviour by Jed Malone.

(g) **What should be your next action?**

Send a Suspicious Activity Report to the National Crime Agency ☐

Tell Brian and Lakmani about your concerns. ☐

On the morning of 16 April, Jed Malone is dismissed for misconduct by BLM & Co and leaves the office. You are temporarily BLM & Co's only accountant. A VAT officer will be coming to the office for a planned visit on the afternoon of 16 April. You are not prepared for this visit and do not believe you can answer any questions from the VAT officer effectively. Brian and Lakmani insist that you must be present and deal with the VAT officer without assistance.

(h) **Which of the following should be your next action?**

Resign from BLM & Co. ☐

Request that the visit by the VAT officer is postponed. ☐

Agree to deal with the VAT officer in line with your employers' instructions. ☐

Because of Jed's misconduct, Brian and Lakmani have asked you to examine his recording of sales ledger transactions in the three months ended 31 March 20X7. You identify the following information:

Sales ledger control account balance at 1 January 20X7: £492,409

From 1 January to 31 March:

- Receipts from credit customers: £934,076
- Sales to credit customers, including VAT: £970,370
- Returns from credit customers, including VAT: £21,177
- Irrecoverable debts written off, including VAT: £4,330.

Amounts owed at 31 March 20X7, as confirmed by credit customers: £487,354.

(i) **Drag each of the four options below to the appropriate column and enter the totals to reconstruct the sales ledger control account for the three months ended 31 March 20X7.**

Sales ledger control account

	£		£
Balance b/d	492,409		
		Balance c/d	487,354
Total		**Total**	

Options:

Cash book	934,076

Sales day book	970,370

Sales return day book	21,177

Journal (irrecoverable debt)	4,330

(j) **Calculate the missing figure in the sales ledger control account.**

£ [   ]

(k) **Which of the following could the missing figure represent?**

Discounts allowed. ☐

Cheque from customer returned unpaid by the bank. ☐

Cash sales. ☐

Task 1.3 (14 marks)

This task is based on the workplace scenario of BLM & Co.

Today's date is 31 January 20X8.

From the cost records you can see that on 1 January BLM & Co had 8,000 kg of raw material inventory. The cost recorded was £18,000. In January the following movements took place:

6 Jan: 4.800 kg purchased for £10.320

13 Jan: 7.200 kg issued to production

The partners want to know how the remaining inventory of 5.600 kg would be valued using different methods of cost accounting.

(a) **Using the FIFO method, value the inventory held on 31 January.**

  £ [ ]

(b) **Using the AVCO method, value the inventory held on 31 January.**

  £ [ ]

BLM & Co manufactures jade sinks in batches of 20. In the last production run in 20X7, the following costs were incurred for the batch:

	£
Direct materials	1,020
Direct labour	960
Prime cost	1,980
Variable production overheads	240
Fixed production overheads	280
Fixed non-production overheads	100
Total costs	2,600

At 31 December 20X7. three jade sinks were held in inventory.

In its financial statements. BLM & Co usually values inventory at full absorption cost.

(c) **Prepare a report for the partners, explaining:**

  (i) **how inventory of unsold sinks is valued differently depending on whether marginal or full absorption cost is used, and**

  (ii) **the effect of using the two different methods mentioned in (i) on the partnership's reported profit in its financial statements.**

To: Lakmani Moore and Brian Moore
From: Sam Jones
Date: 31/1/X8
Subject: Marginal and full absorption costing

As at 31 December 20X7, BLM & Co's closing inventory valuation was £36,800. The partners expect to make sales of £3,190,000 in 20X8, and they expect the inventory valuation to rise by 10% by the year end. The gross margin is expected to be 45%, after deducting direct materials and direct labour.

(d) **How much does BLM & Co expect to spend on direct materials and labour in 20X8? Show your workings.**

Task 1.4 (15 marks)

In the exam you will be able to access relevant extracts from the Code of Ethics via a pop-up window. This information is available in the Appendix which can be found at the back of this book.

This task is based on the workplace scenario of BLM & Co.

Today's date is 28 February 20X8.

Brian has asked you to prepare some financial statements, including a statement of cash flows, and some further documents, including a cash budget. He wants you to do this urgently. He needs to send these to the bank by the end of the week in support of a loan application. Brian tells you that obtaining the loan is very important for the survival of the business, and that the jobs of everyone in the business depend on this. So far, your studies have not covered statements of cash flows or cash budgets.

(a) **Explain the ethical issues that you face as a result of Brian's request. In your answer refer to the conceptual framework of principles, threats and safeguards in the Code of Professional Ethics where relevant.**

You have discussed the matter with Brian and Lakmani but they still wish you to carry out the tasks.

(b) **Explain the specific course of action you should take in order to remain ethical**

You receive the following email from Lakmani Moore:

To: Sam Jones <Sam.Jones@BLMCo.co.uk>
From: Lakmani Moore <Lakmani.Moore@BLMCo.co.uk>
Date: 28/2/X8
Subject: BLM & Co: change in structure

Good morning Sam.

Brian and I are considering starting to operate the business as a limited company.
I would like you to tell me more about the implications of a partnership becoming a limited company.

Please include three sections in your response to me as follows:

(1)   A brief description of a limited company

(2)   A summary of our position as owners if the business becomes a limited company

(3)   Explanations of one key advantage and one key disadvantage of operating as a limited company.

Regards,
Lakmani

(c)   Reply to Lakmani, addressing all the points that have been raised.

To:	
Subject:	
From:	Sam Jones <Sam.Jones@BLMCo.co.uk>
Date:	28/2/X8

Task 2.1 (10 marks)

You are Sam Jones, a part-qualified accounting technician. You work for BLM & Co, a business which manufactures and sells sinks. BLM & Co is owned and run by Brian and Lakmani Moore in partnership.

You cover all aspects of bookkeeping and accounting for the business.

Today's date 31 March 20X6.

BLM & Co has suffered a computer crash. You have been asked to complete the half year sales spreadsheet for the six months ended 31 December 20X7 which was extracted immediately before the crash.

You have been given a spreadsheet which contains information relating to sales in the last six months of 20X7. it contains two worksheets: 'Invoices' and 'Price list'.

Download this spreadsheet file. The spreadsheets referred to in this assessment are available for download either from the AAT website or type www.bpp.com/aatspreadsheets and follow the instructions provided. Save the spreadsheet file in the appropriate location and rename it using the following format: **'your initial-surname-AAT no –dd.mm.yy-Task5'**.
For example: J-Donnovan-123456-12.03xx-Task5

A **high degree of accuracy** is required. You **must save your work as an .XLS or .XLSX file** at regular intervals to avoid losing your work.

- Open this renamed file. In the worksheet called 'Invoices' use a lookup function on the 'Item No' data to calculate the net sales using information from the Price List worksheet.

- Use absolute referencing to calculate the gross sales value of each invoice using the VAT figure provided in cell 12.

  - Check for and remove any duplicate in the voices.
  - If there were any duplicates, enter the number found in cell J2.
  - Make sure all the contents of every cell can be seen.

- Insert a pivot chart and pivot table into a new worksheet of the number of 'Diamond' type sinks sold in each of the six months from July to December.

  - Ensure the pivot table is sorted in chronological month order

  - Format the chart series to show best sales for the period in black and worst sales in red.

  - Add a chart title 'Diamond Sink Sales'.

  - Enlarge the chart so that the whole legend is clearly seen.

  - Produce a trend line and colour it red.

  - Name this worksheet 'Diamond sinks sold'.

- Return to the 'Invoices' worksheet and filter the whole table by net sales to show the bottom five net sales.

  - Insert a subtotal formula in the net sales column to work out the average of the bottom five sales.

- Format this column as GBP currency (£).

- Insert a formula in cell A1 that will always show the current date and time.

- Set the worksheet to show formulas (rather than the resulting values of the formulas) and ensure all the contents can be seen when you set page to landscape.

- Take a screenshot of the worksheet showing formulas and paste it into a new worksheet in your current workbook.

- Name this new worksheet 'Formulas'.

- Return to the Invoices worksheet and remove the 'Show formulas' setting.

- Go to the worksheet called 'Price List' and protect only the range A4:D12 with the password 20xx.

  - Ensure that all other cells are not protected.

At the end of this task you should have one spreadsheet (saved as an .XLS or .XLSX file) to upload to the assessment environment with the following four worksheets: 'Diamond sinks sold', 'Invoices', 'Formulas', and 'Price List'.

••

Below is a checklist for each task in this assessment.

As you complete each task, tick it off the list to show your progress.

Check boxes are provided for your assistance: using them does not constitute formal evidence that a task has been completed.

	Completed
Lookup table	☐
Absolute referencing and duplicate removal	☐
Pivot chart, pivot table, and trendline	☐
Filter	☐
Protection	☐

••

Task 2.2 (16 marks)

You are Sam Jones, a part-qualified accounting technician. You work for BLM & Co, a business which manufactures and sells sinks. BLM & Co is owned and run by Brian and Lakmani Moore in partnership.

You cover all aspects of bookkeeping and accounting for the business.

Today's date is 20 April 20X8.

BLM & Co had originally budgeted to make and sell 5,000 sinks in the quarter to 31 March 20X8. Due to a marketing campaign, however, it actually made and sold 6,000 sinks in the quarter.

The original budget for the quarter to 31 March 20X8 is in the 'Original Budget' worksheet of the provided spreadsheet.

Download the spreadsheet file. The spreadsheet referred to in this assessment are available for download either from the AAT website or type www.bpp.com/aatspreadsheets and follow the instructions provided. Save the spreadsheet file in the appropriate location and rename it in the following format: **'your initial-surname-AAT no-dd.mm.yy-Task6'**.

For example: J-Donnovan-123456-12.03.xx-Task6

A **high degree of accuracy** is required. You **must save your work as an .XLS or .XLSX file** at regular intervals to avoid losing your work.

- Open this renamed file. In the worksheet called 'Original Budget", calculate the percentage to flex this budget in line with the information above and insert this percentage (%) figure into cell D1.

  - In cell D4 enter the title 'Flexed Budget'. Calculate the flexed budget for the relevant entries using absolute referencing where appropriate.

  - In cell E4 enter the title 'Actual Results'. The actual revenue and costs for the quarter are shown in the worksheet headed 'Actual Results'. Use 'copy' and 'paste link' to insert these from the source worksheet into the correct positions in column E of the 'Original Budget' worksheet.

- In cell F4 insert the title 'Variances'. Calculate the variances for the revenue and each cost. Show these in column F.

  - In cell B16 insert the title 'Operating Profit'. Calculate the operating profit for the original, flexed budget, and actual results.

  - Calculate the overall variance in cell F16.

  - Use conditional formatting in column F to show all favourable variances in green and adverse variances in red.

- Put an IF statement in F18 that will show 'Balanced' if the column totals balance, and 'Check' if they do not.

  - Colour cell F18 with a yellow background and a black border.

  - Make sure all column headings are in bold, and adjust all cells so that the contents can be seen.

- Copy the range A3:F15, and paste only the values into a new worksheet. Name this worksheet 'Subtotals'.

  - In the newly created worksheet called 'Subtotals', delete the row that contains the revenue amounts.

  - Produce subtotals for each of: materials, labour, variable overheads and fixed overheads.

  - Show subtotals in original budget, flexed budget, actual results, and variances columns.

- – Hide the detail to only show the subtotals and grand total, not the individual components.

- Return to the worksheet called 'Original Budget'.

  - – Perform a spell check and ensure all the contents of the cells can be seen.

  - – From the variances in cells F5 to F15, identify the most significant favourable variance and the most significant adverse variance. Insert appropriate text in Column H adjacent to each variance, e.g. 'Most significant favourable variance' and 'Most significant adverse variance'.

- Use the pro forma contained in the worksheet called 'Email' to do the following:

  (i) Report the flexed budget, actual operating profit, and total variance to Brian and Lakmani Moore.

  (ii) Explain one possible cause for each of the two variances identified in (e) above.

At the end of this task you should have one spreadsheet (saved as an .XLS or .XLSX file) which in the live assessment, you will upload to the assessment environment. This should have four worksheets titled: 'Original Budget', 'Subtotals', 'Actual Results', and 'Email', with information and data in them.

Email

From:	Sam Jones <Sam.Jones@BLMCo.co.uk>
To:	Lakmani Moore <Lakmani.Moore@BLMCo.co.uk>; Brian Moore <Brian.Moore@BLMCo.co.uk>
Subject:	

Below is a checklist for each task in this assessment.

As you complete each task, tick it off the list to show your progress.

Check boxes are provided for your assistance; using them does not constitute formal evidence that a task has been completed.

BPP
LEARNING MEDIA

Completed

Percentage, flexed budget and actual ☐

Variances, operating profit and conditional formatting ☐

IF statement and formatting ☐

Copy values and subtotals ☐

Identify significant variances ☐

Produce email ☐

··

Task 2.3 (14 marks)

You are Sam Jones, a part-qualified accounting technician. You work for BLM & Co, a business which manufactures and sell sinks. BLM & Co is owned and run by Brian and Lakmani Moore in partnership.

You cover all aspects of bookkeeping and accounting for the business.

Today's date is 31 January 20X9.

You are preparing the final accounts for BLM & Co for the year ended 31 December 20X8.

The statement of profit or loss for BLM & Co shows a profit for the year ended 31 December 20X8 of £250,000.

The business is still operated as a partnership.

You are given the following information arising from the partnership agreement:

- Partners earn commission each month of 1.5% on the sales they personally made in that month, provided these sales are greater than £10,000. They earn no commission in the month otherwise.

- Lakmani is entitled to a salary of £25,000 per annum.

- Brian has taken drawings of £91,200 over the year, and Lakmani has taken £84,400.

- Interest on drawings has been calculated at £300 for Brian and £180 for Lakmani for the year ended 31 December 20X8.

- The residual profit after adjustments is shared between Brian and Lakmani in the ratio 3:2.

Details of the partners' sales are in a separate spreadsheet. Download the spreadsheet file. The spreadsheet referred to in this assessment are available for download either from the AAT website or type www.bpp.com/aatspreadsheets and follow the instructions provided.

Save the spreadsheet file in the appropriate location, and rename it in the following format:

'your initial-surname-AAT no-dd.mm.yy-Task7' in the appropriate folder.

For example: J-Donnovan-123456-12.03.xx-Task7

A **high degree of accuracy** is required. You **must save your work as an .XLS or .XLSX** file at regular intervals to avoid losing your work.

You are required to prepare the appropriation account for BLM & Co for the year ended 31 December 20X8.

- Use the partnership data supplied in the table in the spreadsheet in the following manner:
  - Format all headings to have bold size 12 font.
  - Merge and centre 'Sales' and 'Commission' over their respective columns. Align the month column, including the heading, to the left. Align the other columns, including the name headers, to the right.
  - Use a custom list to sort the whole table from January to December.
  - Use an IF statement to calculate the commission on sales for Brian and Lakmani for each month. Show your results in columns D and E.
  - Total each of the columns B:E.
  - In the shaded area, Custom Format the range B6:E18 in GBP currency with the thousand separator and two decimal places (e.g. £3,200.00).

- (i) Design a partnership appropriation statement in the spreadsheet to appropriate the profit for the year ended 31 December 20X8 between the two partners in accordance with the partnership agreement. Start with the profit for the year, and show clearly:
  - Separate lines for each of the entitlements or charges adjusting this profit. Provide direct references from your answer to (a) where possible.
  - The residual profit available for appropriation.
  - Each partner's share of that residual profit.
  - The total amount distributed to each partner for the year.
  - (ii) Custom format your statement to show GBP currency with the thousand separator, no decimals, and black font for positive. Ensure that any negative figures are Custom Formatted to red with a minus sign.

Lakmani now asks you what figure the profit for the year would need to be if she were to have a total amount distributed to her of £120,000. Assume all other data is unchanged.

- Amend your spreadsheet to show this:
  - Open a new worksheet and name it 'Goal Seek'.
  - Return to the 'BLM 1' worksheet. In your partnership appropriation statement, use What if Goal Seek analysis to amend your data.
  - When the completed Goal Seek dialogue box is showing – but BEFORE you click the OK button – take a screenshot (without pasting). Then complete the Goal Seek analysis.
  - Return to the 'Goal Seek' worksheet and paste the screenshot.

At the end of this task you should have one spreadsheet (saved as an .XLS or .XLSX file) which in the live assessment, you will upload to the assessment environment. This should have two worksheets titled 'BLM 1' and 'Goal seek', with information and data in them.

Below is a checklist for each task in this assessment.

As you complete each task, tick it off the list to show your progress.

Check boxes are provided for your assistance; using them does not constitute formal evidence that a task has been completed.

Completed

Format, Merge, Custom sort, IF statement ☐

Design appropriation statement ☐

Goal seek ☐

AAT AQ2016 SAMPLE ASSESSMENT
Level 3 Synoptic Assessment

ANSWERS

Advanced Diploma Synoptic Assessment (AVSY)
Sample assessment

Task 1.1 (15 marks)

(a) Are these statements true or false?

Statement	True	False
'I have no duty to act in the public interest provided that I act in the interests of Laleham Ltd and the accountancy profession.'	☐	✓
'The ethical code provides detailed rules on how I should act in every possible situation that I might encounter at work'	☐	✓

(b) Show whether or not the ethical code specifically requires Tara to take each of the following actions in order to act in line with the principle of professional behaviour.

Action	Required/not required
Comply with all regulations that affect Laleham Ltd.	Required ▼
Promote the reputation of the profession at every opportunity.	Not required ▼

Wajid has noticed that Tara does not conduct her work thoroughly and she often completes it late. He believes that, as a result of Tara's lack of diligence, she is in breach of one of the fundamental principles.

(c) Which fundamental principles has Tara breached?

Integrity ☐

Professional competence and due care ✓

Objectivity ☐

Tara has been told that she is facing disciplinary procedures because she has behaved unethically.

(d) Show whether or not each organisation below may bring disciplinary procedures against Tara for her unethical behaviour.

AAT | may ▼ | bring disciplinary procedures against Tara.

The National Crime Agency (NCA) | may not ▼ | bring disciplinary procedures against Tara.

Laleham Ltd (Tara's employer) | may ▼ | bring disciplinary procedures against Tara.

Employment regulations require employers to pay workers at least at the National Minimum Wage (NMW).

Laleham Ltd makes high levels of profits. The Chief Executive insists that managers should be paid at a very high rate with regular bonuses, but workers should receive only the NMW, with no entitlement to bonuses.

(e) Show whether the following statements are true or false.

Statement	True	False
The Chief Executive's policy on employee pay raises doubts about the ethical nature of the leadership and culture of Laleham Ltd.	✓	
Because Laleham Ltd complies with the NMW regulations, it is automatically considered to be behaving ethically in relation to its employees.		✓

Ian is an accountant who has just started working for Penton Ltd, reporting to Hettie, who is also an accountant. Ian has discovered a material error in Penton Ltd's last corporation tax return.

(f) What action must Ian now take?

Resign. ☐

Advise HMRC of the error without disclosing any information to Hettie or Penton Ltd. ☐

Tell Hettie about the error and recommend that Penton Ltd disclose the error to HMRC. ✓

Hettie realises that she has inadvertently become involved in Penton Ltd's money laundering operation.

(g) Complete the following statement

Hettie may have a defence against a money laundering charge if she makes an authorised disclosure ▼ to the relevant authority.

Task 1.2 (16 marks)

(a) **What should be shown on the invoice as the tax point of this supply?**

25 March 20X7 ☑

14 April 20X7 ☐

(b) **What other piece of information must be inserted to make this a valid VAT invoice?**

Emporium Ltd's VAT registration number. ☐

BLM & Co's VAT registration number. ☑

(c) **What is the correct amount of VAT that should be included on the invoice?**

£ [435]

(d) **What figure will be inserted in Box 1 of the VAT return for the VAT period ended 31 March 20X7?**

£ [158,198.70]

On reviewing BLM & Co's day books. you have found two errors:

- output VAT of £2,983.50 on a sales invoice was wrongly recorded as sales on 29 March

- a supplier had overstated input VAT by £50 on an invoice received and posted by BLM on 27 March.

You prepare journals to correct these errors.

(e) **Once the journals have been processed, what will be the revised balance carried down on the VAT account?**

£ [64,515.63]

You discover that BLM & Co has been supplying sinks to Malone Ltd, a company owned and run by the brother of your fully-qualified colleague, Jed Malone. When you look at the relevant invoices you realise that Jed has been misrecording VAT so that BLM & Co's sales to Malone Ltd are overstated. As a result, Malone Ltd qualifies for a 15% trade discount on its future purchases from BLM & Co.

(f) **Applying the conceptual framework from the ethical code, which of the following describes the situation faced by Jed Malone when recording sales to his brothers company? Choose ONE option.**

A self-review threat to professional competence and due care. ☐

A familiarity threat to objectivity. ☑

An intimidation threat to professional behaviour. ☐

You conclude that the deliberate misrecording of VAT is unethical behaviour by Jed Malone.

(g) What should be your next action?

Send a Suspicious Activity Report to the National Crime Agency ☐

Tell Brian and Lakmani about your concerns. ☑

On the morning of 16 April, Jed Malone is dismissed for misconduct by BLM & Co and leaves the office. You are temporarily BLM & Co's only accountant. A VAT officer will be coming to the office for a planned visit on the afternoon of 16 April. You are not prepared for this visit and do not believe you can answer any questions from the VAT officer effectively. Brian and Lakmani insist that you must be present and deal with the VAT officer without assistance.

(h) Which of the following should be your next action?

Resign from BLM & Co. ☐

Request that the visit by the VAT officer is postponed. ☑

Agree to deal with the VAT officer in line with your employers' instructions. ☐

(i) Drag each of the four options below to the appropriate column and enter the totals to reconstruct the sales ledger control account for the three months ended 31 March 20X7.

Sales ledger control account

	£		£
Balance b/d	492,409	Cash book	934,076
Sales day book	970,370	Sales returns day book	21,177
		Journal (irrecoverable debt)	4,330
		Balance c/d	487,354
Total	1,462,779	**Total**	1,446,937

(j) Calculate the missing figure in the sales ledger control account.

£ 15,842

(k) Which of the following could the missing figure represent?

Discounts allowed. ☑

Cheque from customer returned unpaid by the bank. ☐

Cash sales. ☐

Task 1.3 (14 marks)

(a) **Using the FIFO method, value the inventory held on 31 January.**

£ 12,120

(b) **Using the AVCO method, value the inventory held on 31 January.**

£ 12,390

(c) (i) When inventory is valued at marginal cost, only the variable costs of producing each item are included in the valuation. This includes the prime cost and the variable production overheads.

For the Jade sink, the marginal cost per unit is £111 ((1980+240)/20) so the 3 sinks held in inventory would be valued together at £333.

When inventory is valued at full absorption cost, a share of fixed production overheads incurred by the business is included in the valuation, so the valuation is higher under absorption costing.

For the Jade sink, the absorption cost per unit is £125 ((1980+240+280)/20) so the 3 sinks held in inventory would be valued together at £375.

Note that, irrespective of method, the non-production overheads are not included in the inventory valuation.

(ii) In the year ended 31 December 20X7, if the partners had valued the Jade sinks at marginal cost rather than full absorption cost, reported profit would have been lower by £42 (375-333), because the share of fixed production overheads was expensed in 20X7, the year of production, rather than being absorbed into inventory, carried forward and expensed in the year of sale.

As at 31 December 20X7, BLM & Co's closing inventory valuation was £36,800. The partners expect to make sales of £3,190,000 in 20X8, and they expect the inventory valuation to rise by 10% by the year end. The gross margin is expected to be 45%. after deducting direct materials and direct labour.

(d) **How much does BLM & Co expect to spend on direct materials and labour in 20X8? Show your workings.**

Sales: 3,190,000
OS: 36,800
Material/labour (balancing figure): 1,758,180
CS (36800*1.1): (40,480)
COS (55%): (1,754,500)
GP (45%): 1,435,500

Task 1.4 (15 marks)

(a)   I do not have the experience, expertise (knowledge and skills), or time to complete the tasks properly.

It would be a breach of the principles of professional competence and due care, and integrity, to attempt to do so immediately.

I am facing familiarity, intimidation and self-interest threats because the partners of BLM & Co are trying to appeal to my loyalty to colleagues and fear of losing my job.

I need to apply relevant safeguards to bring the threat to my principles down to an acceptable level.

(b)   I would tell Brian and Lakmani that I can only complete the tasks they have requested if I have additional training/qualified support/supervision to do so (which will take time).

OR

I would tell Brian and Lakmani that I cannot undertake the task competently so it should be given to someone else/Jed Malone (if he has sufficient expertise)/Addo & Co staff.

(c)

To: Lakmani Moore Lakmani.Moore@BLMCo.co.uk
Subject: BLM & Co: change in structure

Hello Lakmani

Thank you for your email of 28/2/X8.

(1)   A limited company is a business structure which is a separate legal entity distinct from its owners (known as shareholders). It needs to be registered at Companies House. A company's accounts and finances are separate from the personal finances of its owners.

(2)   A company is owned by shareholders, who have equity shares in the company. Persons acting as directors are responsible for running the company. A company must have at least one shareholder and at least one director. You and Brian can remain as the only owners if you own all the shares in the company between you; your ownership will be diluted if you include more shareholders. You can continue to run the company, acting as its only directors, or you may appoint additional directors.

Directors may be paid a salary by the company from its pre-tax profits. Shareholders may receive dividends paid from its after-tax profits. Any after-tax profits that are not paid out as dividends are reinvested in the company on the shareholders behalf.

(3)   The key advantage of operating as a limited company is that of limited liability for the owners. While you as partners in BLM & Co currently have unlimited liability for all the debts of the business, shareholders' liability for any unpaid debts of the company is limited and they only stand to lose their investment in shares. The company as a separate legal entity remains fully liable for its debts.

The key disadvantage of operating as a limited company is that companies are heavily regulated. There are a number of accounting regulations involved with running a limited company, and the statutory requirements of the Companies Act 2006 apply, as do accounting standards. This means that there is a much greater administrative burden than for a partnership. A company must file accounts each year before a certain date and it must file documents when it is set up. All this extra administration bears a cost.

I hope this is useful to you. Please contact me if you have any questions.

Kind regards

Sam

···

Task 2.1 (10 marks)

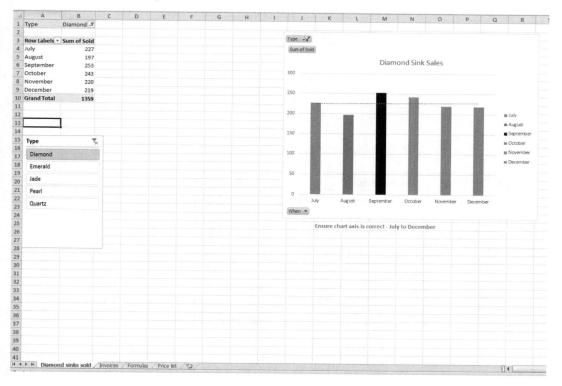

	A	B	C	D	E	F	G	H	I	J
1	23/02/2016 11:35									
2	BLM & Co							VAT	20%	2
3										
4				Sales for sinks for the last 6 months of trading through various outlets						
5										
6	Type	Description	Item No	Sold	When	Where	Invoice No	Net Sale	Gross sale	
17	Emerald	1 Bowl reversible drainer	28654	6	July	Jones & Co	281724	£744.00	£892.80	
69	Quartz	1.5 square reversible	15874	5	July	Elways	281760	£640.00	£768.00	
95	Quartz	1 square reversible	28791	5	August	Internet	281810	£680.00	£816.00	
149	Emerald	1 Bowl reversible drainer	28654	6	Septembe	Elways	281856	£744.00	£892.80	
166	Quartz	1 square reversible	28791	5	Septembe	Zeebras	281881	£680.00	£816.00	
391								£697.60		
392										
393										
394								=SUBTOTAL(1,H17:H166)	£697.60	
395										

1	=NOW()								
2	BLM & Co							VAT	0.2
3									
4					Sales for sinks for the last 6 months of trading through various outlets				
5									
6	Type	Description	Item No	Sold	When	Where	Invoice No	Net Sale	Gross sales
17	Emerald	1 Bowl reversible drainer	28654	6	July	Jones & Co	281724	=D17*VLOOKUP(Invoices!C17,'Price list'!$A$5:$D$12,4,FALSE)	=H17*$I$2+H17
69	Quartz	1.5 square reversible	15874	5	July	Elways	281760	=D69*VLOOKUP(Invoices!C69,'Price list'!$A$5:$D$12,4,FALSE)	=H69*$I$2+H69
95	Quartz	1 square reversible	28791	5	August	Internet	281810	=D95*VLOOKUP(Invoices!C95,'Price list'!$A$5:$D$12,4,FALSE)	=H95*$I$2+H95
149	Emerald	1 Bowl reversible drainer	28654	6	September	Elways	281856	=D149*VLOOKUP(Invoices!C149,'Price list'!$A$5:$D$12,4,FALSE)	=H149*$I$2+H149
166	Quartz	1 square reversible	28791	5	September	Zeebras	281881	=D166*VLOOKUP(Invoices!C166,'Price list'!$A$5:$D$12,4,FALSE)	=H166*$I$2+H166
391								=SUBTOTAL(1,H17:H166)	

	A	B	C	D	E	F	G
1							
2			ONLY Marketing are allowed to alter these prices				
3							
4	Item No	Type	Description	Price			
5	28654	Emerald	1 Bowl reversible drainer	£ 124.00			
6	35698	Jade	1 Bowl & drainer	£ 127.00			
7	15874	Quartz	1.5 square reversible	£ 128.00			
8	28791	Quartz	1 square reversible	£ 136.00			
9	26221	Jade	1.5 Bowl & drainer	£ 145.00			
10	28457	Diamond	1 cubic bowl & drainer	£ 165.00			
11	27894	Emerald	1.5 Bowl reversible drainer	£ 180.00			
12	35789	Pearl	1.5 reversible oval	£ 198.00			
13							
14			Task 5 (e) - Assessors to check that ONLY the above range is protected				
15			You should be able to select every cell except for the above table.				
16							

Task 2.2 (16 marks)

	A	B	C	D	E	F	G	H	I	J
1				20%						
2										
3	BLM & Co: original budget for quarter ended 31 March 20X8									
4	Item		Original Budget £	Flexed Budget	Actual Results	Variances				
5	Revenue		800000	960000	975000	15000	Most significant favourable variance			
6	Materials:	Direct materials 1	90000	108000	105000	3000				
7	Materials:	Direct materials 2	110000	132000	125000	7000				
8	Materials:	Direct materials 3	140000	168000	164700	3300				
9	Direct labour:	Skilled	30000	36000	35000	1000				
10	Direct labour:	Unskilled	70000	84000	81500	2500				
11	Variable overheads:	Supervision	42000	50400	49000	1400				
12	Variable overheads:	Quality Control	60000	72000	70000	2000				
13	Variable overheads:	Production planning	55000	66000	60000	6000				
14	Fixed overheads:	Administration	80000	80000	85000	-5000				
15	Fixed overheads:	Selling and distribution	90000	90000	110000	-20000	Most significant adverse variance			
16	Operating profit	Operating profit	33000	73600	89800	16200				
17										
18										
19						Balanced				

Rows 20–43 empty.

Sheet tabs: Original Budget / Sub Totals / Actual Results / Email

1 2 3	⁄	A	B	C	D	E	F	G	H
	1								
	2								
	3	BLM & Co: original budget for quarter ended 31 March 20X8							
	4	Item		Original Budget £	Flexed Budget	Actual Results	Variances		
+	8	Materials: Total		340000	408000	394700	13300		
+	11	Direct labour: Total		100000	120000	116500	3500		
+	15	Variable overheads: Total		157000	188400	179000	9400		
+	18	Fixed overheads: Total		170000	170000	195000	-25000		
−	19	Grand Total		767000	886400	885200	1200		
	20								
	21								
	22								
	23								
	24								
	25								
	26								
	27								
	28								
	29								
	30								
	31								
	32								
	33								
	34								
	35								
	36								
	37								
	38								
	39								
	40								
	41								
	42								
	43								
	44								
	45								
	46								
	47								
	48								
	49								
	50								
	51								

Original Budget | **Sub Totals** | Actual Results | Email

	A	B	C	D	E	F	G	H	I
1									
2									
3	**BLM & Co: actual results for quarter ended 31 March 20X8**								
4			Actual Results £						
5	Revenue		975000						
6	Materials:	Direct materials 1	105000						
7		Direct materials 2	125000						
8		Direct materials 3	164700						
9	Direct labour:	Skilled	35000						
10		Unskilled	81500						
11	Variable overhead	Supervision	49000						
12		Quality Control	70000						
13		Production planning	60000						
14	Fixed overheads:	Administration	85000						
15		Selling and distributio	110000						
16	Operating profit								
17									
18	Made and sold in quarter: 6,000 sinks								
19									
20									
21									
22									
23									
24									
25									
26									
27									
28									
29									
30									
31									
32									
33									
34									
35									
36									
37									
38									
39									
40									
41									
42									
43									

Original Budget / Sub Totals / **Actual Results** / Email

		Untitled - Message (HTML)
FILE	MESSAGE	INSERT OPTIONS FORMAT TEXT REVIEW DEVELOPER Nuance PDF

	From	Sam Jones <Sam.Jones@BLMCo.co.uk>
Send	To	Lakmani Moore <Lakmani.Moore@BLMCo.co.uk>; Brian Moore <Brian.Moore@BLMCo.co.uk>
	Subject	Variances in quarter to 31 March 20X8

Hi Lakmani and Brian

As promised, please find the explanations below:-

The operating profit variance from the flexed budget was £16,200 favourable. This arose because the budgeted profit when flexed to the actual volume of 6,000 units was £73,600, whereas we achieved an actual profit of £89,800.

The single most significant favourable variance was sales revenue, which was £15,000 favourable. This may have arisen because the selling price per unit was higher, following the marketing campaign.

The single most significant adverse variance was selling and distribution, which was £20,000 adverse. Since this is a fixed cost it was not directly caused by the increase in volume, and so was likely to have been caused by the increased spend on marketing which generated the extra sales, or an increase in salaries.

Task 2.3 (14 marks)

	A	B	C	D	E
1					
2					
3	Sales and commission for year ended 31 December 20X8				
4		Sales		Commission	
5	**Month**	**Brian**	**Lakmani**	**Brian**	**Lakmani**
6	January	£28,000.00	£36,000.00	£420.00	£540.00
7	February	£62,000.00	£57,000.00	£930.00	£855.00
8	March	£71,500.00	£62,000.00	£1,072.50	£930.00
9	April	£63,000.00	£59,750.00	£945.00	£896.25
10	May	£59,200.00	£64,200.00	£888.00	£963.00
11	June	£51,234.00	£58,000.00	£768.51	£870.00
12	July	£55,670.00	£41,000.00	£835.05	£615.00
13	August	£9,540.00	£56,000.00	£0.00	£840.00
14	September	£49,300.00	£3,257.00	£739.50	£0.00
15	October	£52,000.00	£57,276.00	£780.00	£859.14
16	November	£43,000.00	£46,540.00	£645.00	£698.10
17	December	£37,500.00	£28,927.00	£562.50	£433.91
18		£581,944.00	£569,950.00	£8,586.06	£8,500.40
19					

21				
22	Assessors - Table should contain all these elements before Goal Seek			
23	(b) Partnership appropriation statement for year ended 31 December 20X8			This table should not be seen in the learner's answers unless the learner has not performed the Goal Seek.
24		Brian	Lakmani	Total
25	Profit for the year			£250,000
26	Salary		£25,000	£25,000
27	Interest on drawings	-£300	-£180	-£480
28	Commission	£8,586	£8,500	£17,086
29	Residual profit available for appropriation			£208,394
30	Profit share	£125,036	£83,357	£208,394
31	Total amount distributed to each part	£133,322	£116,678	£250,000
32				
33	Assessors - Table should contain all these elements before Goal Seek			
34	(c) Partnership appropriation statement after Goal Seek for year end 31 December 20X8			
35		Brian	Lakmani	Total
36	Profit for the year			£258,305
37	Salary		£25,000	£25,000
38	Interest on drawings	-£300	-£180	-£480
39	Commission	£8,586	£8,500	£17,086
40	Residual profit available for appropriation			£216,699
41	Profit share	£130,019	£86,680	£216,699
42	Total amount distributed to each part	£138,305	£120,000	£258,305
43				
44				
45				
46				
47				
48				
49				
50				

BLM 1 / Goal seek

BPP
LEARNING MEDIA

	Brian	Lakmani	Total	
6 © Partnership appropriation after Goal Seek for year end 31 December 20X8				
9 Profit for the year			£250,000	
10 Salary		£25,000	£25,000	
11 Interest on drawings	-£300	-£180	-£480	
13 Commission	£8,586	£8,500	£17,086	
14 Residual profit available for distribution			£208,394	
15 Profit share	£125,036	£83,357	£208,394	
16 Total profit appropriated to each partne	£133,322	£116,678	£250,000	

Goal Seek

Set cell: $C$42

To value: 120000

By changing cell: $D$36

OK   Cancel

BPP PRACTICE ASSESSMENT 1
LEVEL 3 SYNOPTIC
ASSESSMENT

Time allowed: 3 hours

Level 3 Synoptic Assessment
BPP practice assessment 1

Task 1

The following statements have been made by trainee accountants in relation to the ethical code and the fundamental principles.

(a) Show whether the below statements are true or false?

Statement	True	False
'It doesn't matter whether or not people might think my actions are unethical, it is whether or not I actually am that counts'	☐	☐
'As long as I comply with the principle of integrity, compliance with the other principles will be implied as a result'	☐	☐
'The ethical code applies to my role as a professional and my working life. My private life, on the other hand, is just that – private!'	☐	☐
'As a professional accountant, it is more important for me to be ethical as I work in the public interest.'	☐	☐

Professional accountants are required to undertake continuing professional development (CPD).

(b) Which of the following fundamental principles is safeguarded by CPD?

	✓
Integrity	☐
Objectivity	☐
Professional competence and due care	☐

Marion, a professional accountant in practice, gives Larch Ltd an opinion on the application of accounting principles to the company's specific transactions. Marion knew that she was forming her opinion on the basis of inadequate information.

(c) Show whether or not the following fundamental principles have been breached by Marion.

Action	Yes/No
Integrity	▼
Professional competence and due care	▼
Professional behaviour	▼

Dipika is an accountant employed by Natural Beauty, a company which develops, manufactures and sells luxury bath and body products. One of the company's top selling products is a body polish which it claims uses all natural ingredients. The exfoliating quality of the polish is achieved using sea salt and fine sand.

During the course of her work, Dipika discovers that, in order to reduce costs, the company has begun to replace some of the sand with microbeads. Mircrobeads are tiny plastic beads which pollute both the ocean and the food chain for human consumption. The use of microbeads in banned in a number of countries, but they have not yet been banned by the country in which Natural Beauty operates. They are not 'natural' ingredients and the packaging has not been updated to reflect this.

(d) Show whether the below statements are true or false?

Statement	True	False
Natural Beauty may have broken the law	☐	☐
Natural Beauty has acted unethically	☐	☐

(e) Which of the below actions should Dipika now take?

	✓
Take the issue directly to the press as it is in the public interest to disclose this via the media	☐
She should do nothing, the issue is not of a financial nature and therefore outside the scope of her expertise and ethical requirements	☐
Discuss the findings with her immediate manager and share her concerns regarding the company's use of mircobeads	☐

(f) If Dipika discloses this issue through appropriate channels, either internally or externally, would any protection against dismissal be offered to Dipika under the Public Information Disclosure Act 1998 (PIDA)?

	✓
No, she as disclosure of the matter would be inappropriate in this situation	☐
Yes, as she has reasonable grounds to believe that the environment is being damaged and disclosure was made in good faith	☐
No, PIDA only protects individuals who are disclosing serious organised crimes such as money laundering	☐

Task 2

The tasks are based on the following workplace scenario of Clodlands Ltd:

You are Cedric, a part-qualified accounting technician employed by an accountancy firm.

Your friend Chipo has recently begun to trade through a new company, Clodlands Ltd, which owns and lets several areas of land including two houses.

Chipo has now registered Clodlands Ltd for VAT. She has become a client of your employer and you assist with the company's VAT under the supervision of your manager, Katya.

Katya has put a reference in the file to HMRC's guidance at www.gov.uk/government/publications/vat-notice-706-partial-exemption/vat-notice-706-partial-exemption#introduction and asks you to look at this.

(a) **Katya has explained to Chipo that the business is 'partially exempt'. This means what?**

Statement	True	False
Clodlands Ltd will be able to reclaim input tax relating to taxable supplies	☐	☐
Clodlands Ltd may be able to reclaim input tax relating to exempt supplies depending on de minimis tests	☐	☐
Clodlands Ltd may charge a reduced rate of VAT on taxable supplies	☐	☐
Clodlands Ltd makes a mixture of taxable and exempt supplies	☐	☐
Clodlands Ltd need not have registered for VAT	☐	☐

(b) **For each of the following supplies by Clodlands Ltd, Chipo wants to know whether she must provide an invoice, whether she must charge 20% VAT, and whether any VAT will be borne by her customer.**

	Invoice	VAT	Borne by customer
	Yes/No	20%/0	Yes/none
A standard-rated let to an unregistered first-time car-boot seller	▼	▼	▼
A standard-rated let to a registered trader for a Saturday market	▼	▼	▼
An exempt residential let to unregistered private individuals	▼	▼	▼

Task 3

Boo Boosters distributes a popular range of car seats for children. They are bought from the manufacturer and then shipped to various online retailers and independent specialist stores across the UK.

(a) **Complete the inventory record card for May using the FIFO method. Round to two decimal places if required.**

Date	Receipts (units)	Total cost £	Quantity sold	Balance (units)	Total cost £
Balance as at 1 May				800	12,000
5 May	750	10,940			
10 May			900		
18 May	1,000	14,140			
20 May			900		

(b) **Complete the inventory record card for May using the AVCO method.**

Date	Receipts (units)	Total cost £	Quantity sold	Balance (units)	Total cost £
Balance as at 1 May				800	12,000
5 May	750	10,940			
10 May			900		
18 May	1,000	14,140			
20 May			900		

There has been an error in the accounting records whereby the discounts received on new car seats has been incorrectly recorded as follows

Account	Debit	Credit
Discounts received	750	
Purchase ledger control account		750

(c) **What type of error is this? Choose the ONE most suitable answer from the table below.**

Description	✓
Error of commission	
Reversal of entries	
Error of omission	
One-sided entry	

(d) **Which ONE of the following statements about a Limited Liability Partnership is NOT correct?**

Description	✓
An LLP is a separate legal entity	
The LLP must be registered with the Registrar of Companies	
There is no upper limit to the number of partners a LLP can have	
The LLP must file annual returns, accounts and an annual corporation tax return	

Task 4

It is Monday morning when a partner calls you into his office for a private meeting. He explains that he has a number of expenses relating to personal expenditure that he would like to put through the company's books of accounts. He hands you a file containing a year's worth of private bank statements and requests you to identify any expenditure relating to his expensive family holidays and post as an expense to the business travel account. Your response is you have learnt at college that only valid business expenditure should be recorded through the business's books of account. However, his reasoning is that the holidays are there to help him relax from the stress of running a business so it is only fair this is recorded as a business expense. The director implies that as a thank you he may able to obtain two tickets for two seats for the finals at a tennis tournament. When you return to your desk you complete an Internet search and are surprised to discover these tickets are currently selling in excess of £500 each.

(a) **Outline any potential ethical issues that this work request can bring. In your answer refer to the Code of Professional Ethics highlighting specific threats that may apply.**

(b) Identify the most appropriate course of action in these circumstances.

You have received the following email from one of your colleagues:

To: You@.accounts

From: **Colleague@.accounts**

Subject: Partnership accounts

Hi,

I am a new joiner at the partnership and will be working on the partnership end of year financial statements. I have just started my accountancy studies and have only covered sole traders. We have not covered the types of accounts and financial statements used in partnerships. This is all new to me!

Please can you help me get started?

Thank you,

Kind regards,

Colleague

(c) Reply to your colleague outlining the accounts and statements used in a partnership arrangement. Your answer should be suitable for someone with no knowledge of partnerships.

· ·

Task 5

You have been given a spreadsheet Grades20X6.xls which shows the results of 38 students enrolled on a course at a further education college during the year 20X6. It contains two worksheets: 'Grades' and 'Result'.

Download this spreadsheet file from www.bpp.com/aatspreadsheets and save in the appropriate location. Rename it using the following format: **'your initial-surname-AAT no –dd.mm.yy-Task5.3'**.

For example: J-Donnovan-123456-12.03xx-Task5.3

A **high degree of accuracy** is required. You must **save your work as an .XLS or .XLSX file** at regular intervals to avoid losing your work.

- Open the renamed spreadsheet and open the grades worksheet
    - Change the title of column G to 'average'
    - Use a formula in cell G2 to calculate the mean score achieved by Alexander
    - Apply this formula to all students

Students who have achieved less than 50% in any of the individual exams are considered to be at risk of not passing the course and are referred for help in the relevant area.

- Use an IF statement in column I along with a lookup function in column H to determine if any students need to be referred.

    - The IF statement should return the values 0 for a referral and 1 for a pass. A pass will be achieved if 50% or more is gained in every subject. A referral will be made if less than 50% is achieved in one or more exams.

    - The lookup function should designate either 'PASS' or 'REFER' to each student based on the outcome of the IF statement

- Improve the look and usability of the spreadsheet

    - Hide your workings so that the lookup references are not visible

    - Use conditional formatting to highlight any REFER values

    - Use the freeze panes function to keep the top row of the spreadsheet visible at all times

The five lowest scoring students will automatically be offered the chance of help even if they have not been referred for any specific subjects.

- Use the rank feature to determine which five students should be offered additional help

    - Highlight the rows relating to the students who should be offered help using the fill feature.

    - Password protect the entire workbook and using the password Grades16

••

Task 6

You are Sarah-Jane Smith, a part-qualified accounting technician. You work for Winter Co, which manufactures and installs bathrooms.

You cover all aspects of bookkeeping and accounting for the business. You report to Emma Neesome, the Chief Finance Officer.

Today's date is 15 October 20X1.

Emma has asked you to do some breakeven analysis, based on the budgeted figures for the next quarter. Forecast sales are 5,000 units and sales price is $300. Cost figures are as follows:

	$
Direct materials	400,000
Direct labour	200,000
Assembly	300,000
Installation	450,000

60% of assembly costs and 80% of installation costs are variable.

Emma has told you the company's target margin of safety is 30% and its target profit is $140,000.

Download the spreadsheet file from the www.bpp.com/aatspreadsheets. Save the spreadsheet file in the appropriate location and rename it in the following format: 'your initial-surname-AAT no-dd.mm.yy-Task1'. For example: H-Darch-123456-12.03.xx-Task1

A **high degree of accuracy** is required. You must **save your work as an .XLS or.XLSX file** at regular intervals to avoid losing your work.

1. Open the renamed file. Calculate total revenue and enter it in cell B2.

2. Enter total direct materials in cell B4 and total direct labour in cell B5.

3. Calculate variable assembly and packaging costs and enter them in cells B6 and B7.

4. Calculate total variable costs and enter them in cell B8.

5. Calculate variable costs per unit, using the budgeted sales volume of 5,000, and enter it in cell B9

6. Calculate contribution per unit, using the budgeted sales price of $300, and enter it in cell B10.

7. Calculate fixed assembly and packaging costs and enter them in cells B12 and B13.

8. Calculate total fixed costs and enter them in cell B14.

9. Calculate the breakeven point in units and enter it in cell B15, giving your answer to the nearest unit. Use conditional formatting to show this figure in green if it is less than the budgeted sales volume and red if it is more than the budgeted sales volume.

10. Calculate the breakeven point in revenue terms and enter it in cell B16.

11. Calculate the contribution/sales ratio and enter it in cell B17, showing it to 2 decimal places.

12. Calculate the margin of safety in units and enter it in cell B18, giving your answer to the nearest unit.

13. Calculate the margin of safety in % terms and enter it in cell B19, showing it to 2 decimal places. Highlight this figure with a yellow background and black border. Put an IF statement in cell C19 to show HIGHER if it is greater than the target margin of safety of 30%, LOWER if it is less than the target margin of safety.

14. Calculate the volume of sales needed to achieve the target profit of $140,000and enter it in cell B20, giving your answer to the nearest unit. Highlight this figure with a yellow background and black border. Put an IF statement in cell C20 to show LESS if the budgeted sales volume of 5,000 units is lower than the volume of sales needed to achieve the target profit, MORE if the budgeted sales volume Is higher.

15. Perform a spell check and ensure that the contents of all cells can be seen.

16. Use the proforma email to do the following:

    - Comment on the results of your calculations
    - Give two problems with breakeven analysis

To:	Emma Neesome
From:	Sarah-Jane Smith
Date:	15 October 20X1
Subject:	Breakeven analysis

Task 7

You are preparing the final accounts of a sole trader trading as Most Lotus and have been given the following final trial balance.

Most Lotus

Trial Balance as at 31 January 20X6

	Dr £	Cr £
Bank	7,230	
Capital		10,000
Payables		3,000
Receivables	2,780	
Discount received		200
Discounts allowed	1,950	
Drawings	5,000	
Fittings at cost	2,500	
Electricity	1,350	
Insurance	1,800	
Other expenses	40,200	
Motor vehicles at cost	15,000	
Cost of sales	160,850	
Allowance for doubtful debts		100
Accumulated depreciation		
Fittings		500
Motor vehicles		3,000
Rent	27,500	
Sales		300,900
Wages	42,000	
Closing inventory	6,000	
Depreciation expense fittings	250	
Depreciation expense motor vehicles	1,500	
Prepayments	2,890	
Accruals		1,100
	318,800	318,800

Open a spreadsheet and save in an appropriate location using the following format **'your initial-surname-task 2.3'**

You should aim for a **high degree of accuracy.** You **should save your work as an .XLS or .XLSX file** at regular intervals to avoid losing your work.

Using your saved spreadsheet you are required to prepare a statement of profit and loss and a statement of financial position for Most Lotus for the year ended 31 January 20X6.

Prepare your statements on separate worksheets.

Your statements should be prepared using appropriate formula and formatted in the following manner:

- All headings in bold using size 12 font

- Figures to be presented with thousand separators and no decimals

- Headings merged and centred over their respective columns

- Currency (£) symbol entered to denote currency columns

- Use top and double bottom borders on totals

- Name your SPL worksheet tab ML1 and format tab in yellow

- Name your SOFP worksheet tab ML2 and format tab in green

- Apply conditional formatting to highlight any amounts in the SOFP in excess of £10,000 with a red border

The owner is concerned regarding the cash flow of the business and has asked you to prepare a 2-D pie chart to show the current assets of the business.

You are required to prepare a 2-D pie chart to clearly show the requested non-current asset information.

- To the right of your statement of financial position statement prepare a 2-D pie chart to show the current assets of the business

- Title your chart **Most Lotus Current Assets** and ensure your chart has an appropriate legend

Finally resave your spreadsheet as **'your initial-surname-task 2.3 finished'**

BPP PRACTICE ASSESSMENT 1
LEVEL 3 SYNOPTIC ASSESSMENT

ANSWERS

Level 3 Synoptic Assessment
BPP practice assessment 1

Task 1

(a)

Statement	True	False
'It doesn't matter whether or not people might think my actions are unethical, it is whether or not I actually am that counts'	☐	✓
'As long as I comply with the principle of integrity, compliance with the other principles will be implied as a result'	☐	✓
'The ethical code applies to my role as a professional and my working life. My private life, on the other hand, is just that – private!'	☐	✓
'As a professional accountant, it is more important for me to be ethical as I work in the public interest.'	✓	☐

(b)

	✓
Integrity	☐
Objectivity	☐
Professional competence and due care	✓

(c)

Action	Yes/No
Integrity	Yes
Professional competence and due care	Yes
Professional behaviour	No

(d)

Statement	True	False
Natural Beauty may have broken the law	☐	✓
Natural Beauty has acted unethically	✓	☐

(e)

	✓
Take the issue directly to the press as it is in the public interest to disclose this via the media	☐
She should do nothing, the issue is not of a financial nature and therefore outside the scope of her expertise and ethical requirements	☐
Discuss the findings with her immediate manager and share her concerns regarding the company's use of mircobeads	☑

(f)

	✓
No, she as disclosure of the matter would be inappropriate in this situation	☐
Yes, as she has reasonable grounds to believe that the environment is being damaged and disclosure was made in good faith	☑
No, PIDA only protects individuals who are disclosing serious organised crimes such as money laundering	☐

Task 2

(a)

Statement	True	False
Clodlands Ltd will be able to reclaim input tax relating to taxable supplies	☑	☐
Clodlands Ltd may be able to reclaim input tax relating to exempt supplies depending on de minimis tests	☑	☐
Clodlands Ltd may charge a reduced rate of VAT on taxable supplies	☐	☑
Clodlands Ltd makes a mixture of taxable and exempt supplies	☑	☐
Clodlands Ltd need not have registered for VAT	☐	☑

(b)

	Invoice	VAT	Borne by customer
	Yes/No	20%/0	Yes/none
A standard-rated let to an unregistered first-time car-boot seller	Yes	Yes	None
A standard-rated let to a registered trader for a Saturday market	Yes	Yes	Yes
An exempt residential let to unregistered private individuals	Yes	No	None

Task 3

(a)

Date	Receipts (units)	Total cost £	Quantity sold	Balance (units)	Total cost £
Balance as at 1 May				800	12,000
5 May	750	10,940		1,550	22,940
10 May			900	650	9,481
18 May	1,000	14,140		1,650	23,621
20 May			900	750	10,602.50

Workings

Sale of 900 units on 10 May: 800 units at (£12,000/800) £15 per unit = £12,000
100 units at (£10,940/750) £14.59 per unit = £1,459

Total value of inventory sold on 10 May £13,459
Value of inventory left on 10 May = £22,940 - £13,459 = £9,481

Sale of 900 units on 20 May: 650 units at £14.59 per unit = £9,483.50
250 units at (£14,140/1,000) £14.14 per unit = £3,535

Total value of inventory sold on 20 May = £13,018.50
Value of inventory left on 20 May = £10,602.50

(b)

Date	Receipts (units)	Total cost £	Quantity sold	Balance (units)	Total cost £
Balance as at 1 May				800	12,000
5 May	750	10,940		1,550	22,940
10 May			900	650	9,620
18 May	1,000	14,140		1,650	23,760
20 May			900	750	10,800

Workings

Average cpu as at end of 5 May: $\dfrac{12,000 + 10,940}{1,550} = £14.80$

Units remaining at 10 May = 650 units $\times$ £14.80 = £9,620

New receipt, average cost per unt at end of 18 May: $\dfrac{£9,620 + £14,140}{1,650} = £14.40$

Units left at end of 20 May = 750 $\times$ £14.40 = £10,800

(c)

Description	✓
Error of commission	
Reversal of entries	✓
Error of omission	
One-sided entry	

(d)

Description	✓
An LLP is a separate legal entity	
The LLP must be registered with the Registrar of Companies	
There is no upper limit to the number of partners a LLP can have	
The LLP must file annual returns, accounts and an annual corporation tax return	✓

Task 4

(a) When preparing financial statements only valid business expenditure is allowed to be recorded as a business expense. This is because the business is a single entity (not legal entity) and its financial affairs need to be kept separate from the owner or owners own personal dealings. Recording invalid expenses would misrepresent the results of the company and would also understate taxable profits. This can be viewed as money laundering and is a criminal offence. If the partners' own family holiday costs were recorded through the partnership this would be dishonest and a breach of the integrity principle. There is a self-interest threat the objectivity principle as I may be influenced by the promise of the tennis tickets. Due to the value of the tennis tickets this could be seen as a bribe and is a criminal offence under the Bribery Act.

(b) I must refuse to comply with the partner's request and as this can be seen as money laundering. I need to prepare an internal report to disclose this matter to the partnership Money Laundering Reporting Officer.

A reasonable third party would view the tennis tickets as a bribe and must not be accepted.

(c) To: Colleague@accounts

From: You@accounts

Subject: Partnership accounts

Hi,

Welcome to the partnership and thank you for contacting on this matter.

A partnership has many similarities to a sole trader as accounting principles and concepts will be the same however there are some important differences to account for two or more people sharing the business.

Here is a summary of the important differences.

Capital accounts

When an individual starts a business they will have a capital account to record the money invested in the business. This is similar to partnerships where each partner will have a separate capital account to record permanent capital invested in the partnership. An important point here is that partnership capital accounts only record long term capital investment.

Current accounts

Each partner will also have separate current account and these are used to record shorter term transactions arising from the partnership and show amounts owing to or from the partnership. Typical credit entries on a current account can be salaries, interest on capital and share in any profits made. These are amounts owed to the individual partner. A typical debit entry will be drawings where a partner extracts money from the partnership similar to a sole trader taking drawings from a business. Any drawings made by a partner will reduce the amount owed to the partner by the partnership.

Appropriation account

The appropriation account shows the total amount of profit made by the partnership with deductions for partner's salaries and interest on capital and adjustments for any interest charged on drawings. The residue amount is then available for sharing between the partners in the agreed partnership sharing ratios.

Statement of financial position

This financial statement shows the assets and liabilities of the partnership. The bottom part of the statement of financial position will show the current and capital accounts for each partner.

I hope this helps.

Please let me know if I can clarify any of the above.

Regards,

Task 5

- Open the renamed spreadsheet and open the grades worksheet

  - Change the title of column G to 'average'
  - Use a formula in cell G2 to calculate the mean score achieved by Alexander
  - Apply this formula to all students

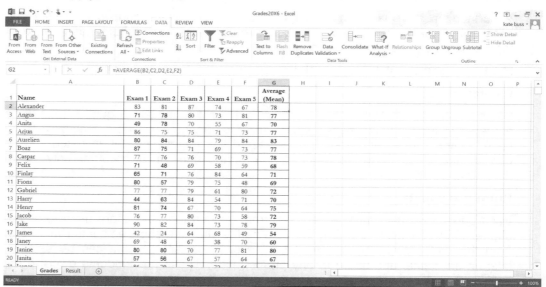

- Use an IF statement in column I along with a lookup function in column H to determine if any students need to be referred.

  - The IF statement should return the values 0 for a referral and 1 for a pass. A pass will be achieved if 50% or more is gained in every subject. A referral will be made if less than 50% is achieved in one or more exams.

BPP
LEARNING MEDIA

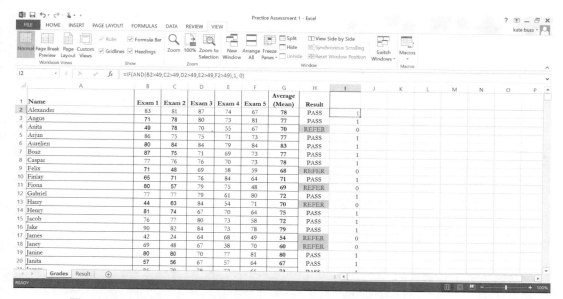

- The lookup function should designate either 'PASS' or 'REFER' to each student based on the outcome of the IF statement

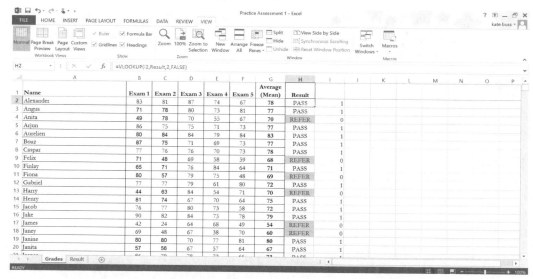

- Improve the look and usability of the spreadsheet

  - Hide your workings so that the lookup references are not visible

  - Use conditional formatting to highlight any REFER values

  - Use the freeze panes function to keep the top row of the spreadsheet visible at all times

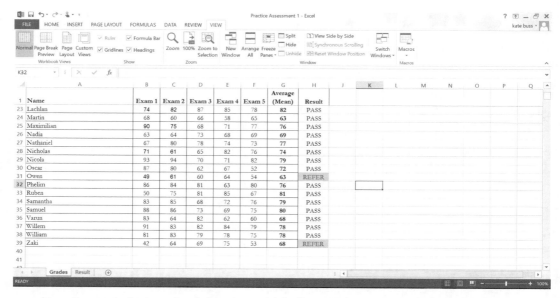

- Use the rank feature to determine which five students should be offered additional help

  - Re-order the students to show in order of rank using the sort function

  - Highlight the rows relating to the students who should be offered help in grey using the fill feature.

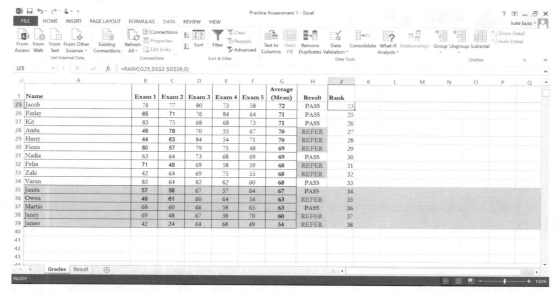

- Password protect the entire workbook and using the password Grades16

Task 6

To:	Emma Neesome
From:	Sarah-Jane Smith
Date:	15 October 20X1
Subject:	Breakeven analysis

Hi Emma

I've carried out the breakeven calculations that you asked me to carry out. They show that the breakeven sales volume is 2,917 units and the breakeven sales revenue is $875,000. We should achieve a contribution/sales ratio of 0.24. The margin of safety in units is 2,083, in % terms 41.67%, which is greater than our target margin of 30%. We should also exceed our target profit of $140,000, as the sales volume required to achieve this profit is 4,861 units, lower than our budgeted sales volume of 5,000 units.

Two problems with breakeven analysis are:

- It assumes selling price is constant
- It assumes all costs can be split into fixed and variable elements

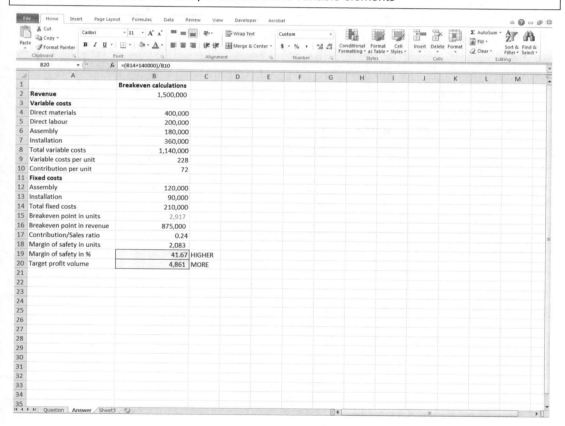

	A	B	C
		Breakeven calculations	
1			
2	Revenue	1,500,000	
3	Variable costs		
4	Direct materials	400,000	
5	Direct labour	200,000	
6	Assembly	180,000	
7	Installation	360,000	
8	Total variable costs	1,140,000	
9	Variable costs per unit	228	
10	Contribution per unit	72	
11	Fixed costs		
12	Assembly	120,000	
13	Installation	90,000	
14	Total fixed costs	210,000	
15	Breakeven point in units	2,917	
16	Breakeven point in revenue	875,000	
17	Contribution/Sales ratio	0.24	
18	Margin of safety in units	2,083	
19	Margin of safety in %	41.67	HIGHER
20	Target profit volume	4,861	MORE

B20 fx =(B14+140000)/B10

Task 7

	A	B	C	D	E	F	G	H
1				Most Lotus				
2				Statement of Profit or Loss				
3				For the year ended 31 January 20X6				
4								
5					£		£	
6	Sales revenue						300,900	
7	Cost of sales						160,850	
8	Gross profit						140,050	
9	Discounts received						200	
10	Adjusted gross profit						140,250	
11								
12	Less expenses							
13	Electricity				1,350			
14	Insurance				1,800			
15	Other expenses				40,200			
16	Rent				27,500			
17	Wages				42,000			
18	Discounts allowed				1,950			
19	Depreciation expense fittings				250			
20	Depreciation expense motor vehicles				1,500			
21							116,550	
22	Net profit						23,700	
23								
24								

| ML1

Suggested formulas

	A	B	C	D	E	F	G	H
1				Most Lotus				
2				Statement of Profit or Loss				
3				For the year ended 31 January 20X6				
4								
5					£		£	
6	Sales revenue						300900	
7	Cost of sales						160850	
8	Gross profit						=G6-G7	
9	Discounts received						200	
10	Adjusted gross prof						=G8+G9	
11								
12	Less expenses							
13	Electricity				1350			
14	Insurance				1800			
15	Other expenses				40200			
16	Rent				27500			
17	Wages				42000			
18	Discounts allowed				1950			
19	Depreciation exper				250			
20	Depreciation exper				1500			
21							=SUM(E13:E20)	
22	Net profit						=G10-G21	
23								
24								

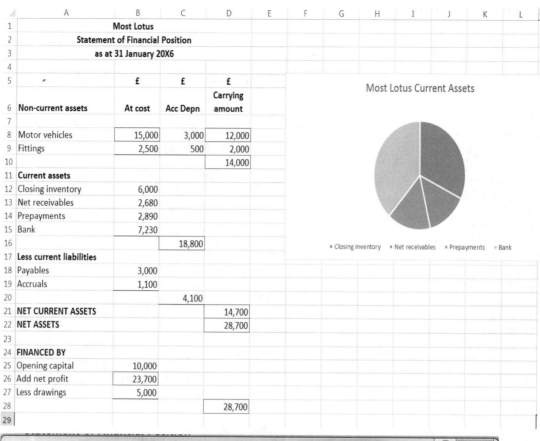

	A	B	C	D
1		Most Lotus		
2		Statement of Financial Position		
3		as at 31 January 20X6		
4				
5		£	£	£
6	Non-current assets	At cost	Acc Depn	Carrying amount
7				
8	Motor vehicles	15,000	3,000	12,000
9	Fittings	2,500	500	2,000
10				14,000
11	Current assets			
12	Closing inventory	6,000		
13	Net receivables	2,680		
14	Prepayments	2,890		
15	Bank	7,230		
16			18,800	
17	Less current liabilities			
18	Payables	3,000		
19	Accruals	1,100		
20			4,100	
21	NET CURRENT ASSETS			14,700
22	NET ASSETS			28,700
23				
24	FINANCED BY			
25	Opening capital	10,000		
26	Add net profit	23,700		
27	Less drawings	5,000		
28				28,700
29				

Most Lotus Current Assets

Closing inventory · Net receivables · Prepayments · Bank

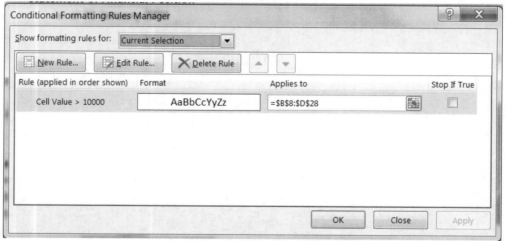

Conditional Formatting Rules Manager

Show formatting rules for: Current Selection

New Rule... | Edit Rule... | Delete Rule

Rule (applied in order shown)	Format	Applies to	Stop If True
Cell Value > 10000	AaBbCcYyZz	=$B$8:$D$28	☐

OK | Close | Apply

ML2

BPP PRACTICE ASSESSMENT 2
LEVEL 3 SYNOPTIC ASSESSMENT

Time allowed: 3 hours

PRACTICE ASSESSMENT 2

Level 3 Synoptic Assessment
BPP practice assessment 2

Task 1

(a) Complete the following sentence.

A professional accountant who complies with the law, brings no disrepute on the profession and is perceived as being ethical by other people has complied with the fundamental principle of [▼   ].

Picklist

confidentiality
due care
integrity
objectivity
professional behaviour
professional competence

The requirement for ethical business practices means that sustainable development and corporate social responsibility are becoming increasingly important.

(b) Which of the below is true in respect of the accountant's role in respect to the above?

	✓
Sustainability and CSR are not financial matters and sit outside the remit of the professional accountant	☐
Sustainability and CSR form part of the accountant's obligation to work in the public interest	☐
Sustainability and CSR are only key considerations for accountants working in particular industries, such as the renewable energy industry	☐

Danny is a professional accountant working in practice. Whilst carrying out some work for his client, Inge, he has acted outside the limits of his professional expertise.

As a result of the work carried out by Danny, Inge has now incurred a regulatory fine.

(c) Show whether Inge might be able to seek compensation from Danny for this loss on each of the following grounds.

Action	Yes/No
Professional negligence	▼
Breach of contract	▼
Fraud under false representation	▼

Sparkys Limited, a small home electricals company who you have worked with for a number of years, has unexpectedly requested your practice to help in selling a number of residential properties that they have recently acquired.

(d)   Explain whether customer due diligence should be carried before accepting this work.

Statement	True	False
Due diligence procedures are not necessary as this situation relates to an existing client.	☐	☐
You should report this matter urgently to the relevant authorities. There is clearly something amiss.	☐	☐

You are a newly qualified accounting technician working in practice. Your colleague Piers has been off work sick for the past week and your line manager asks you to go through his in-tray and deal with anything that needs urgent attention.

In Piers' in-tray you find a letter addressed to Piers from one of his clients, Martin. In this the letter Martin asks Piers to include a revenue figure in his tax return which is much lower than the actual revenue received by the client. Martin offers Piers 'the £1,000 you need to clear your gambling debt' in return for inclusion of this incorrect figure. Martin also suggests that if this is not done by the end of the month, he will inform the firm of the other ways in which Piers has helped him to present suitable figures in the past.

(e)   Complete the following sentence

As a result of this letter, Piers faces threats of [　　　　▼] and [　　　　▼] to his professional ethics.

Picklist

advocacy
familiarity
intimidation
self-interest
self-review

(f)   Show whether or not the following of Piers' fundamental principles are threatened by the letter.

Action	Yes/No
Integrity	▼
Objectivity	▼
Confidentiality	▼
Professional competence and due care	▼
Professional behaviour	▼

(g) Which of the following actions would it be most appropriate for you to take on discovery of this letter?

	✓
Hide the letter back in the in-tray and pretend you never saw it; it would not do for you to get caught up in this mess	☐
Report the misconduct immediately to the AAT	☐
Discuss the situation with your immediate line manager	☐

Task 2

The following tasks are based on the following workplace scenario of Elsewares.

You are Ethan, a part-qualified accounting technician. You are employed by an accountancy firm where you assist clients including Elsewares with bookkeeping and VAT compliance.

Elsewares has been run for many years by Elsie as a sole trader.

You have the complete figures for Elseware's transactions for the most recent quarter:

- All goods are standard rated
- All required paperwork has been kept
- Net sales to UK customers were £3,800
- Goods bought from UK suppliers cost £1,400 net of VAT
- £648 was spent by Elsewares on exempt UK postage
- Goods were sold to individual customers in France for a total of £2,592
- Goods were sold to businesses in Germany for a total of £4,780
- Goods were sold to a business in India for a total of £560
- Elsie introduced extra capital of £1,500 into the business

Enter the figures for boxes 6 to 9 of the online VAT return for the quarter. Show your workings.

(link to www.gov.uk/government/publications/vat-notice-70012-filling-in-your-vat-return/vat-notice-70012-filling-in-your-vat-return#how-to-fill-in-each-box-on-your-return)

VAT Return for the quarter		£
Total value of sales and all other outputs excluding any VAT. Include your box 8 figure. WHOLE POUNDS ONLY	for Box 6	
Total value of purchases and all other inputs excluding any VAT. Include your box 9 figure. WHOLE POUNDS ONLY	for Box 7	
Total value of all supplies of goods and related costs, excluding any VAT, to other EC Member States. WHOLE POUNDS ONLY	for Box 8	
Total value of all acquisitions of goods and related costs, excluding any VAT, from other EC Member States. WHOLE POUNDS ONLY	for Box 9	

Task 3

James and Suzy have been the owners of a partnership business for many years, sharing profits and losses in the ratio 3:2, with James receiving the larger share.

On 1 January 20X7, the partnership agreement was changed so that James and Suzy will share profits and losses in the ratio 2:1, with James receiving the larger share.

Goodwill was valued at £84,800 at this date. No entries for goodwill have yet been made in the partnership accounting records.

(a) Show the entries required to introduce the goodwill into the partnership accounting records on 1 January 20X7.

Account name		Amount £	Debit	Credit
	▼			
	▼			
	▼			

Picklist

Balance b/d
Balance c/d
Bank
Capital – James
Capital – Suzy
Current – James
Current – Suzy
Drawings
Goodwill

(b) Which of the following should be included in a partnership agreement? Choose ONE:

	✓
The partnership appropriation account.	
Capital and current accounts for each partner.	
Salaries and wages to be paid to all employees.	
The rate at which interest is to be allowed on capital.	

The partnership manufactures and sells cake tins. They are considering buying a new piece of equipment to launch an improved model, the K47, and have asked you to calculate the number of units they need to sell in the first year to breakeven.

K47 Cake Tin

Selling price   £6.25 per unit
Variable costs   £1.00 per unit (materials)
                  £1.25 per unit (labour)

Fixed costs   £28,000 per year

It takes 1 hour to produce 10 units. The factory operates 50 weeks of the year, with 40 productive hours per week.

(c) Calculate the number of units to be produced and sold in the first year in order for the partnership to breakeven on the K47. Show your workings.

(d) Using the information in part (c), calculate the maximum revenue which can be generated from the K47 in the first year. Show your workings.

(e) Based on your answers in (c) and (d), what would be the profit on the K47 at the end of the first year.

··

Task 4

You are currently working on the year-end financial statements. The work involves the collection of revenue and costs from three divisions. One of your colleagues has mentioned that to speed up communication between divisions he has been using a social media site to transfer and share financial information. He has suggested that you should also do so as the present company policy of password protected data transfer is slow and inconvenient.

(a) Referring to the Code of Professional Ethics explain the ethical principles that are at risk here.

(b) What actions should you take to reduce the risks to the ethical principles?

Your worst fears have been realised as the financial data your colleague uploaded onto the Internet has been deleted and lost. A back-up copy has not been made.

You have receive the following email:

To: You@accounts

From: Colleague@acounts

Subject: Missing information

Hi,

I have lost some important financial information. The information I need are amounts paid for trade purchases and sales revenue. I need these figures for the year-end statement of profit or loss.

I have been able to recover that opening payables amounted to £5,400 and closing payables were £4,800. Amounts paid from our bank account to our trade suppliers amounted to £108,000.

If it is any help the sales team have informed me that we operate on a 20% mark-up on cost and inventory values were negligible.

Please help.

Regards,

(c) Reply to your colleagues email explaining the approach that is required and also supply the sales and purchase figures that your colleague is requesting.

··

Task 5

You have been given a spreadsheet RegionalSales_Quarter1.xls which shows sales figures during the quarter January – March 20X6 for a company which operates in three regions, North, South and Central. It contains four worksheets: 'North', 'South', 'Central' and 'PriceList'.

Download this spreadsheet file and save in the appropriate location. Rename it using the following format: **'your initial-surname-AAT no –dd.mm.yy-Task5.3'**.

For example: J-Donnovan-123456-12.03xx-Task5.3

A **high degree of accuracy** is required. You **must save your work as an .XLS or .XLSX file** at regular intervals to avoid losing your work.

- Open the renamed spreadsheet and open the north worksheet

    - In cell C3 create a formula which includes a lookup function to calculate the value of units sold in January by the North team

    - Apply this formula to all other relevant cells in this column

    - Create similar formulas including lookup functions in cells E3 and G3 and copy this down to all relevant cells in these columns

    - Use autosum at the bottom of columns C, E and G to calculate the total for each month

- Repeat the above steps for the South and Central regions

- Insert a new sheet and rename it 'Jan-Mar Total Sales'

    - Reorder the worksheets so that the new total sales worksheet is in the left-most position

    - Produce summary sheet data in this new worksheet where the rows are the three regions and the columns are the months in order to summarise total value of sales

- Produce a 2D pie chart of the total sales value to illustrate the proportions of total value of sales contributed by each of the three regions.

    - Change the title of the chart to 'Regional Sales'

    - Format the chart options to include gradient fill

Task 6

You are Harry Sullivan, a part-qualified accounting technician. You work for Henniswoode Co, which manufactures kitchen utensils.

You cover all aspects of bookkeeping and accounting for the business. You report to Sarah Foster, the Chief Executive.

Today's date is 12 November 20X2.

Sarah has asked you to do a comparison between the actual overheads for the year 31 October 20X2 and the overheads absorbed, using the basis of labour hours. The information you need is attached.

Download the spreadsheet file from www.bpp.com/aatspreadsheets. Save the spreadsheet file in the appropriate location and rename it in the following format: 'your initial-surname-AAT no-dd.mm.yy-Task1'. For example: H-Darch-123456-12.03.xx-Task1

A **high degree of accuracy** is required. You must **save your work as an .XLS or.XLSX file** at regular intervals to avoid losing your work.

1. Open the renamed file. In cells B3-B11, identify the basis you will use to allocate the overheads given in rows 3-11.

2. Allocate the overheads in each department using the bases that you have chosen.

3. In cells D12-G12 subtotal the overheads allocated to each department.

4. Put an IF statement in cell H12 that will show 'Balanced' if the column totals add to the same total as the total in cell C12 and 'Check' if they do not.

5. Reallocate the overheads allocated to the stores department in row 13, using the information given. Show the overheads allocated to other departments as positive figures and the overheads allocated away from stores as a negative figure. Confirm the accuracy of what you have done by totalling in cell C13 the figures in cells D13-G13. The total should be a nil figure.

6. In cells D14-F14 subtotal the overheads allocated to the two production departments and the maintenance department.

7. Reallocate the overheads allocated to the maintenance department in Row 15, using the information given. Show the overheads allocated to other departments as positive figures and the overheads allocated away from maintenance as a negative figure. Confirm the accuracy of what you have done by totalling in cell C15 the figures in cells D15-F15. The total should be a nil figure.

8. In cells D16-E16 subtotal the overheads allocated to the two production departments.

9. Insert the budgeted labour hours for the two production departments in cells D17 and E17.

10. Calculate the overhead absorption rate for the two production departments and insert the figures in cells D18 and E18.

11. Colour cells D18 and E18 with a yellow background and black border.

12. Calculate the amount of overheads absorbed by actual production, using the information given about actual labour hours. Show this figure in cell C19.

13. Calculate the over or under absorption of overheads and show this figure in cell C20. If there has been an over-absorption of overheads, show this figure as a positive figure in green. If there has been an under-absorption of overheads, show this figure as a negative figure in red.

14. Enter the figure for absorbed overheads in cell B26 and calculate what the profit would have been using this figure in cell B27.

15. Enter the figure for over and under absorption of overheads in cell B28 and calculate the actual profit in cell B29.

16. Tidy up the calculation by showing all negative figures in brackets and all figures with comma for 000s.

17. Perform a spell check and ensure that all the contents of the cells can be seen.

18. Use the proforma email to do the following:

- Report the actual profit and amount of overheads over and under absorbed, explaining why the over or under absorption has occurred

- Give one advantage and one disadvantage of using absorption costing

To:	Sarah Foster
From:	Harry Sullivan
Date:	12 November 20X2
Subject:	Absorption of overheads

Task 7

As part of your role as an accounting technician you have been requested to prepare a partnership profit appropriation account for the Awesome Partnership for the year ended 30 June 20X6.

The following information is available to you:

The partnership has three partners; Andy, Wahid and Erin and profits are shared 3:3:2 respectively

Salaries:

Andy £17,500
Wahid £15,000
Erin £10,000

Interest of 15% is paid on capital balances at the end of the year.

Capital balances as at 30 June 20X6
Andy £30,000 Credit balance
Wahid £45,000 Credit balance
Erin £35,000 Credit balance

Net profit for the year ended 30 June 20X6 amounted to £100,000 before any partnership distributions.

Open a spreadsheet and save in an appropriate location using the following format **'your initial-surname-task 2.3'**

You should aim for a **high degree of accuracy**. You **should save your work as an .XLS or .XLSX file** at regular intervals to avoid losing your work.

Using your saved spreadsheet you are required to prepare a profit appropriation account for the Awesome Partnership for the year ended 30 June 20X6.

Your partnership profit appropriation account should be prepared using appropriate formula and formatted in the following manner:

- Account heading in bold, italics using size 14 font
- Heading merged and centred over respective columns
- Figures to be presented with thousand separators and no decimals
- Insert currency (£) symbols where relevant
- Use top and double bottom borders on account totals
- Name your appropriation worksheet tab AWE1 and format tab in blue

The partnership is considering using a spreadsheet to help with valuation and location of inventory held in the store room. The store room is split into two sections named '1' and '2'. Wahid has explained to you that the business sells many products but he would like you to prepare a pilot spreadsheet for just four products, A to D containing two 'look-up' formulae to show the current price of a product and also their location in the store room.

The following information is available:

Product	Price	Location in store room
A	£25.00	1
B	£27.80	1
C	£28.40	2
D	£30.00	2

Open a new worksheet and enter the information above.

You are required to prepare a worksheet that can quickly show both price and location of a product using appropriate look-up formulae.

- Use grey infill for any non-active areas of your worksheet
- Custom format in GBP currency to two decimal places

Finally resave your spreadsheet as **'your initial-surname-task 2.3 finished'**

BPP PRACTICE ASSESSMENT 2
LEVEL 3 SYNOPTIC ASSESSMENT

ANSWERS

Level 3 Synoptic Assessment
BPP practice assessment 2

Task 1

(a)

A professional accountant who complies with the law, brings no disrepute on the profession and is perceived as being ethical by other people has complied with the fundamental principle of | professional behaviour |.

(b)

	✓
Sustainability and CSR are not financial matters and sit outside the remit of the professional accountant	☐
Sustainability and CSR form part of the accountant's obligation to work in the public interest	✓
Sustainability and CSR are key considerations for accountants working in particularly industries, such as the renewable energy industry	☐

(c)

Action	Yes/No
Professional negligence	Yes
Breach of contract	Yes
Fraud under false representation	No

(d)

Statement	True	False
Due diligence procedures are not necessary as this situation relates to an existing client.	☐	✓
You should report this matter urgently to the relevant authorities. There is clearly something amiss.	☐	✓

(e)

As a result of this letter, Piers faces threats of | self-interest | and | intimidation | to his professional ethics.

(f)

Action	Yes/No
Integrity	Yes
Objectivity	Yes
Confidentiality	No
Professional competence and due care	No
Professional behaviour	Yes

(g)

	✓
Hide the letter back in the in-tray and pretend you never saw it; it would not do for you to get caught up in this mess	☐
Report the misconduct immediately to the AAT	☐
Discuss the situation with your immediate line manager	☑

Task 2

Solution

VAT Return for the quarter		£
Total value of sales and all other outputs excluding any VAT. Include your box 8 figure. WHOLE POUNDS ONLY £3,800 + £2,592 x 100/120 = 2,160 + £4,780 + £560 =	for Box 6	11,300
Total value of purchases and all other inputs excluding any VAT. Include your box 9 figure. WHOLE POUNDS ONLY £1,400 + £648 =	for Box 7	2,048
Total value of all supplies of goods and related costs, excluding any VAT, to other EC Member States. WHOLE POUNDS ONLY £2,592 x 100/120 = 2,160 + £4,780 =	for Box 8	6,796
Total value of all acquisitions of goods and related costs, excluding any VAT, from other EC Member States. WHOLE POUNDS ONLY	for Box 9	0

....

Task 3

(a)

Account name	Amount £	Debit	Credit
Goodwill	84,800	✓	
Capital – James*	50,880		✓
Capital – Suzy**	33,920		✓

Workings

*James £84,800/5 × 3 = £50,880
**Suzy £84,800/5 × 2 = £33,920

(b)

	✓
The partnership appropriation account.	
Capital and current accounts for each partner.	
Salaries and wages to be paid to all employees.	
The rate at which interest is to be allowed on capital.	✓

(c) Breakeven point

$$\frac{£28,000}{6.25 - (1.25 + 1.00)} = 7,000 \text{ units}$$

(d) Maximum revenue

£125,000

Workings

Maximum number of hours in a week = 40

Maximum number of units to be produced in a week = 40 hours x 10 units (10 units per hour) = 400 units

Maximum units in a year = 400 units per week x 50 weeks of production in a year = 20,000 units per year

Maximum revenue in a year = 20,000 units x £6.25 = £125,000

(e) Profit at the end of year 1

£52,000

Workings

Revenue (from part d)	£125,000
Less fixed costs	£28,000
Less variable costs (20,000 × £2.25)	£45,000
Profit	£52,000

Task 4

(a) The two ethical principles most at risk here are confidentiality and professional behaviour. Organisations have a professional and legal obligation to keep data and information secure and confidential. Typically this will require strict access policies and the use of password protection. My colleague's use of social media to transfer company information is risking a breach of confidentiality and is against company policy. In respect of the Data Protection Act It is likely to be illegal as well. The second principle at risk here is professional behaviour. It were to be public knowledge that the company was using this method of transferring sensitive information this would bring disrepute to the company and the accountancy profession.

(b) I must refuse to share and exchange information in this way and only communicate information as per company policies on information and data. I should also report this matter to my supervisor as this is a serious breach of company policy and can have wider legal implications and affect respect for the accountancy profession.

(c) To: Colleague@accounts

From: You@accounts

Subject: Missing information

Hi,

Firstly I must remind you that we do have responsibility to keep proper books of accounts that would be able to supply this information.

However, when there are incomplete records we can use various techniques to reconstruct the missing information from the records we do have. Incomplete records can occur when proper records have not been kept or in unusual circumstances through fire, flood or system crashes.

Amounts that are missing can be reconstructed by the use of raw data, for example paying-in stubs, bank statements, invoices and credit notes. When opening and closing balances are known balancing figures can sometimes be inserted into workings to discover missing amounts. Other methods can include the use of percentage mark-ups and margins to calculate missing figures. This can include the reconstruction of sales revenue, cost of sales and gross profit figures.

Trade payments

The bank statement shows that £108,000 has actually been paid to trade suppliers however this has to be adjusted for the opening and closing balances to show how much should go into the statement of profit or loss. This is part of the matching or accruals concept.

£108,000 plus amounts outstanding at the end of the year = £108,000 + £4,800 = £112,800 less £5,400 that relates to the previous year = £112,800 - £5,400 = £107,400

£107,400 is the amount to be included in the statement of profit or loss for trade purchases.

Sales revenue

As we operate on a 20% plus cost basis sales revenue is £107,400 × 1.20 = £128,880.

Please keep information and data safer in future.

Regards,

••

Task 5

- Open the renamed spreadsheet and open the north worksheet
  - In cell C3 create a formula which includes a lookup function to calculate the value of units sold in January by the North team

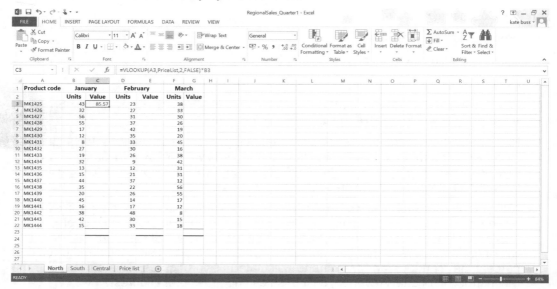

‒ Apply this formula to all other relevant cells in this column

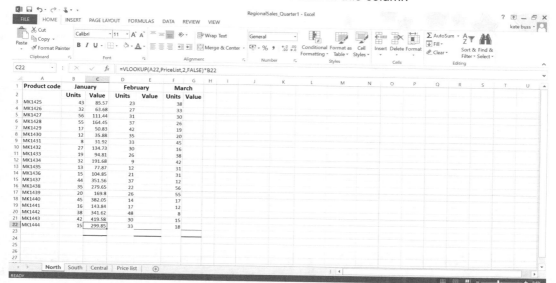

‒ Create similar formulas including lookup functions in cells E3 and G3 and copy this down to all relevant cells in these columns

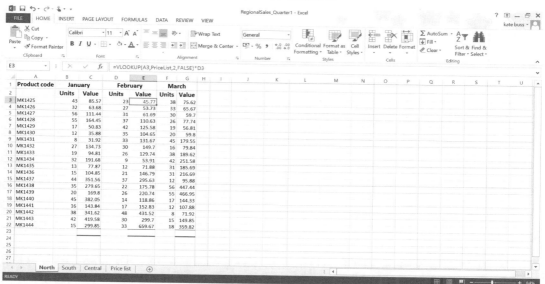

BPP practice assessment 2: answers

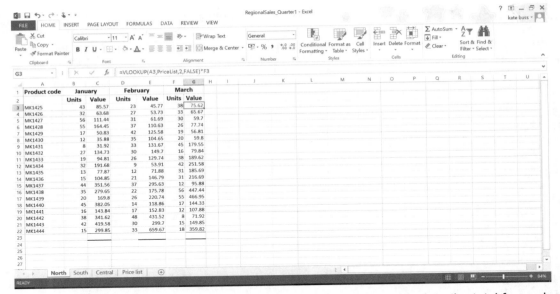

- Use autosum at the bottom of columns C, E and G to calculate the total for each month

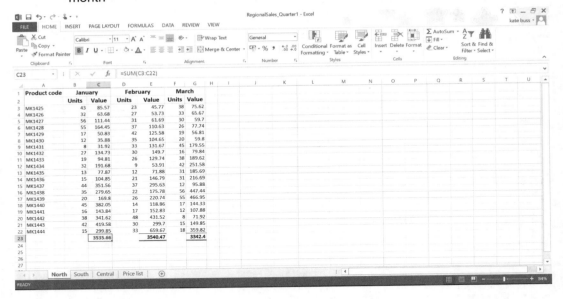

- Repeat the above steps for the South and Central regions

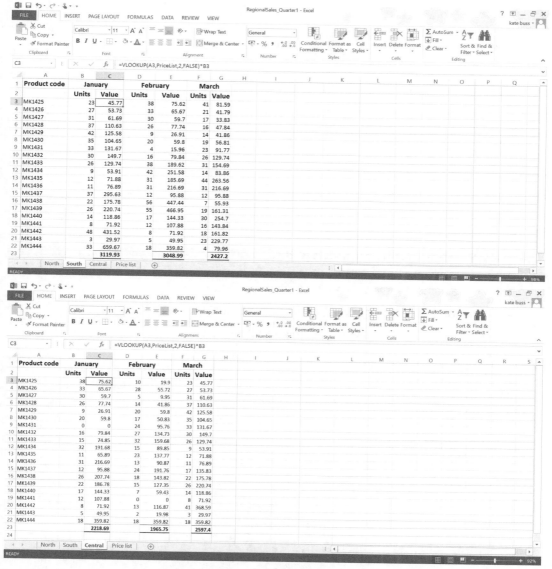

- Insert a new sheet and rename it 'Jan-Mar Total Sales'

  - Reorder the worksheets so that the new total sales worksheet is in the left-most position

  - Produce summary sheet data in this new worksheet where the rows are the three regions and the columns are the months in order to summarise total value of sales

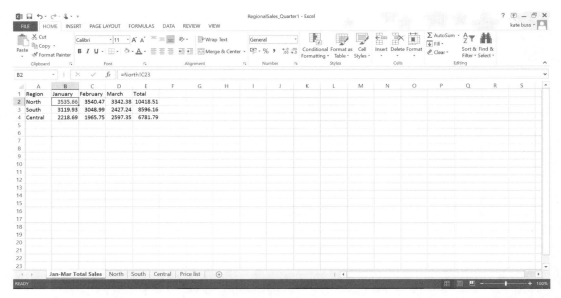

- Produce a 2D pie chart of the total sales value to illustrate the proportions of total value of sales contributed by each of the three regions.

  - Change the title of the chart to 'Regional Sales'

  - Format the chart options to include gradient fill

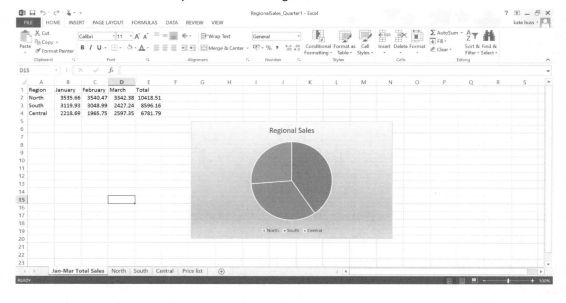

Task 6

To:	Sarah Foster
From:	Harry Sullivan
Date:	12 November 20X2
Subject:	Absorption of overheads

Hi Sarah

The actual profit for the year was £966,000. This is calculated after taking into account an over-absorption of overheads of £2,414. This means that actual overheads were less than overheads absorbed, on the basis of total labour hours worked.

One advantage of absorption costing is that it should ensure that all overheads are covered. One disadvantage with using absorption costing is that the method of absorption can be arbitrary.

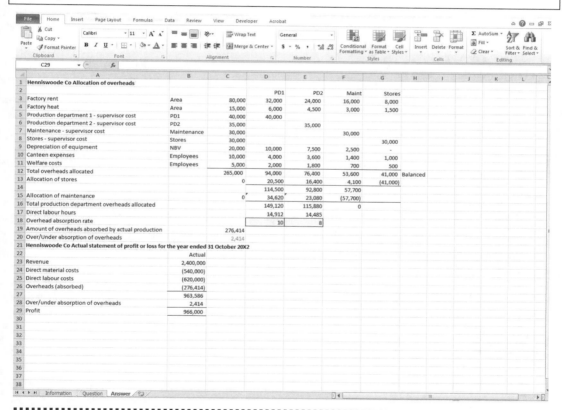

	A	B	C	D	E	F	G
1	Henniswoode Co Allocation of overheads						
2				PD1	PD2	Maint	Stores
3	Factory rent	Area	80,000	32,000	24,000	16,000	8,000
4	Factory heat	Area	15,000	6,000	4,500	3,000	1,500
5	Production department 1 - supervisor cost	PD1	40,000	40,000			
6	Production department 2 - supervisor cost	PD2	35,000		35,000		
7	Maintenance - supervisor cost	Maintenance	30,000			30,000	
8	Stores - supervisor cost	Stores	30,000				30,000
9	Depreciation of equipment	NBV	20,000	10,000	7,500	2,500	-
10	Canteen expenses	Employees	10,000	4,000	3,600	1,400	1,000
11	Welfare costs	Employees	5,000	2,000	1,800	700	500
12	Total overheads allocated		265,000	94,000	76,400	53,600	41,000 Balanced
13	Allocation of stores		0	20,500	16,400	4,100	(41,000)
14				114,500	92,800	57,700	
15	Allocation of maintenance		0	34,620	23,080	(57,700)	
16	Total production department overheads allocated			149,120	115,880	0	
17	Direct labour hours			14,912	14,485		
18	Overhead absorption rate			10	8		
19	Amount of overheads absorbed by actual production		276,414				
20	Over/Under absorption of overheads		2,414				
21	Henniswoode Co Actual statement of profit or loss for the year ended 31 October 20X2						
22		Actual					
23	Revenue	2,400,000					
24	Direct material costs	(540,000)					
25	Direct labour costs	(620,000)					
26	Overheads (absorbed)	(276,414)					
27		963,586					
28	Over/under absorption of overheads	2,414					
29	Profit	966,000					

Task 7

	A	B	C	D	E	F	G	H
1	Interest on capital		15%					
2								
3			*Profit appropriation account*					
4			£	£			£	
5					Profit for the year		100,000	
6	Salaries							
7	Andy		17,500					
8	Wahid		15,000					
9	Erin		10,000					
10				42,500				
11	Interest on capital							
12	Andy	30,000	4,500					
13	Wahid	45,000	6,750					
14	Erin	35,000	5,250					
15				16,500				
16								
17	Balance c/d			41,000				
18				100,000			100,000	
19	Profit share				Profit for apropriation		41,000	
20	Andy	0.375	15,375					
21	Wahid	0.375	15,375					
22	Erin	0.25	10,250					
23			41,000				41,000	
24								

AWE1

Suggested formulas

	A	B	C	D	E	F	G	H
1	Interest on capital		0.15					
2								
3			*Profit appropriation account*					
4			£	£			£	
5					Profit for the year		100000	
6	Salaries							
7	Andy		17500					
8	Wahid		15000					
9	Erin		10000					
10				=SUM(C7:C9)				
11	Interest on capital							
12	Andy	30000	=B12*C$1					
13	Wahid	45000	=B13*C$1					
14	Erin	35000	=B14*C$1					
15				=SUM(C12:C14)				
16								
17	Balance c/d			=G5-D10-D15				
18				=D10+D15+D17			=G5	
19	Profit share				Profit for apropriation		=D17	
20	Andy	=3/8	=B20*G$19					
21	Wahid	=3/8	=B21*G$19					
22	Erin	0.25	=B22*G$19					
23			=SUM(C20:C22)				=C23	
24								
25								

	A	B	C	D	E	F	G	H
1	Product	Price	Location		Price	£27.80		
2	A	£25.00	1		Location	1		
3	B	£27.80	1					
4	C	£28.40	2					
5	D	£30.00	2					
6								
7	Product		B					
8								
9								
10								
11								

Suggested formulas

	A	B	C	D	E	F	G
1	Product	Price	Location		Price	=VLOOKUP(C7,A1:E5,2,FALSE)	
2	A	25	1		Location	=VLOOKUP(C7,A1:C5,3,FALSE)	
3	B	27.8	1				
4	C	28.4	2				
5	D	30	2				
6							
7		Product	B				
8							
9							

BPP PRACTICE ASSESSMENT 3
LEVEL 3 SYNOPTIC ASSESSMENT

Time allowed: 3 hours

PRACTICE ASSESSMENT 3

Level 3 Synoptic Assessment
BPP practice assessment 3

Task 1

The AAT is sponsored by four professional bodies.

(a) Which TWO of the below are sponsoring bodies of the AAT?

	✓
CCAB	☐
CIMA	☐
CIPFA	☐
ACCA	☐

(b) Complete the following statement

The FRC aims to promote ethical [▼] and increased [▼]
in the accountancy profession in the UK.

Picklist

accounting
compliance
confidence
financial reporting
practices

(c) Are these statements true or false?

Statement	True	False
The need to act ethically is most important for accountants employed in the public sector as they are more open to criticism if this money is perceived to be spent inappropriately.	☐	☐
The Code of Professional Ethics sets out the required standards of professional behaviour with guidance on how these standards can be achieved	☐	☐
The Code of Professional Ethics adopts a principles-based approach in order to allow individuals to choose appropriate behaviour and to remove the need for professional judgements to be made.	☐	☐

You have recently terminated your relationship with a client after discovering a number of errors in their VAT return that they refused to correct.

(d) **You withdrew from this engagement to safeguard against which threat to your fundamental principles?**

	✓
Familiarity	☐
Self-interest	☐
Intimidation	☐

You have now been approached by the client's new accountant who has asked you why the agreement ended.

(e) **Which of the fundamental principles does this threaten?**

	✓
Professional behaviour	☐
Confidentiality	☐
Objectivity	☐

You have just found out that, as result of the discovery of previously withheld information, that the financial statements of a client are materially misstated. Several months ago you issued an unqualified audit report and confirmed that the statements presented a true and fair view.

(f) **Which of the below statements are true?**

	✓
You failed to comply with the ethical principle of professional competence and due care at the time of the audit.	☐
You failed to comply with the ethical principle of integrity at the time of the audit.	☐
You complied with the ethical principles at the time of the audit	☐

(g) Which of the following actions should now be taken?

	✓
You should make a note on the audit file for next year. The report on these financial statements has already been issued and it is too late to retract it.	☐
You should issue a revised audit report immediately.	☐
You should securely destroy the new information to prevent damage to your reputation as a professional accountant.	☐

Task 2

The following tasks are based on the following workplace scenario of InTime:

You are Ignacio, a part-qualified accounting technician. You are employed by InTime, a business repairing and selling clocks and watches. You assist with bookkeeping and VAT compliance.

There are several exceptions to the general rules on time of supply.

(a) Where a VAT invoice is issued on a date in advance of the date of supply, the tax point will be the [   ] of the two dates

Where full payment is made on a date in advance of the date of supply, the tax point will be the [   ] of the two dates

If part payment is made before the supply takes place, this [   ] create a tax point. If the remainder is paid before the supply takes place, there will be [   ]. Where payment is split, [   ] to show the full invoice in one VAT return.

Where an invoice is issued after the supply has taken place, this may create a tax point. The invoice date becomes the tax point if it is within [   ] after the supply.

Picklist

14 days
30 days
another tax point
earlier
it is necessary
it may not be correct
later
no effect
will
will not

(b) There are time limits on issuing invoices.

Normally an invoice must be issued within [blank] of a supply of goods, or [blank] of a supply of services.

Where payment is received in advance, an invoice must be issued within [blank] of the [blank].

Picklist

14 days
30 days
payment
supply

(c) Draft a short note to explain the difference between a basic and actual tax point, giving one example of each relating to a sale of goods by InTime.

Task 3

You are preparing the statement of financial position for the Fenland Trading partnership for the year end 31 December 20X7.

The partners are Jenny and John.

You have the final trial balance below. All the necessary year-end adjustments have been made, except for the transfer of £44,550 profit to the current accounts of the partners. Partners share profits and losses in the ratio 60:40, with Jenny taking the larger share.

(a) Calculate the balance of each partner's current account after sharing profits. Indicate whether these balance are DEBIT or CREDIT by writing either word in the appropriate field (the answer fields are not case sensitive).

	Balance	Debit/Credit
Current account: Jenny £	£	
Current account: John	£	

(b) Prepare a statement of financial position for the partnership as at 31 December 20X7. You need to use the partners' current account balances that you have just calculated in (a). Do NOT use brackets, minus signs or dashes.

Fenland Trading

Trial balance as at 31 December 20X7

	Debit £	Credit £
Accruals		1,400
Bank	13,460	
Capital account – Jenny		22,000
Capital account – John		14,000
Carriage inwards	6,852	
Cash	320	
Closing inventory	24,380	24,380
Current account – Jenny	1,562	
Current account – John	1,412	
Depreciation charges	7,080	
Interest paid	294	
Office equipment at cost	35,400	
Office equipment accumulated depreciation		14,160
Office expenses	41,576	
Opening inventory	25,870	
Purchases	146,388	
Purchases ledger control account		17,635
Sales		269,127
Sales ledger control account	40,083	
Travel expenses	6,297	
VAT		2,872
Wages	14,600	
Total	365,574	365,574

Fenland Trading

Statement of financial position as at 31 December 20X7

	£	£	£
Non-current assets	Cost	Accumulated Depreciation	Carrying amount
▼			
Current assets			
▼			
▼			
▼			
▼			
▼			
Total current assets			
Current liabilities			
▼			
▼			
▼			
▼			
▼			
Total current liabilities			
Net current assets			
Net assets			
Financed by:	Jenny	John	Total
▼			
▼			

Picklist

Accruals
Bank
Capital accounts
Carriage inwards
Cash
Current accounts
Expenses
Inventory
Office equipment
Purchases
Sales
Trade payables
Trade receivables
VAT
Wages

(c) **Fenland Trading uses the FIFO method of inventory valuation. Select which ONE of the following statements is an ADVANTAGE of using this method of valuation by ticking in the relevant box.**

Reason	✓
Inventory is valued at a price which most closely represents the current market value	
It complies with IAS 2 *Accounting for Inventory*	
It is easy to calculate when there is a high volume of stock movement in and out of the business	
Fluctuations in prices are smoothed out, making it easier to analyse the data for decision making	

(d) **Which ONE of the following is NOT an accounting characteristic**

	✓
Relevance	
Prudence	
Comparability	
Ease of understanding	

Task 4

It is just after the year-end and you are currently working on the inventory value to go into the extended trial balance. For many years the company has used a weighted average

cost (WAVCO) method in the calculation of inventory values but this year one of the directors has requested you to use a 'last in first out' (LIFO) method. The reason given for this was that purchase costs increased considerably towards the end of the year so this would reflect 'economic reality' and we can change back to WAVCO next year when costs have settled down to a more normal level. The director also mentioned that he is in the process of considering the approval of your annual leave request.

(a) Identify and explain the ethical principles at risk here along with any associated threats to that principle.

(b) What actions should you take in these circumstances?

Your company runs regular continuing professional development (CPD) events and you have been asked to run a session on the need to prepare financial statements along with the ethical principles that are important in their preparation.

(c) Prepare speaker notes for your presentation. Your notes need to include examples of the ethical principles and how they can relate to the preparation of financial statements.

....

Task 5

You have been given a spreadsheet JobCosting.xls which shows the estimated cost for a job. It contains five worksheets: 'costing', 'materials', 'labour', 'overheads' and 'decision'.

Download this spreadsheet file from www.bpp.com/aatspreadsheets and save in the appropriate location. Rename it using the following format: **'your initial-surname-AAT no –dd.mm.yy-Task5'**.

For example: J-Donnovan-123456-12.03xx-Task5 A **high degree of accuracy** is required. You **must save your work as an .XLS or .XLSX file** at regular intervals to avoid losing your work.

- Open the renamed spreadsheet and open the costing worksheet

    - Use a formula in cell D3 to calculate the cost of material 3 to be charged to the job. The formula should refer to the table 'materials' which is held on the materials worksheet.

    - Apply this formula to other materials charged to this job

    - Use autosum to calculate the total direct materials charged to the job

- Create a formula in cell E8 to calculate the cost of labour from department A to be charged to the job. The formula should refer to the table 'labour' which is held in the labour worksheet.

    - Apply this formula to calculate the cost of labour from other departments charged to this job

    - Use autosum to calculate the total direct labour charged to the job.

- Create a formula in cell E12 to calculate the overheads charged to this job.

  - Add a formula to cell E14 to calculate the total production cost for this job

  - Format the numbers to include thousand separators

Jobs which cost less than £10,000 will be accepted. If the projected cost is greater than this, then the job will be rejected

- Use an IF statement in cell G16 along with a lookup function in column E16 to determine if the job will be accepted or rejected.

  - The IF statement should return the values 1 for accept and 2 for reject. The lookup function should designate either 'ACCEPT' or 'REJECT' based on the outcome of the IF statement

  - Use conditional formatting in cell G16 so that if the outcome is ACCEPT the cell will be highlighted green and if the outcome is REJECT the cell will be highlighted red

  - Hide column G

There has been an issue with the supply of the materials used in this costing. If this is not resolved soon, it is predicted that the cost of materials is likely to rise. The predicted cost of materials 3 and 9 are £4 and £8 per kg if this situation were to arise.

- Use the scenario manager function to determine the impact that this would have on the job costing

  - Name the original scenario 'costing' and the potential scenario 'costing 2'

  - Show the impact of the scenario on the costing worksheet to show whether or not the job would still be accepted.

Task 6

You are Tegan Jovanka, a part-qualified accounting technician. You work for Miller Inc, a company that manufactures precision equipment for workshops.

You cover all aspects of bookkeeping and accounting for the business. You report to John Stevens, the Finance Director.

Today's date is 6 December 20X3.

John Stevens has asked you to carry out an analysis of the company's overheads because he is not satisfied with the accuracy of the current absorption basis used, which is labour hours. He wants to see the results of using machine hours to absorb overheads, and using ABC to calculate absorbed overheads.

The information relating to the next accounting period that you need to carry out this analysis is attached.

Download the spreadsheet file from the www.bpp.com/aatspreadsheets. Save the spreadsheet file in the appropriate location and rename it in the following format: 'your initial-surname-AAT no-dd.mm.yy-Task1'. For example: H-Darch-123456-12.03.xx-Task1

A **high degree of accuracy** is required. You must **save your work as an .XLS or.XLSX file** at regular intervals to avoid losing your work.

1. Open the renamed file. Enter the total machine hours for each product in the period in cells C3-F3 and the total machine hours in cell G3.

2. Use the total machine hours figure in your calculation of the absorption rate per machine hour, Enter this figure in B4 and show it to 2 decimal places.

3. Show the total overheads absorbed per unit on a machine hour basis for each product in cells C5-F5, showing these figures to two decimal places.

4. Enter the total labour hours for each product in the period in cells C7-F7 and the total labour hours in cell G7.

5. Use the total labour hours figure in your calculation of the absorption rate per labour hour. Enter this figure in B8 and show it to 2 decimal places.

6. Show the total overheads absorbed per unit on a labour hour basis for each product in cells C9-F9, showing these figures to two decimal places.

7. Enter the number of set-ups for each product in the period in cells C11-F11 and the total number of set-ups in cell G11.

8. Use the total number of set-ups in your calculation of the cost per set-up. Enter this figure in B12 and show it to 2 decimal places.

9. Show the total set-up costs absorbed for each product in cells C13-F13.

10. Enter the number of requisitions for each product in the period in cells C14-F14 and the total number of requisitions in cell G14.

11. Use the total number of requisitions in your calculation of the stores receipt cost per requisition. Enter this figure in B15 and show it to 2 decimal places.

12. Show the total stores receipt costs absorbed for each product in cells C16-F16.

13. Enter the number of units produced for each product in the period in cells C17-F17 and the total number of units produced in cell G17.

14. Use the total number of units produced in your calculation of the quality control cost per unit produced. Enter this figure in B18 and show it to 2 decimal places.

15. Show the total quality control costs absorbed for each product in cells C19-F19.

16. Enter the number of orders executed for each product in the period in cells C20-F20 and the total number of orders executed in cell G20.

17. Use the total number of orders executed in your calculation of the materials handling and despatch costs per order executed. Enter this figure in B21 and show it to 2 decimal places.

18. Show the total materials handling and despatch costs absorbed for each product in cells C22-F22.

19. Total the overheads absorbed on an ABC basis for each of the products and enter these totals in cells C23-F23.

20. Calculate the overheads absorbed per unit on an ABC basis and enter these figures in cells C24-F24, showing them to 2 decimal places.

21. Summarise the results, by showing the absorbed cost per unit under each of the three methods in cell range C26-F28.

22. Highlight the product with the highest absorbed cost per unit for each method by showing the cost with a red background and black borders round each cell. Highlight the product with the lowest absorbed cost per unit for each method by showing the cost with a green background and black borders round each cell.

23. Tidy up the calculation by showing all negative figures in brackets and all figures with comma for 000s.

24. Perform a spell check and ensure that all the contents of the cells can be seen.

25. Use the proforma email to do the following:

    • Compare the results of the different methods of absorbing overheads
    • Give two advantages of activity-based costing

To:	John Stevens
From:	Tegan Jovanka
Date:	6 December 20X3
Subject:	Overhead analysis

· ·

Task 7

You are in the process of preparing the final accounts for Velocity Ltd for the year ended 31 March 20X6.

You are given the following trial balance for the company with adjustments shown.

	Ledger balances		Adjustments	
	£	£	£	£
Bank	4,750			
Share capital and reserves		5,000		
Closing inventory			2,760	2,760
Non-current assets at cost	125,000			
Accumulated depreciation		17,500		
Depreciation charge	2,500			
Long term loan		7,500		
General expenses	56,780			
Interest paid	375			
Opening inventory	3,000			
Prepayments			1,120	
Accruals				520
Purchase ledger control		2,320		

Sales ledger control	1,950			
Sales		318,405		
Purchases	155,770			
Suspense	600		450	1,050
	350,725	350,725	4,330	4,330

Open a spreadsheet and save in an appropriate location using the following format **'your initial-surname-task 2.3'**

You should aim for a **high degree of accuracy**. You **should save your work as an .XLS or .XLSX file** at regular intervals to avoid losing your work.

Using your saved spreadsheet you are required to extend the above trial balance for Velocity Ltd for the year ended 31 March 20X6.

Your extended trial balance should be prepared using appropriate formula and needs to be presented and formatted in the following manner:

- Two new columns to be inserted for each of statement of profit or loss and statement of financial position entries
- All heading to be merged and centred over appropriate columns
- Insert additional rows as required to extend your trial balance
- Figures to be presented with thousand separators and no decimals
- Insert currency (£) symbols where relevant
- Use top and double bottom borders on column totals
- Name your appropriation worksheet tab ETB and format tab in red

The company is expanding into a grocery delivery service however the directors are becoming concerned about the number of parking fines drivers are accumulating.

The following information is available for the year ended 31 March 20X6.

Delivery driver		
First name	Last name	Parking fines
Ted	Greenfield	£40
Jane	Featherstone	£150
Frankie	Sing	£75
Ben	Cruz	£125
Sally	Leung	£60

Open a new worksheet and enter the information above.

You are required to:

• Custom sort the data into last name order (A down to Z)

• Use data validation to circle any parking fines in excess of £100

• Prepare a bar chart to show drivers and fines. Your chart should be titled "Driver parking fines" and have an appropriate legend

• Your chart should be positioned below your data

• Name your worksheet tab Fines and format tab in yellow

Finally resave your spreadsheet as **'your initial-surname-task 2.3 finished'**

BPP PRACTICE ASSESSMENT 3
LEVEL 3 SYNOPTIC ASSESSMENT

ANSWERS

Level 3 Synoptic Assessment
BPP practice assessment 3

Task 1

(a)

	✓
CCAB	☐
CIMA	✓
CIPFA	✓
ACCA	☐

(b)

The FRC aims to promote ethical | financial reporting | and increased | confidence |
in the accountancy profession in the UK.

(c)

Statement	True	False
The need to act ethically is most important for accountants employed in the public sector as they are more open to criticism if this money is perceived to be spent inappropriately.	☐	✓
The Code of Professional Ethics sets out the required standards of professional behaviour with guidance on how these standards can be achieved	✓	☐
The Code of Professional Ethics adopts a principles-based approach in order to allow individuals to choose appropriate behaviour and to remove the need for professional judgements to be made.	☐	✓

(d)

	✓
Familiarity	☐
Self-interest	☐
Intimidation	✓

(e)

	✓
Professional behaviour	☐
Confidentiality	☑
Objectivity	☐

(f)

	✓
You failed to comply with the ethical principle of professional competence and due care at the time of the audit.	☐
You failed to comply with the ethical principle of integrity at the time of the audit.	☐
You complied with the ethical principles at the time of the audit	☑

(g)

	✓
You should make a note on the audit file for next year. The report on these financial statements has already been issued and it is too late to retract it.	☐
You should issue a revised audit report immediately.	☑
You should securely destroy the new information to prevent damage to your reputation as a professional accountant.	☐

Task 2

(a) Where a VAT invoice is issued on a date in advance of the date of supply, the tax point will be the [earlier] of the two dates

Where full payment is made on a date in advance of the date of supply, the tax point will be the [earlier] of the two dates

If part payment is made before the supply takes place, this [will] create a tax point. If the remainder is paid before the supply takes place, there will be [another tax point] . Where payment is split, [it may not be correct] to show the full payment in one VAT return.

Where an invoice is issued after the supply has taken place, this may create a tax point. The invoice date becomes the tax point if it is within [14 days] after the supply.

(b) Normally an invoice must be issued within 30 days of a supply of goods, or 30 days of a supply of services.

Where payment is received in advance, an invoice must be issued within 30 days of the payment .

(c) The tax point is the time of a supply for VAT.

The basic tax point will always be the date of the physical supply. For example, the date a clock is delivered to a customer's house.

An actual tax point may override the basic tax point in some circumstances. For example, full payment in advance of delivery of a clock would create an actual tax point.

If the basic tax point is earlier, no actual tax point arises.

....

Task 3

(a)

	Balance	Debit/Credit
Current account: Jenny £	£ 25,168	credit
Current account: John £	£ 16,408	credit

Workings

Jenny: (£44,550 × 60%) – £1,562 = £25,168

John: (£44,550 × 40%) – £1,412 = £16,408

(b) **Fenland Trading**

Statement of financial position as at 31 December 20X7

	£	£	£
Non-current assets	Cost	Accumulated Depreciation	Carrying amount
Office equipment	35,400	14,160	21,240
Current assets			
Inventory		24,380	
Trade receivables		40,083	
Cash		320	
Bank		13,460	
Total current assets		78,243	
Current liabilities			
Trade payables	17,635		
VAT	2,872		
Accruals	1,400		
Total current liabilities		21,907	
Net current assets			56,336
Net assets			77,576
Financed by:	**Jenny**	**John**	**Total**
Capital accounts	22,000	14,000	36,000
Current accounts	25,168	16,408	41,576
	47,168	30,408	77,576

(c)

Reason	✓
Inventory issued is valued at a price which most closely represents the current market value	
It complies with IAS 2 *Accounting for Inventory*	✓
It is easy to calculate when there is a high volume of stock movement in and out of the business	
Fluctuations in prices are smoothed out, making it easier to analyse the data for decision making	

Option 1 is a benefit of LIFO. Option 3 and option 4 are benefits of the weighted average cost valuation method.

(d)

	✓
Relevance	
Prudence	✓
Comparability	
Ease of understanding	

Prudence is one of the four accounting principles. The missing accounting characteristics are materiality and reliability.

....

Task 4

(a) The ethical principles at risk can include objectivity and integrity. The financial statements should be prepared without bias or any undue influence. It would be unfair to change the valuation method for one year as this would be against the accounting concept of consistency in the use of accounting policies. In this case using a LIFO valuation method would mean lower costs accounted for in the closing inventory value resulting in an inflated profit figure. Intentionally changing the inventory method for this purpose would be dishonest and in breach of the integrity principle. The threats here are intimidation through the possible refusal of my annual leave request and also a self-interest threat for the director in manipulating profits higher. An added issue here is that the LIFO method is not normally allowed for inventory valuation.

(b) It can be possible to change accounting policies provided that there is a valid reason for doing so, for example a change in how an industry is regulated or if it was found that the current policies did not provide a fair reflection of the results of a business. In this case it appears the only reason is to manipulate profits on a short-term basis therefore I should refer this matter onto my immediate supervisor for authorisation to make this change in the valuation method. When I contact my supervisor I should also mention the impact the change will make on reported profits and also that LIFO is not normally considered an appropriate valuation method.

(c) The purpose of the financial statements is to show the financial performance of the business during the reporting period. This is reported through the statement of profit or loss. The financial statements will also show the financial status of the business through the statement of financial position. This statement shows the assets and liabilities of the business including the capital invested into the business by its owner or owners as in the case of a partnership.

The financial statements can be used by a variety of users and these can include; employees, customers, suppliers, potential investors, banks and also the tax authorities.

It is important that the financial statements are prepared on an ethical basis. The Code of Professional Ethics identifies five ethical principles and these are:

Integrity

This is where the financial statements are prepared with honesty and transparency. An example can be accounting for sales revenue and costs correctly so that the tax authorities receive the correct amount of tax.

Confidentiality

The financial results of sole traders and partnerships are confidential to those who only have authority to have access to this information. There are circumstances when confidentiality can be breached and these include when it is in the public interest or if there is a legal requirement to do so. An example can be having policies not to take financial information out of the office on data storage devices to reduce the risk of breaches of confidentiality.

Professional behaviour

This ethical principle is all about acting in a way that would be expected of a professional accountant and by not bringing disrepute on the accountancy profession, a business or an individual. An example can be acting in appropriate manner when having meetings with the owner or owners of a business.

Professional competence and due care

Having professional competence means having the skills and knowledge to prepare financial statements and being up-to-date with any new developments. This can be achieved by undertaking regular continuing professional development (CPD), for example through attending seminars and reading accountancy journals. Due care is about taking the correct level of care and attention in the completion of work. An example here can be having sufficient time to prepare the financial statements so work is not rushed and is error free.

Objectivity

The objectivity principle is about completing work without bias and without any undue influence. It is important to prepare the financial statements on a fair basis without any intention to report results in one particular way. An example can be using appropriate depreciation rates that will have a direct impact on profits or losses and carrying values of assets.

··

Task 5

- Open the renamed spreadsheet and open the costing worksheet

    - Use a formula in cell D3 to calculate the cost of material 3 to be charged to the job. The formula should refer to the table 'materials' which is held on the materials worksheet.

    - Apply this formula to other materials charged to this job

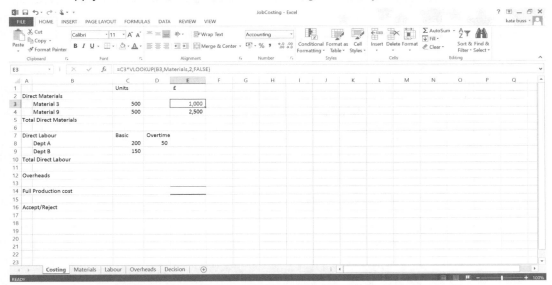

    - Use autosum to calculate the total direct materials charged to the job

BPP practice assessment 3: answers

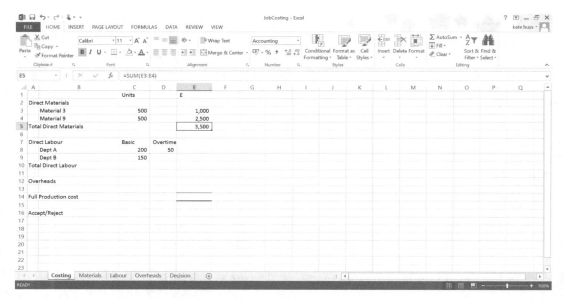

- Create a formula in cell E8 to calculate the cost of labour from department A to be charged to the job. The formula should refer to the table 'labour' which is held in the labour worksheet.

  - Apply this formula to calculate the cost of labour from other departments charged to this job

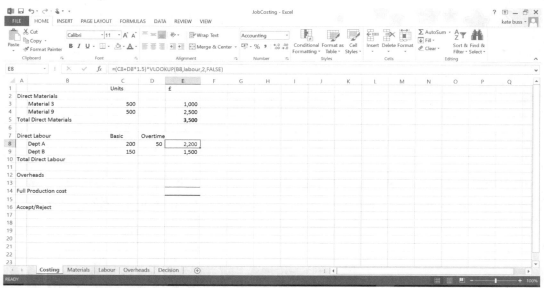

  - Use autosum to calculate the total direct labour charged to the job.

- Create a formula in cell E12 to calculate the overheads charged to this job.

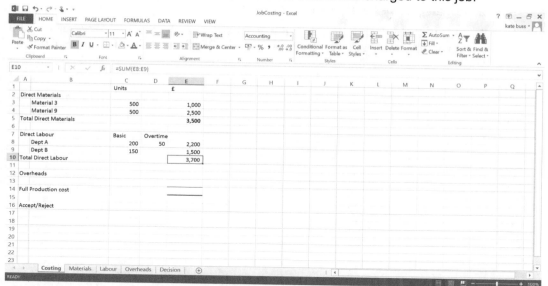

- Add a formula to cell E14 to calculate the total production cost for this job

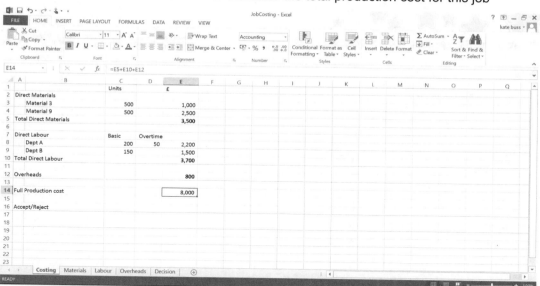

- Format the numbers to include thousand separators

- Use an IF statement in cell G16 along with a lookup function in column E16 to determine if the job will be accepted or rejected.

  - The IF statement should return the values 1 for accept and 2 for reject. The lookup function should designate either 'ACCEPT' or 'REJECT' based on the outcome of the IF statement

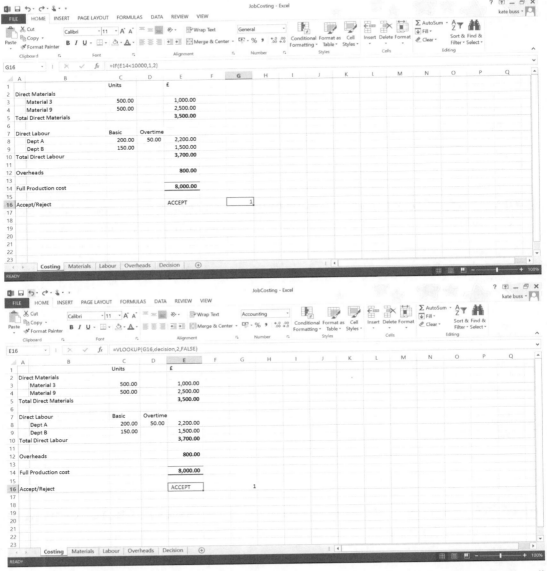

  - Use conditional formatting in cell G16 so that if the outcome is ACCEPT the cell will be highlighted green and if the outcome is REJECT the cell will be highlighted red

  - Hide column G

BPP
LEARNING MEDIA

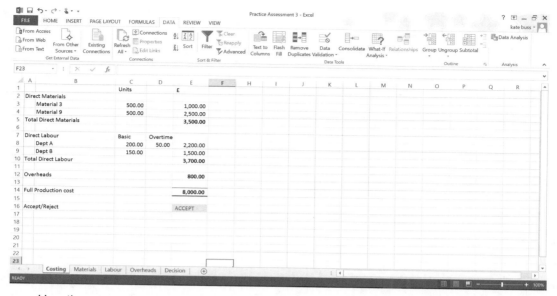

- Use the scenario manager function to determine the impact that this would have on the job costing

  - Name the original scenario 'costing' and the potential scenario 'costing 2'

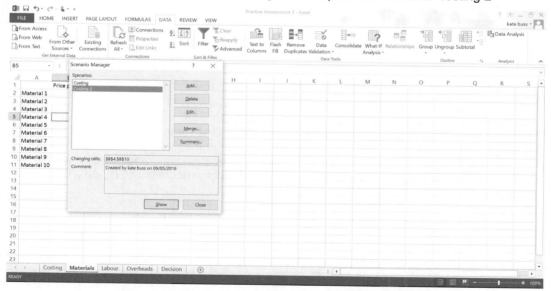

  - Show the impact of the scenario on the costing worksheet to show whether or not the job would still be accepted.

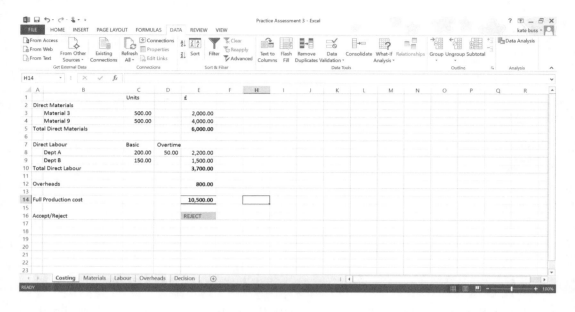

Task 6

To:	John Stevens
From:	Tegan Jovanka
Date:	6 December 20X3
Subject:	Overhead analysis

I have carried out the overhead analysis you requested. Under all methods product AB absorbs the most overheads per unit, but the difference in overhead absorbed between it and the other products under ABC is much less than under the machine or labour hour methods, showing the importance of the different activities that the products generate. Under each method a different product absorbs the least overhead per unit, GH on a machine hours basis, EF on a labour hours basis and CD on an ABC basis.

Two advantages of using ABC are:

- It is concerned with all overhead costs
- It shows what drives overhead costs

	A	B	C	D	E	F	G
1			AB	CD	EF	GH	Total
2	**Overheads Machine hours**						
3	Total Machine hours		700	1,500	1,600	1,200	5,000
4	Overhead absorption rate	4.80					
5	Overheads absorbed per unit		33.60	14.40	19.20	9.60	
6	**Overheads Labour hours**						
7	Total Labour hours		800	1,000	400	1,800	4,000
8	Overhead absorption rate	6.00					
9	Overheads absorbed per unit		48.00	12.00	6.00	18.00	
10	**ABC**						
11	Set-ups		4	7	6	8	25
12	Cost per set-up	200.00					
13	Set-up costs		800	1,400	1,200	1,600	
14	Requisitions		10	60	50	80	200
15	Stores receipt cost per requisition	37.50					
16	Stores receipt costs		375	2,250	1,875	3,000	
17	Number of units		100	500	400	600	1,600
18	Quality control cost per unit produced	3.75					
19	Quality control costs		375	1,875	1,500	2,250	
20	Orders executed		4	32	28	36	100
21	Materials handling and despatch cost per order executed	55.00					
22	Materials handling and despatch costs		220	1,760	1,540	1,980	
23	Total overheads absorbed		1,770	7,285	6,115	8,830	
24	Overheads absorbed per unit		17.70	14.57	15.29	14.72	
25	**Summary**						
26	Machine hours basis		33.60	14.40	19.20	9.60	
27	Labour hours basis		48.00	12.00	6.00	18.00	
28	ABC basis		17.70	14.57	15.29	14.72	

Task 7

	A	B	C	D	E	F	G	H	I	J
1						Statement of		Statement of		
2		Ledger balances		Adjustments		profit or loss		financial position		
3		£	£	£	£	£	£	£	£	
4	Bank	4,750						4,750		
5	Share capital and reserves		5,000						5,000	
6	Closing inventory			2,760	2,760		2,760	2,760		
7	Non-current assets at cost	125,000						125,000		
8	Accumulated depreciation		17,500						17,500	
9	Depreciation charge	2,500				2,500				
10	Long term loan		7,500						7,500	
11	General expenses	56,780				56,780				
12	Interest paid	375				375				
13	Opening inventory	3,000				3,000				
14	Prepayments			1,120				1,120		
15	Accruals				520				520	
16	Purchase ledger control		2,320						2,320	
17	Sales ledger control	1,950						1,950		
18	Sales		318,405				318,405			
19	Purchases	155,770				155,770				
20	Suspense	600		450	1,050					
21	Profit or loss for the year					102,740			102,740	
22		350,725	350,725	4,330	4,330	321,165	321,165	135,580	135,580	
23										

ETB

Suggested formulas

	A	B	C	D	E	F	G	H	I
1									
2		Ledger balances		Adjustments		Statement of profit or loss		Statement of financial position	
3		£	£	£	£	£	£	£	£
4	Bank	4750						4750	
5	Share capital and reserves		5000						5000
6	Closing inventory			2760	2760		2760	2760	
7	Non-current assets at cost	125000						125000	
8	Accumulated depreciation		17500						17500
9	Depreciation charge	2500				2500			
10	Long term loan		7500						7500
11	General expenses	56780				56780			
12	Interest paid	375				375			
13	Opening inventory	3000				3000			
14	Prepayments			1120				1120	
15	Accruals				520				520
16	Purchase ledger control		2320						2320
17	Sales ledger control	1950						1950	
18	Sales		318405				318405		
19	Purchases	155770				155770			
20	Suspense	600		450	1050				
21	Profit or loss for the year					102740			=F21
22		=SUM(B4:B20)	=SUM(C4:C20)	=SUM(D6:D20)	=SUM(E6:E20)	=SUM(F4:F21)	=SUM(G4:G21)	=SUM(H4:H21)	=SUM(I4:I21)
23									

	A	B	C	D	E	F	G
1	**First name**	**Last name**	**Fines**				
2	Ben	Cruz	£125				
3	Jane	Featherstone	£150				
4	Ted	Greenfield	£40				
5	Sally	Leung	£60				
6	Frankie	Sing	£75				
7							

Delivery driver fines

Fines

✓ *fx* | 125

B

nan

rsto
ield

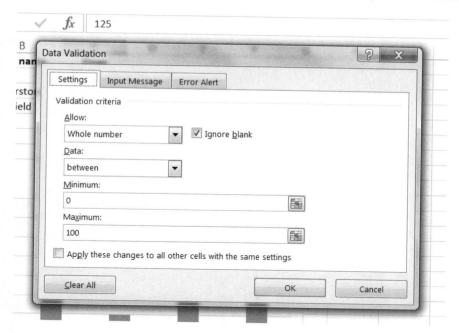

Data Validation ? X

| Settings | Input Message | Error Alert |

Validation criteria

Allow:

Whole number ▼ ☑ Ignore blank

Data:

between ▼

Minimum:

0

Maximum:

100

☐ Apply these changes to all other cells with the same settings

Clear All   OK   Cancel

Appendix: Reference materials for the synoptic assessment

The information in this section is for use alongside the AAT's practice assessment and the sample assessments in this Question Bank.

This will be available to you in the assessment in pop-up windows.

Code of Professional Ethics

Code of Professional Ethics – Part A

Introduction – 100

Section 100 – Introduction and code of fundamental principles

100.1 A distinguishing feature of the accountancy profession is its acceptance of the responsibility to act in the public interest. Therefore, your responsibility as a member is not exclusively to satisfy the needs of an individual client or employer. In acting in the public interest, members shall observe and comply with the ethical requirements set out in this *Code.*

100.2 This *Code* is in three parts. Part A establishes the code of fundamental principle of professional ethics for members and provides a conceptual framework for applying those principles. The conceptual framework provides guidance on fundamental ethical principles. Member are required to apply this conceptual framework to enable them to identify threats to compliance with the fundamental principles, to evaluate their significance and, if such threats are not clearly insignificant, to apply safeguards to eliminate them or reduce them to an acceptable level such that compliance with the fundamental principles is not compromised.

100.3 Part B and C describe how the conceptual framework applies in certain situations. They provide examples of safeguards that may be appropriate to address threats to compliance with the fundamental principles. They also describe situations where safeguards are not available to address the threats and where the activity or relationship creating the threats shall be avoided. Part B applies to members in practice. Part C applies to members in business. Members in practice may also find Part C relevant to their particular circumstances.

100.4 In this *Code* the use of the word 'shall' imposes a requirements on the member to comply with the specific provision in which 'shall' has been used. Compliance is required unless an exception is permitted by this *Code.*

Fundamental principles – 100.5

100.5 A member shall comply with the following fundamentals principles:

(i) **Integrity**: to be straight forward and honest in all professional and business relationships.

(ii) **Objectivity**: to not allow bias, conflict of interest or undue influence of others to override professional or business judgements.

(iii) **Professional competence and due care**: to maintain professional knowledge and skill at the level required to ensure that a client or employer receives competent professional service based on current developments in practice, legislation and techniques. A member shall act diligently and accordance with applicable technical and professional standards when providing professional services.

(iv) **Confidentiality**: to, in accordance with the law, respect the confidentiality of information acquired as a result of professional and business relationships and not disclose any such information to third parties without proper and specific authority unless there is legal or professional right or duty to disclose. Confidential information acquired as a result of professional and business relationships shall not be used for the personal advantage of the member or third parties.

(v) **Adopt professional behaviour**: to comply with the relevant laws and regulation and avoid any action that brings our profession into disrepute.

Each of these fundamentals principles is discussed in more detail in Sections 110-150.

Conceptual framework approach – 100.6

100.6 The circumstances in which members operate may give rise to specific threats to compliance with the fundamental principles. It is impossible to define every situation that create such threats and specify the appropriate mitigating action. In addition, the nature of engagements and work assignments may differ and consequently different threats may exist, requiring the application of different safeguards. Therefore, this *Code* establishes a conceptual framework approach assists members in complying with the ethical requirements of this *Code* and meeting their responsibility to act in the public interest. It accommodates many variations in circumstances that create threats to compliance with the fundamental principles and can deter a professional accountant from concluding that a situation is permitted if it is not specifically prohibited.

100.7 When a member identifies threats to compliance with the fundamental principles and, based on an evaluation of those threats, determines that they are not at an acceptable level, the member shall determine whether appropriate safeguards are available and can be applied to eliminate the threats or reduce them to an acceptable level. In making that determination, the member shall exercise professional judgement and take into account whether a reasonable and informed third party, weighing all the specific facts and circumstances available to the member at the time, would be likely to conclude that the threats would be eliminated or reduced to an acceptable level by the application of the safeguards, such that compliance with the fundamental principles is not compromised.

100.8 A member shall evaluate any threats to compliance with the fundamental principles when the member knows, or could reasonably be expected to know, of circumstances or relationships that may compromise compliance with the fundamental principles.

100.9 A member shall take qualitative as well as quantitative factors into account when considering the significance of a threat. When applying the conceptual framework, a member may encounter situations in which threats cannot be eliminated or reduced to an acceptable level, either because the threat is too significant or because appropriate safeguards are not available, or cannot be applied. In such situations, a member shall decline or discontinue the specific professional service involved or, when necessary, resign from the engagement (in the case of a member in practice) or the employing organisation (in the case of a member in business).

100.10 Sections 290 and 291 (as detailed within the associated document *Code of Professional Ethics: independence provisions relating to review and assurance engagements*) contain provisions with which a member shall comply if the member identifies a breach of an independence provision of the *Code*. If a member identifies a breach of any other provisions of this *Code*, the member shall evaluate the significance of the breach and its impact on the member's ability to comply with the fundamental principles. The member shall take whatever actions that may be available, as soon as possible, to satisfactorily address the consequences of the breach. The member shall determine whether to report the breach, for example, to those who may have been affected by the breach, a member body, relevant regulator or oversight authority.

100.11 When a member encounters unusual circumstances in which the application of a specific requirement of the *Code* would result in a disproportionate outcome or an outcome that may not be in public interest, it is recommended that the member consult with AAT on the issue.

Threats and safeguards – 100.12

100.12 Threats may be created by a broad range of relationships and circumstances. When a relationship or circumstance create a threat, such a threat could compromise, or could be perceived to compromise, a member's compliance with the fundamental principles. A circumstance may create more than one threat, and a threat may affect compliance with more than one fundamental principle.

Threats fall into the following categories:

(i) self-interest threats, which may occur where a financial or other investment will inappropriately influence the member's judgement or behaviour

(ii) self-review threats, which may occur when a previous judgement needs to be re-evaluated by the member responsible for that judgement

(iii) advocacy threats, which may occur when a member promotes a position or opinion to the point that subsequent objectivity may be compromised

(iv) familiarity threats, which may occur when, because of a close or personal relationship, a member becomes too sympathetic to the interests of others

(v) intimidation threats, which may occur when a member may be deterred from acting objectively by threats, whether actual or perceived.

Parts B and C of this Code explain how these categories of threats may be created for members in practice and members in business respectively. Members in practice may also find Part C relevant to their particular circumstances.

Threats and safeguards – 100.13 to 100.16

100.13 Safeguards are actions or other measures that may eliminate threats or reduce them to an acceptable level. These fall into two broad categories:

(i)   safeguards created by the profession, legislation or regulation

(ii) safeguards in the work environment.

100.14 Safeguards created by the profession, legislation or regulation include, but are not restricted to:

(i)   educational, training and experience requirements for entry into the profession

(ii)   continuing professional development requirements

(iii) corporate governance regulations

(iv)   professional standards

(v)   professional or regulatory monitoring and disciplinary procedures

(vi)   external review of the reports, returns, communications or information produced by a member and carried out by a legally empowered third party.

100.15 Parts B and C of this Code, respectively, discuss safeguards in the work environment for members in practice and members in business.

100.16 Certain safeguards may increase the likelihood of identifying or deterring unethical behaviour. Such safeguards, which may be created by the accounting profession, legislation, regulation or an employing organisation, include, but are not restricted to:

(i)   effective, well publicised complaints systems operated by the employing organisation, the profession or a regulator, which enable colleagues, employers and members of the public to draw attention to unprofessional or unethical behaviour

(ii) an explicitly stated duty to report breaches of ethical requirements.

Conflicts of interest – 100.17

100.17 A member may be faced with a conflict of interest when undertaking a professional activity. A conflict of interest creates a threat to objectivity and may create threats to the other fundamental principles. Such threats may be created when:

(i)   the member undertakes a professional activity related to a particular matter for two or more parties whose interests with respect to that matter are in conflict or

(ii) the interest of the member with respect to a particular matter and the interests of a party for whom the member undertakes a professional activity related to that matter are in conflict.

100.18 Parts B and C of this *Code* discuss conflicts of interest for members in practice and members in business respectively.

Ethical conflict resolution – 100.19

100.19 In evaluating compliance with the fundamental principles, a member may be required to resolve conflict in the application of fundamental principles.

100.20 When initiating either a formal or informal conflict resolution process, a member shall consider the following, either individually or together with others, as part of the resolution process:

(i)   relevant facts
(ii) ethical issues involved
(iii) fundamental principles related to the matter in question
(iv) established internal procedures
(v)   alternative courses of action.

Having considered these factors, a member shall determine the appropriate course of action that is consistent with the fundamental principles identified. The member shall also weigh the consequences of each possible course of action. If the matter remains unresolved, the member may wish to consult with other appropriate persons within the firm or employing organisation for help in obtaining resolution.

100.21 Where a matter involves a conflict with, or within, an organisation, a member shall determine whether to consult with those charged with governance of the organisation, such as the board of directors or the audit committee.

100.22 It may be in the best interests of the member to document the substance of the issue and details of any discussions held or decisions taken concerning that issue.

100.23 If a significant conflict cannot be resolved, a member may consider obtaining professional advice from the relevant professional body or legal advisers on a confidential basis and thereby obtain guidance on ethical issues without breaching confidentiality. For example, a member may suspect that he or she has encountered a fraud and may need to discuss confidential information in order to satisfy themselves as to whether their suspicions are justified. In such circumstances, the member shall also consider the requirement under the anti-money laundering legislation to submit a report to NCA or to the firm's Money Laundering Reporting Officer (MLRO).

100.24 If, after exhausting all relevant possibilities, the ethical conflict remains unresolved, a member shall, where possible, refuse to remain associated with the matter creating the conflict. The member shall determine whether, in the circumstances, it is appropriate to withdraw from the engagement team or specific assignment, or to resign altogether from the engagement, the firm or the employing organisation.

Communicating with those charged with governance – 100.25

100.25 When communicating with those charged with governance in accordance with the provisions of this *Code*, the member or firm shall determine, having regard to the nature and importance of the particular circumstances and matter to be communicated, the appropriate person(s) within the entity's governance structure with whom to communicate. If the member or firm communicates with a subgroup of those charged with governance – for example, an audit committee or an individual – the member or firm shall determine whether communication with all those charged with governance is also necessary so that they are adequately informed.

Integrity – 110

Section 110 – Integrity

110.1 The principle of integrity imposes an obligation on all members to be straightforward and honest in professional and business relationships. Integrity also implies fair dealing and truthfulness.

110.2 A member shall not be associated with reports, returns, communications or other information where they believe that the information:

(i) contains a false or misleading statement

(ii) contains statements or information furnished recklessly

(iii) omits or obscures information required to be included where such omission or obscurity would be misleading.

When a member becomes aware that they have been associated with such information they shall take steps to be disassociated from the information.

110.3 A member will not be considered to be in breach of paragraph 110.2 if the member provides a modified report in respect of a matter contained in paragraph 110.2.

Objectivity – 120

Section 120 – Objectivity

120.1 The principle of objectivity imposes an obligation on all members not to compromise their professional or business judgement because of bias, conflict of interest or the undue influence of others.

120.2 A member may be exposed to situations that may impair objectivity. It is impractical to define and prescribed all such situations. Relationships that bias or unduly influence the professional judgement of the member shall be avoided. A member shall not perform a professional service if a circumstance or relationship biases or unduly influences their professional judgement with respect to that services.

Professional competence and due care – 130

Section 130 – Professional competence and due care

130.1 The principle of professional competence and due care imposes the following obligations on members:

(i) to maintain professional knowledge and skill at the level required to ensure that clients or employers receive competent professional service and

(ii) to act diligently in accordance with applicable technical and professional standards when providing professional services.

130.2 Competent professional service requires the exercise of sound judgement in applying professional knowledge and skills in the performance of such service. Professional competence may be divided into two separate phrases:

(i) attainment of professional competence and
(ii) maintenance of professional competence.

130.3 The maintenance of professional competence requires continuing awareness and understanding of relevant technical, professional and business developments. Continuing professional development (CPD) develops and maintains the capabilities that enable a member to perform competently within the professional environment. To achieve this, the AAT Council expects all members to undertake CPD in accordance with the *AAT Policy on Continuing Professional Development*. This requires members to assess, plan, action and evaluate their learning and development needs. Members in practice should also refer to paragraph 200.3.

130.4 Diligence encompasses the responsibility to act in accordance with the requirements of an assignment, carefully thoroughly and on a timely basis.

130.5 A member shall take reasonable steps to ensure that those working under the member's authority in a professional capacity have appropriate training and supervision.

130.6 Where appropriate, a member shall make clients, employers or other users of the professional services aware of limitations inherent in the services to avoid the misinterpretation of an expression of opinion as an assertion of fact.

Confidentiality 140.1 to 140.6

Section 140 – Confidentiality

In general terms, there is a legal obligation to maintain the confidentiality of information which is given or obtained in circumstances giving rise to a duty of confidentiality. There are some situation where the law allows a breach of this duty.

The following sections help to explain what this means in practice for members as well as giving guidance on the standards required of members from an ethical perspective.

140.1 The principle of confidentiality imposes an obligation on members to refrain from:

(i) disclosing outside the firm or employing organisation confidential information acquired as a result of professional and business relationships without proper and specific authority or unless there is a legal or professional right or duty to disclose and

(ii) using confidential information acquired as a result of professional and business relationships to their personal advantage or the advantage of third parties.

Information about a past, present, or prospective client's or employer's affairs, or the affairs of clients of employers, acquired in a work context, is likely to be confidential if it is not a matter of public knowledge.

140.2 A member shall maintain confidentiality even in a social environment. The member shall be alert to the possibility of inadvertent disclosure, particularly in circumstances involving close or personal relations, associates and long established business relationships.

140.3 A member shall maintain confidentially of information disclosed by a prospective client or employer.

140.4 A member shall maintain confidentiality of information within the firm or employing organisation.

140.5 A member shall take all reasonable steps to ensure that staff under their control and persons from whom advice and assistance is obtained respect the principle of confidentiality. The restriction on using confidential information also means not using it for any purpose other than that for which it was legitimately acquire.

140.6 The need to comply with the principle of confidentiality continues even after the end of relationships between a member and a client or employer. When a member changes employment or acquires a new client, the member is entitled to use prior experience. The member shall not, however, use or disclose any confidential information either acquired or received as a result of a professional or business relationship.

Confidentiality 140.7 to 140.8

Section 140 – Confidentiality

140.7 The following are circumstances where members are or may be required to disclose confidential information or when such disclosure may be appropriate:

(i) where disclosure is permitted by law and is authorised by the client or the employer (or any other person to whom an obligation of confidence is owed)

(ii) where disclosure is required by law, for example:

    (a) production of documents or other provision of evidence in the course of legal proceedings or

    (b) disclosure to the appropriate public authorities (for example, HMRC) of infringements of the law that come to light

    (c) disclosure of actual or suspected money laundering or terrorist financing to the member's firm's MLRO or to NCA if the member is a sole practitioner, or

(iii) where there is a professional duty or night to disclose, which is in the public interest, and is not prohibited by law. Examples may include:

    (a) to comply with the quality review of an IFAC member body or other relevant professional body

    (b) to respond to an inquiry or investigation by AAT or relevant regulatory or professional body

    (c) to protect the member's professional interests in legal proceedings

    (d) to comply with technical standards and ethics requirements.

This is a difficult and complex area and members are therefore specifically advised to seek professional advice before disclosing confidential information under (c) above.

140.8 In deciding whether to disclose confidential information, members should consider the following points:

(i) whether the interest of all parties, including third parties, could be harmed even though the client or employer (or other person to whom there is a duty of confidentiality) consents to the disclosure of information by the member

(ii) whether all the relevant information is known and substantiated, to the extent that this is practicable. When the situation involves unsubstantiated facts, incomplete information or unsubstantiated conclusions, professional judgement should be used in determining the type of disclosure to be made, if any

(iii) the type of communication or disclosure that may be made and by whom it is to be received; in particular, members should be satisfied that the parties to whom the communication is addressed are appropriate recipients.

Members who are in any doubt about their obligations in a particular situation should seek professional advice.

Professional behaviour – 150

Section 150 – Professional behaviour

150.1 The principle of professional behaviour imposes an obligation on members to comply with relevant laws and regulations and avoid any action that may bring disrepute to the profession. This includes actions which a reasonable and informed third party, having knowledge of all relevant information, would conclude negatively affect the good reputation of the profession.

Members should note that conduct reflecting adversely on the reputation of AAT is a ground for disciplinary action under *AAT's Disciplinary Regulations*.

150.2 An example of this principle is that in marketing and promoting themselves and their work, members shall be honest and truthful. They may bring the profession into disrepute if they:

(i) make exaggerated claims for the services they are able to offer, the qualifications they possess, or experience they have gained

(ii) make disparaging references or unsubstantiated comparison to the work of others.

Taxation

Taxation – 160.1 to 160.9

Section 160 – Taxation

160.1   Members performing taxation services in the UK, Ireland and in other member states of the EU will be dealing with compliance and advice on direct and indirect taxes based on income, gains, losses and profits. The administrative authorities and the legal basis for direct and indirect taxes vary substantially.

160.2   It is beyond the scope of this *Code* to deal with detailed ethical issues relating to taxation services encountered by members. The guidance that follows consists therefore of general principles for members which apply to both direct and indirect taxation

160.3   A member providing professional tax services has a duty to put forward the best position in favour of a client or an employer. However, the service must be carried out with professional competence, must not in any way impair integrity or objectivity and must be consistent with the law.

160.4   A member shall not hold out to a client or an employer the assurance that any tax return prepared and tax advice offered are beyond challenge. Instead the member shall ensure that the client or the employer is aware of the limitation attaching to tax advice and services so that they do not misinterpret an expression of opinion as an assertion of fact.

160.5   A member shall only undertake taxation work on the basis of full disclosure by the client or employer. The member, in dealing with the tax authorities, must act in good faith and exercise care in relation to facts or information presented on behalf of the client or employer. It will normally be assumed that facts and information on which business tax computations are based were provide by the client or employer as the taxpayer, and the latter bears ultimate responsibility for the accuracy of the facts, information and tax computations. The member shall avoid assuming responsibility for the accuracy of facts, etc. outside his or her own knowledge.

160.6   When a member submits a tax return or tax computation for a taxpayer client or employer, the member is acting as an agent. The nature and responsibilities of the member's duties should be made clear to the client or employer, in the case of the former, by a letter of engagement.

160.7   Tax advice or opinions of material consequence given to a client or an employer shall be recorded, either in the form of a letter or in a memorandum for the files.

160.8   In the case of a member in practice acting for a client, the member shall furnish copies of all tax computations to the client before submitting them to HMRC.

160.9   When a member learns of a material error or omission in a tax return of a prior year, or of a failure to file a required tax return, the member has a responsibility to advise promptly the client or employer of the error or omission and recommend that disclosure be made to HMRC. If the client or employer, after having had a reasonable time to reflect, does not correct the error, the member shall inform the client or employer in writing that it is not possible for the member to act for them in connection with that return or other related information submitted to the authorities. Funds dishonestly retained after discovery of an error or omission become criminal property and their retention amounts to money laundering by the client or employer. It is also a criminal offence in the UK for a person, including an accountant, to become concerned in an arrangement which he knows or suspects facilities (by whatever means) the acquisition, retention, use or control of criminal property by or on behalf of another person. Other EU states have equivalent provisions. In each of these situations, the member shall comply with the duty to report the client's or employer's activities to the relevant authority, as explained in the following paragraph.

Taxation – 160.10 to 160.11

Section 160 – Taxation

160.10 (i) A member in practice whose client refuses to make disclosure of an error or omission to HMRC, after having had notice of it and a reasonable time to reflect, is obliged to report the client's refusal and the facts surrounding it to the MLRO if the member is within a firm, or to the appropriate authority (NCA in the UK) if the member is a sole practitioner. The member shall not disclose to the client or anyone else that such a report has been made if the member knows or suspects that to do so would be likely to prejudice any investigation which might be conducted following the report.

(ii) In circumstances where the employer of a member in business refuses to make disclosure of an error or omission to HMRC:

(a) where the employed member in business has acted in relation to the error or omission, he or she should report the employer's refusal and the surrounding facts, including the extent of the member's involvement, to the appropriate authority as soon as possible, as this may provide the member with a defence to the offence of facilitating the retention of criminal property

(b) where the employed member in business has not acted in relation to the error or omission, he or she is not obliged to report the matter to the authorities. However, if the member does make a report to the appropriate authority, such report will not amount to a breach of the member's duty of confidentiality.

(iii) Where a member in business is a contractor who is a 'relevant person' for the purposes of the Money Laundering Regulations 2007 in the UK or equivalent legislation in another EU State or other overseas jurisdictions, the member shall act in accordance with paragraph 160.10(i) above, as though he were a member in practice. However, where the member in business is not such a relevant person, he should act in accordance with paragraph 160.10(ii) above.

All members have a responsibility to make themselves familiar with anti-money laundering and terrorist financing legislation and any guidance issued by AAT in this regard.

160.11 The tax authorities in many countries have extensive powers to obtain information. Members confronted by the exercise of these powers by the relevant authorities should seek appropriate legal advice.

See FA2015 Tax reference material below:

Rates of VAT and tax points

Rates of VAT

There are three rates of VAT, depending on the goods or services the business provides. The rates are:

- standard – 20%. The standard-rate VAT fraction for calculating the VAT element of a gross supply is 20/120 or 1/6

- reduced – 5%

- zero – 0%

Tax points

The time of supply, known as the 'tax point', is the date when a transaction takes place for VAT purposes.

This date is not necessarily the date the supply physically takes place.

Generally, a registered business must pay or reclaim VAT in the (usually quarterly) VAT period, or tax period, in which the time of supply occurs, and it must use the correct rate of VAT in force on that date.

This means knowing the time of supply/tax point for every transaction is important, as it must be put on the right VAT return.

Tax points

Time of supply (tax point) for goods and services

The time of supply for VAT purposes is defined as follows:

- For transactions where no VAT invoice is issued, the time of supply is normally the date the supply takes place (as defined below).

- For transactions where there is a VAT invoice, the time the supply is normally the date the invoice is issued, even if this is after the date the supply took place (as defined below).

To issue VAT invoice, it must be sent (by post, email etc) or given to the customer for them to keep. A tax point cannot be created simply by preparing an invoice. However there are exceptions to these rules on time of supply, detailed below.

Date the supply takes place

For goods, the time when the goods are considered to be supplied for VAT purposes is the date when one of the following happens.

- The supplier sends the goods to the customer.

- The customer collects the goods from the supplier.

- The goods (which are not either sent or collected) are made available for the customer to use, for example if the supplier is assembling something on the customer's premises.

For services, the date when the services are supplied for VAT purposes is the date when the service is carried out and all the work – except invoicing – is finished.

Exceptions regarding time of supply (tax point)

The above general principles for working out the time of supply do not apply in the following situations:

- For transactions where a VAT invoice is issued, or payment is received, in advance of the date of supply, the time of supply is the date the invoice is issued or the payment is received, whichever is the earlier.

- If the supplier receives full payment before the date when the supply takes place and no VAT invoice has yet been issued, the time of supply is the date the payment is received.

- If the supplier receives part-payment before the date when the supply takes place, the time of supply becomes the date the part-payment is received but only for the amount of the part-payment (assuming no VAT invoice has been issued before this date – in which case the time of supply is the date the invoice is issued). The time of supply for the remainder will follow the normal rules – and might fall in a different VAT period, and so have to go onto a different VAT Return.

- If the supplier issues a VAT invoice more than 14 days after the date when the supply took place, the time of supply will be the date the supply took place, and not the date the invoice is issued. However, if a supplier has genuine commercial difficulties in invoicing within 14 days of the supply taking place, they can contact HMRC to ask for permission to issue invoices later than 14 days and move the time of supply to this later date.

VAT invoices

What a VAT invoice must show

A VAT invoice must show:

- an invoice number which is unique and follows on from the number of the previous invoice – any spoiled or cancelled serially numbered invoice must be kept to show to a VAT officer at the next VAT inspection

- the seller's name or trading name, and address

- the seller's VAT registration number

- the invoice date

- the time of supply or tax point if this is different from the invoice date

- the customer's name or trading name, and address

- a description sufficient to identify the goods or services supplied to the customer.

For each different type of item listed on the invoice, the business must show.

- the unit price or rate, excluding VAT
- the quantity of goods or the extent of the services
- the rate of VAT that applies to what is being sold
- the total amount payable, excluding VAT
- the rate of any cash discount or settlement discount for prompt payment
- the total amount of VAT charged.

If the business issues a VAT invoice that includes zero-rated or exempt goods or services, it must:

- show clearly that there is no VAT payable on those goods or services
- show the total of those values separately.

Completing the VAT return

Completing the VAT Return, box by box

Box 1 – VAT due in this period on sales and other outputs.

Include the VAT due on all goods and services you supplied in the period covered by the return. This is your 'output VAT' (or 'output tax') for the period. VAT may also be due on supplies outside the mainstream of your business.

Some examples are:

- fuel used for private motoring where VAT is accounted for using a scale charge

Points to remember when filling in box 1:

- deduct any VAT on credit notes issued by you
- you can sometimes include VAT underdeclared/overdeclared on previous returns
- you must not declare zero-rated exports or supplies to other EC Member States

Box 2 – VAT due in this period on acquisitions from other Member States of the European Community (EC)

Show the VAT due on all goods and related costs purchased from VAT registered suppliers in other EC Member States. You may also be entitled to reclaim this amount as input VAT and do so by including the relevant figure within the total at box 4.

Box 3 – Total VAT due

Show the total VAT due, that is, boxes 1 and 2 added together.

Box 4 – VAT reclaimed in this period on purchases and other inputs (including acquisitions from the (EC)

Show the total amount of deductible VAT charged on your business purchases. This is referred to as your 'input VAT' (or 'input tax') for the period.

You can reclaim VAT:

- you can reclaim on acquisitions of goods from VAT registered suppliers in other EC Member States (this must correspond with the amount declared within box 2)
- you are claiming back as bad debt relief

Points to remember when filling in box 4 make sure you do not include VAT:

- you pay on goods bought wholly for your personal use
- on business entertainment expenses

Other points to remember:

- deduct VAT on any credit notes issued to you

- you can sometimes include VAT underdeclared/overdeclared on previous returns

- if you are partly exempt your recovery of input VAT is subject to partial exemptions rules.

Box 5 – Net VAT to be paid to HMRC or reclaimed

Take the figures in boxes 3 and 4. Deduct the smaller from the larger and enter the difference in box 5.

Box 6 – Total value of sales and all other outputs excluding any VAT

Show the total value of all your business and sales and other specific outputs but leave out any VAT.

Some examples are:

- zero-rate, reduced-rate and exempt supplies
- exports
- supplies to other EC Member States (that is any figure entered in box 8)
- deposits for which an invoice has been issued

Box 7 – Total value of purchases and all other inputs excluding any VAT

Show the total value of your purchases and expenses but leave out any VAT.

You must include the value of:

- imports

- acquisitions from VAT registered suppliers in other EC Member States (that is any figure entered in box 9)

Box 8 – Total value of all supplies of goods and related costs, excluding any VAT, to other EC Member States

Show the total value of all supplies of goods to other EC Member States and directly related costs, such as freight and insurance, where these form part of the invoice or contract price. Leave out any VAT.

Box 9 – Total value of acquisitions of goods and related costs, excluding any VAT, from other EC Member States

Show the total value of all acquisitions of goods from VAT registered suppliers in other EC Member States and directly related costs, such as freight and insurance, where these form part of the invoice or contract price, but leave out any VAT.